THE JOY OF LOOKING

GREAT PHOTOGRAPHS
from the Library of Congress

Photographer unidentified, *Old Zÿds, the Kolk (canal)*, Amsterdam, ca. 1890–1900. Photochrom print.

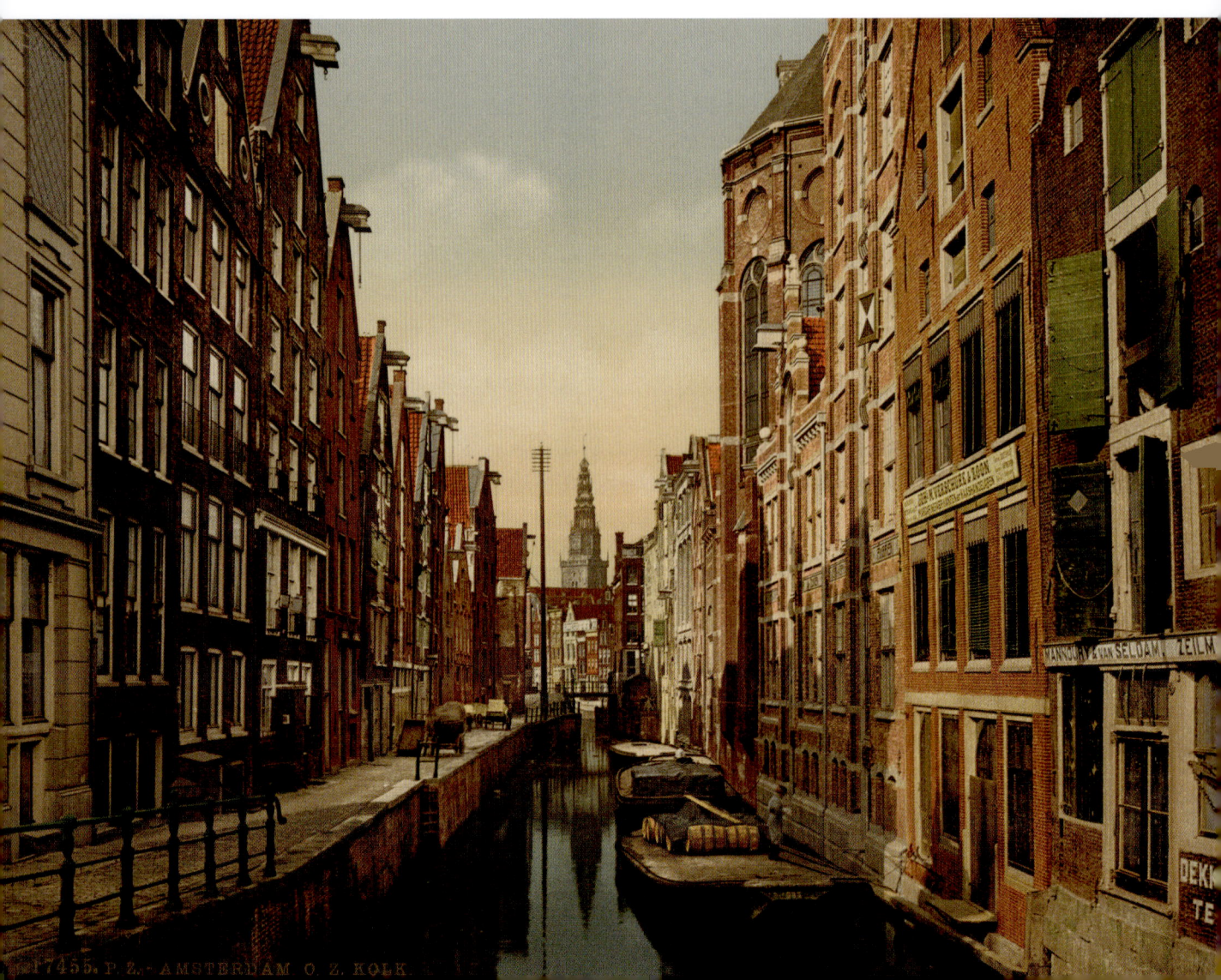

THE JOY OF LOOKING

GREAT PHOTOGRAPHS
from the Library of Congress

Edited by Aimee Hess and Hannah Freece

Foreword by Carla D. Hayden,
Librarian of Congress

Washington, DC

© 2023 Library of Congress
ISBN 978-0-8444-9584-2

Library of Congress Cataloging-in-Publication Data

Names: Library of Congress, author. | Hess, Aimee, editor. | Freece,
  Hannah, 1987- editor. | Hayden, Carla Diane, 1952- writer of foreword.
Title: The joy of looking : great photographs from the Library of Congress
  / edited by Aimee Hess and Hannah Freece ; foreword by Carla D. Hayden, Librarian of Congress.
Description: Washington, DC : Library of Congress, [2023] | Series: Collection close-up | "Most of the
images in this book come from the Library's Prints & Photographs Division, but photographs can be found
throughout the Library's collections, often in unexpected places. Here you will see pictures from the
Veterans History Project, which preserves personal accounts of America's war veterans, and from the
Manuscript, Rare Book & Special Collections, and Motion Picture, Broadcast, & Recorded Sound Divisions as
well"--Foreword. | Includes index.
Identifiers: LCCN 2022055226 | ISBN 9780844495842 (paperback)
Subjects: LCSH: Library of Congress--Photograph collections--Catalogs. | Photographs--Catalogs. |
Photography--United States--History--Sources.
Classification: LCC TR6.U62 W374 2023 | DDC 770--dc23/eng/20221117
LC record available at https://lccn.loc.gov/2022055226

Contents

Beverly Willis (1928–), *San Francisco Ballet Building Civic Center*, 1978–1983. Transparency.

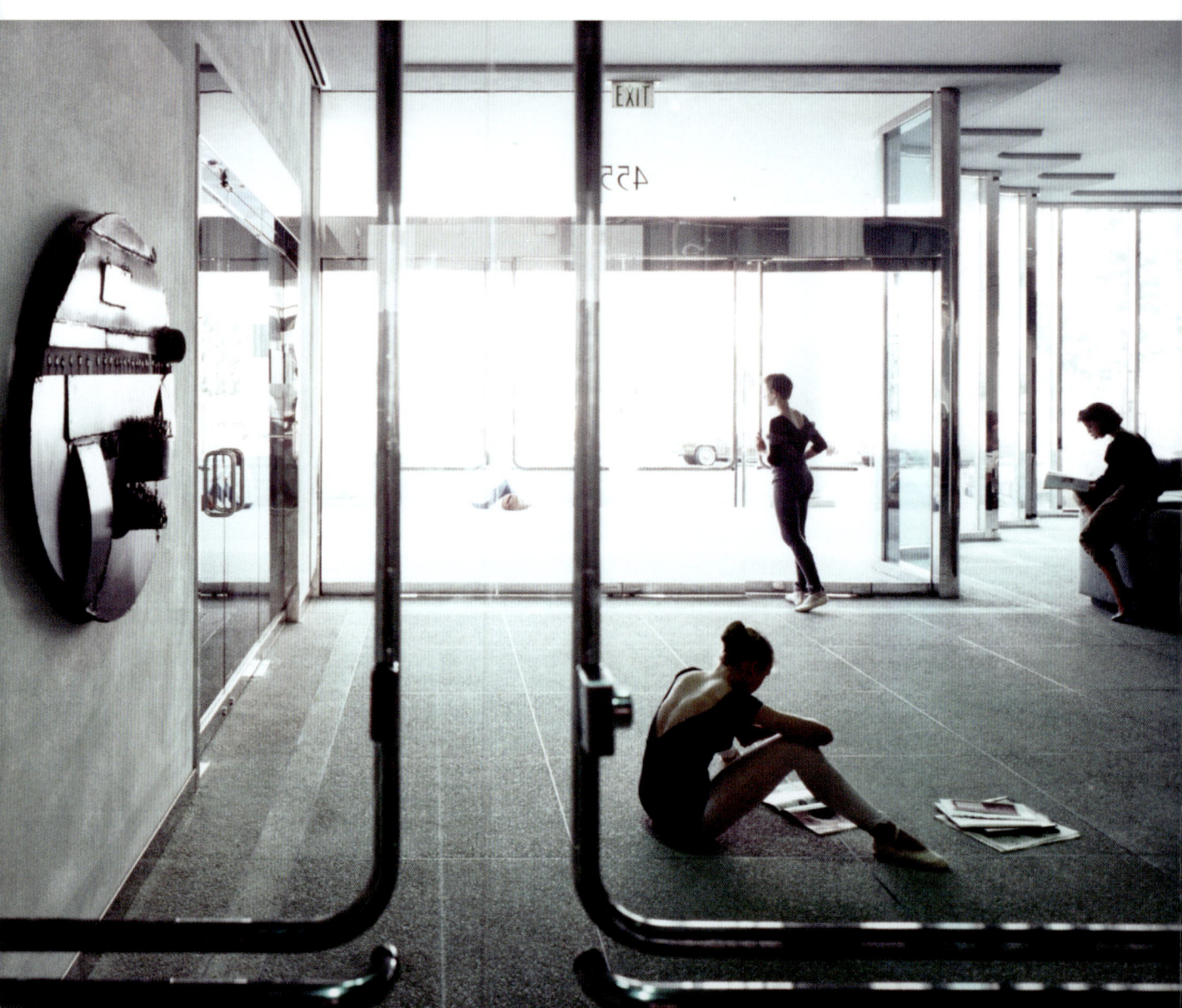

Foreword

In the twenty-first century, we are inundated with photographic imagery, whether in print, online, or saved on the cell phone in your pocket. What makes you stop and take a second look at a photograph? Is it the composition, the arrangement of shapes, the balance of light and dark? Is it the expression on someone's face, how an emotion has been captured? Maybe it poses a question: what is being depicted? Are you surprised by what you see? Perhaps it is simply beauty.

Since photography's invention in the early nineteenth century, the medium has produced countless thought-provoking images. The Library of Congress—the world's largest library—holds more than seventeen million photographs in its collections, ranging from some of the earliest images ever taken to photographs by artists working today. In *The Joy of Looking: Great Photographs from the Library of Congress*, the Library presents a selection of striking and fascinating photographs, ones that deserve a closer look and can offer endless new details or insights when revisited.

Both familiar and less well-known photographs appear here. Dorothea Lange's portrait of Florence Owens Thompson, commonly known as "Migrant Mother," is widely celebrated for humanizing the plight of struggling migrant workers during the

Great Depression. Others, like street photographer Anthony Angel's lively series of two women sitting on a New York City park bench, were unknown during the photographer's lifetime and deserve greater attention.

While entire books could be written about each photographer whose work is featured here, only minimal captions are included, along with the photographs' original titles when known, to let the images speak for themselves. If a photo or an artist catches your eye, I encourage you to follow your curiosity and seek out resources to learn more about the photographer and their body of work.

Most of the images in this book come from the Library's Prints & Photographs Division, but photographs can be found throughout the Library's collections, often in unexpected places. Here you will see pictures from the Veterans History Project, which preserves personal accounts of America's war veterans, and from the Manuscript, Rare Book & Special Collections, and Motion Picture, Broadcast & Recorded Sound Divisions as well. I invite you to explore all the Library has to offer in our Collection Close-Up series, and to visit in person or online at www.loc.gov.

Carla D. Hayden

Librarian of Congress

Photographs

Best known for his photographs of the civil rights movement, Bob Adelman captured a diverse audience at the "People Wall," a moving grandstand in the IBM Pavilion at the New York World's Fair. Audience members look in all directions in this playful view of the viewers.

Bob Adelman (1930–2016), *People Wall, World's Fair,* New York City, 1964. Gelatin silver print. © Bob Adelman.

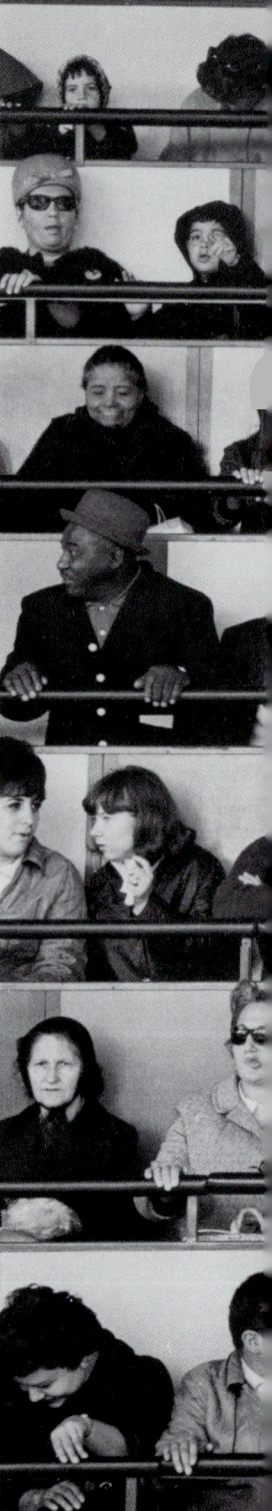

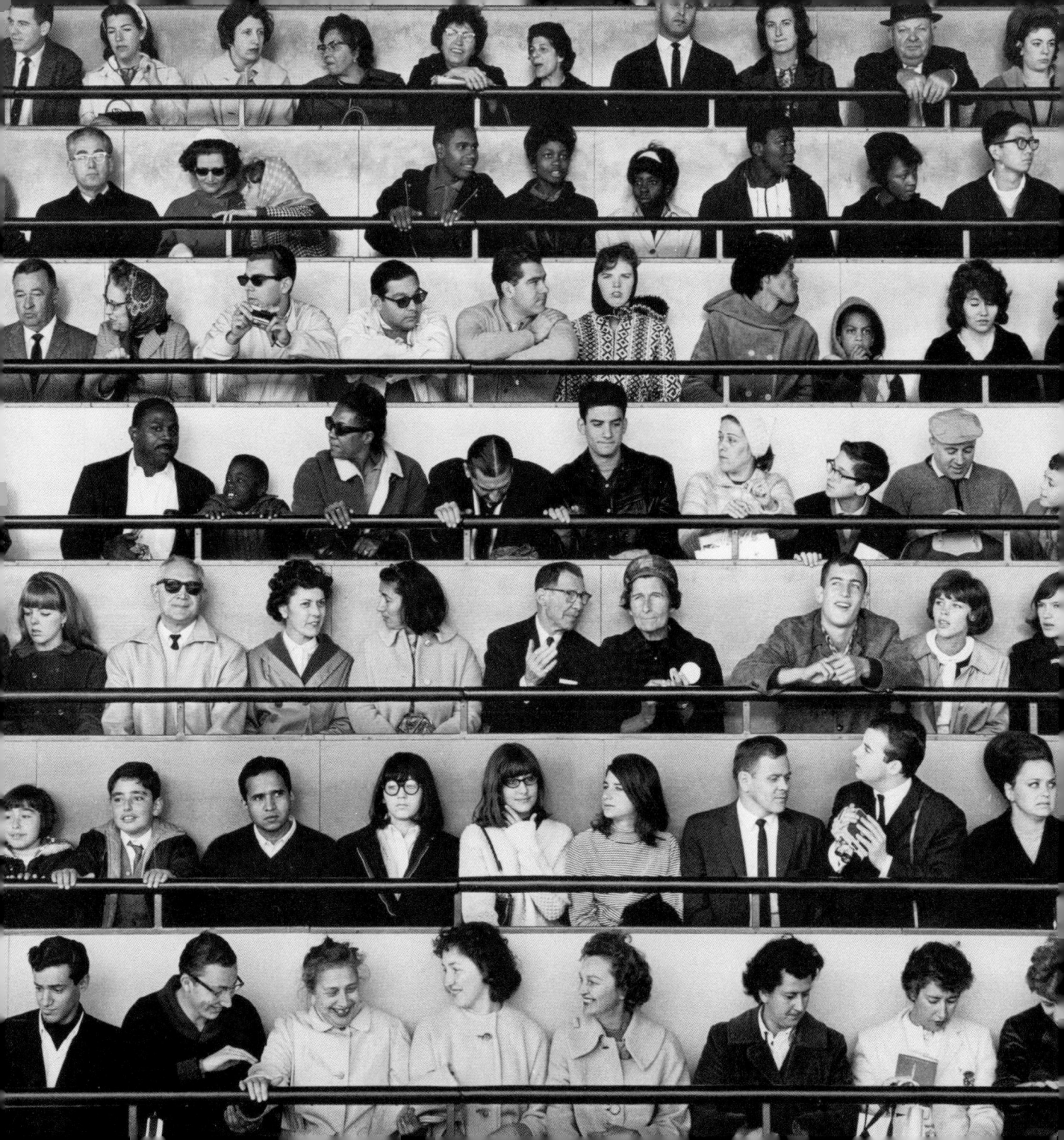

Shooting from below,
F. S. Lincoln highlighted
the gleaming curvature
of a model Chrysler
in the company's
showroom. The lights on
the ceiling shine onto
the mirror-like floor,
casting a reflected road
beneath the car.

F. S. (Fay Sturtevant)
Lincoln (1894–1975),
Chrysler Salon, New
York City, 1937. Gelatin
silver print.

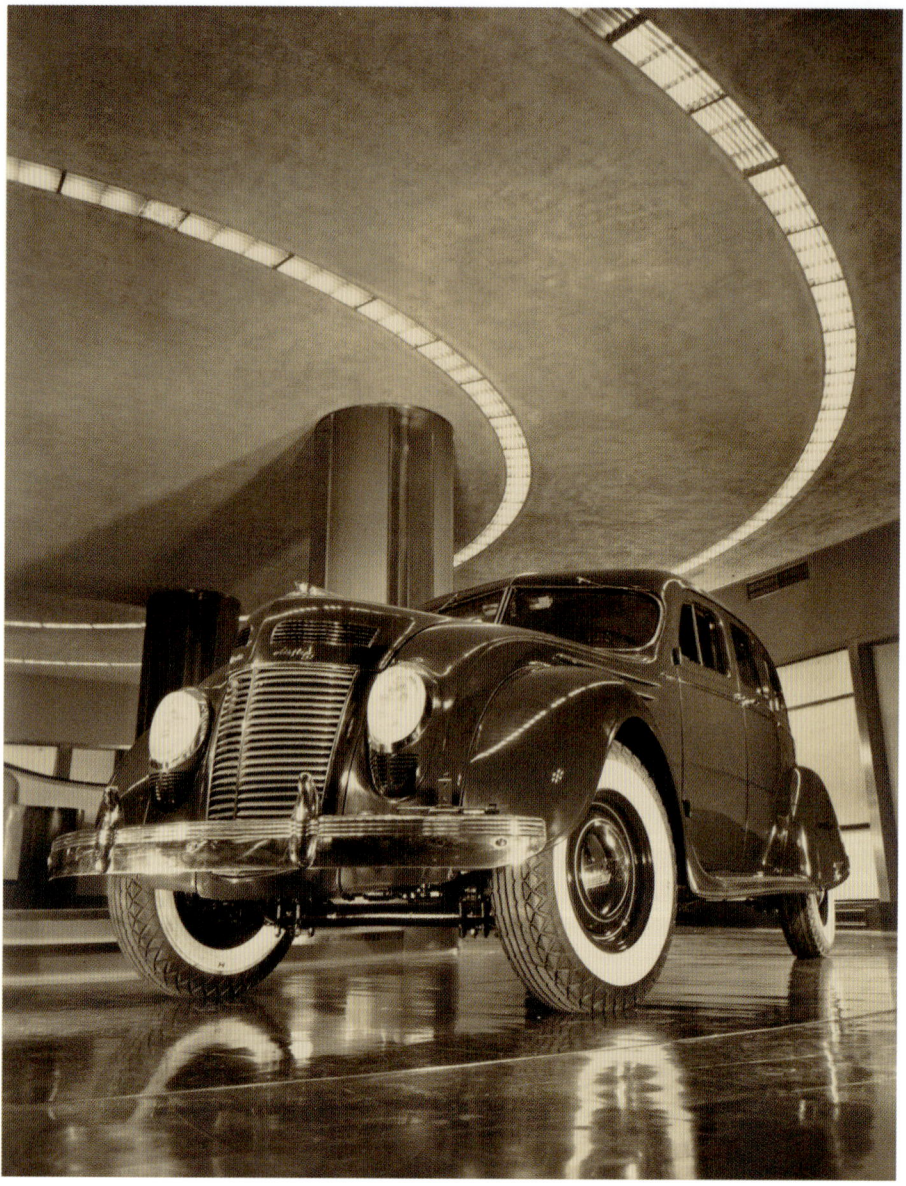

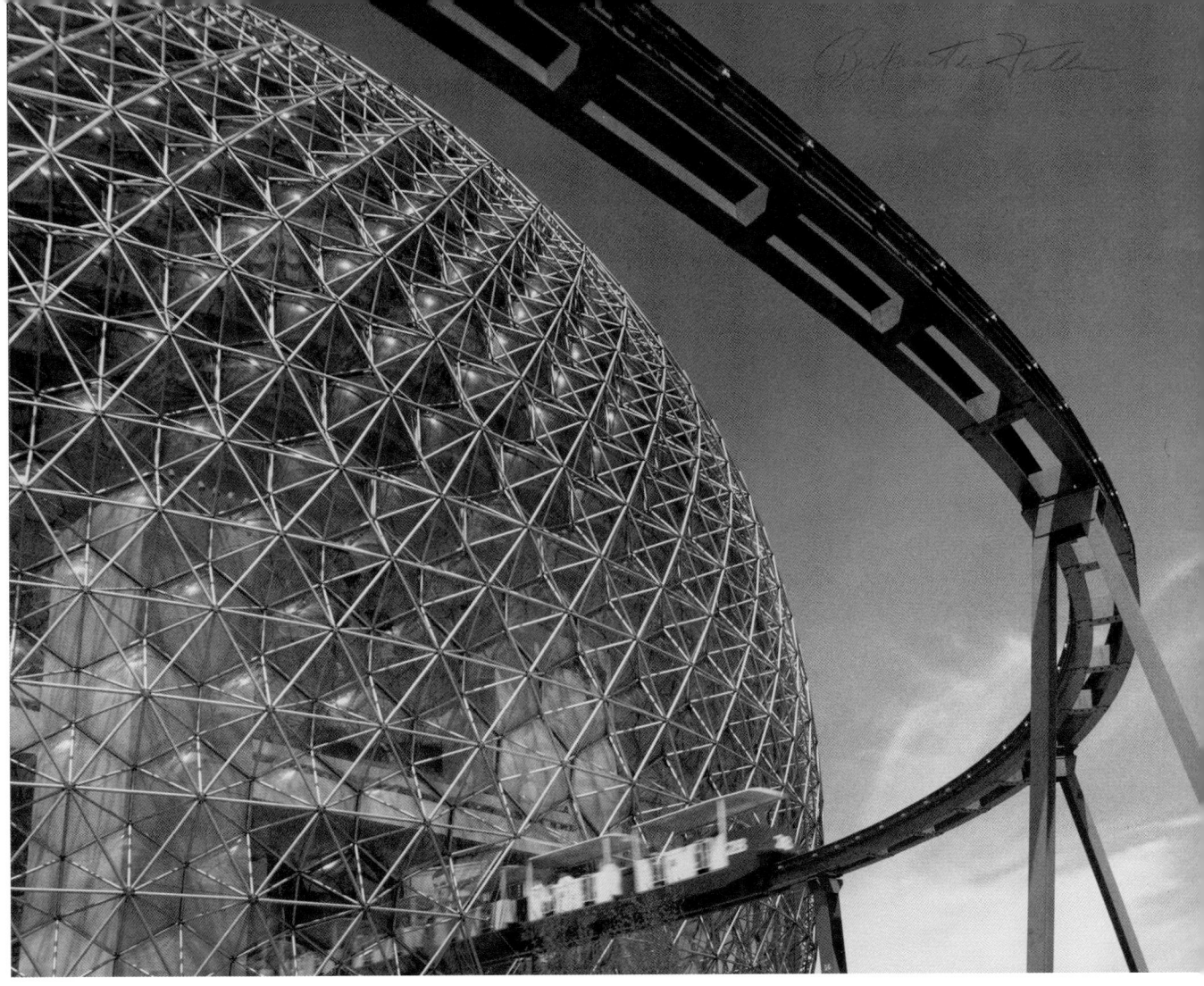

Bill Engdahl, working for influential architectural photography firm Hedrich Blessing, captured the futuristic promise of the United States pavilion at Expo 67 in Montreal. Pierced by the monorail track, the enormous geodesic dome was designed by iconoclastic architect Buckminster Fuller, who signed the upper right corner of this print.

Bill Engdahl (1925–1997), Expo '67, Montreal, Quebec, Canada, 1967. Gelatin silver print.

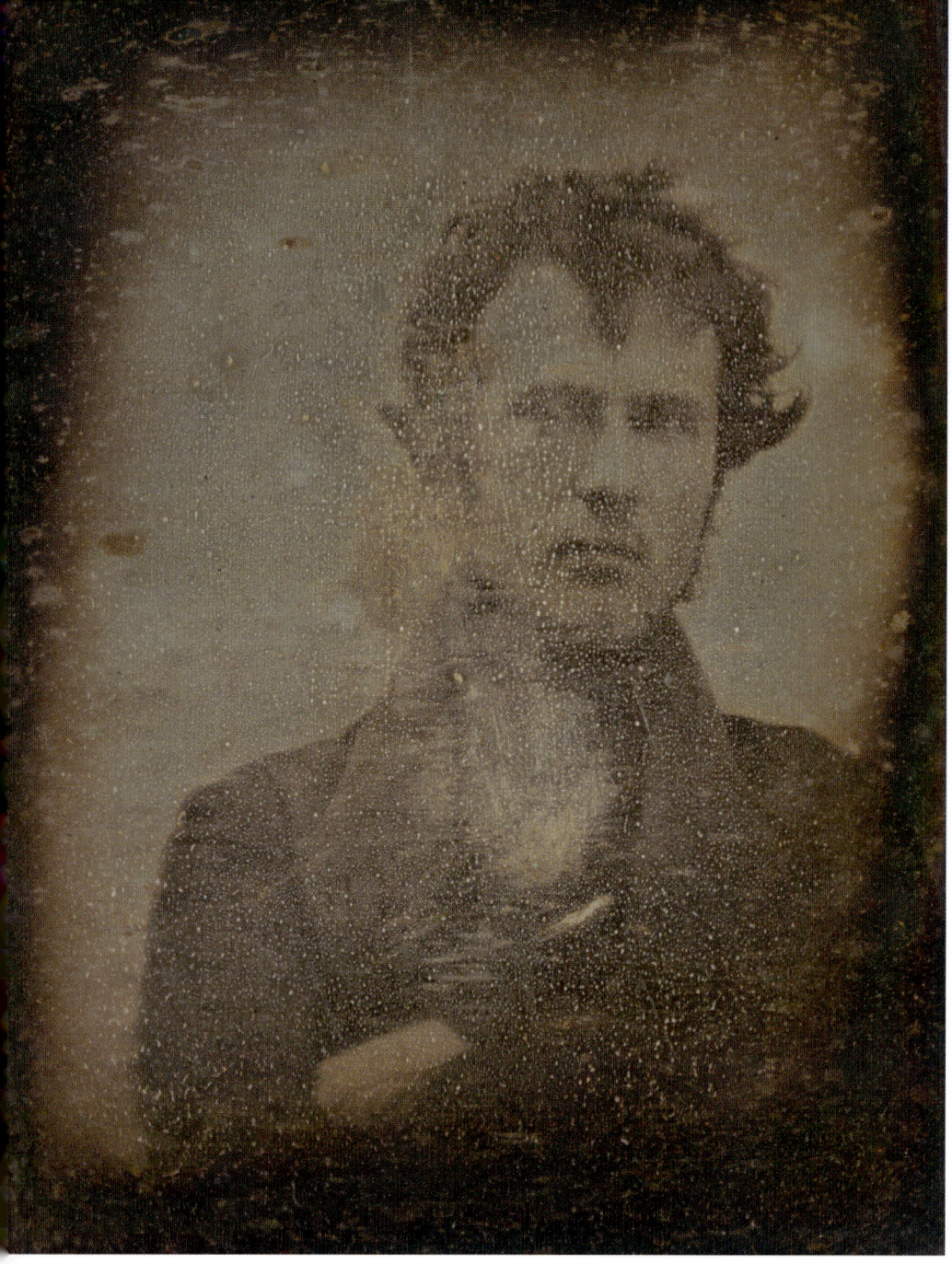

Just months after Louis Daguerre announced his invention of a photographic method in France, Robert Cornelius took this self-portrait outside his family's Philadelphia lamp and chandelier store, using a box fitted with a lens from an opera glass. Cornelius faces the lens with arms crossed and a quizzical expression, anticipating what would become the first American photographic self-portrait.

Robert Cornelius (1809–1893), *Self-Portrait*, Philadelphia, 1839. Approximate quarter-plate daguerreotype.

O. Winston Link hauled extensive equipment around the Norfolk & Western railway lines to take his dramatic nighttime photographs of the last steam engines on the rails. In this self-portrait with assistant George Thom, Link is nearly overshadowed by the many flashbulbs, reflectors, lanterns, and even miner's headlamps he used to capture the iconic locomotives.

| O. Winston Link (1914–2001), *Winston Link and George Thom with Night Flash Equipment*, March 1956. Gelatin silver print.
© O. Winston Link Museum and Winston Conway Link.

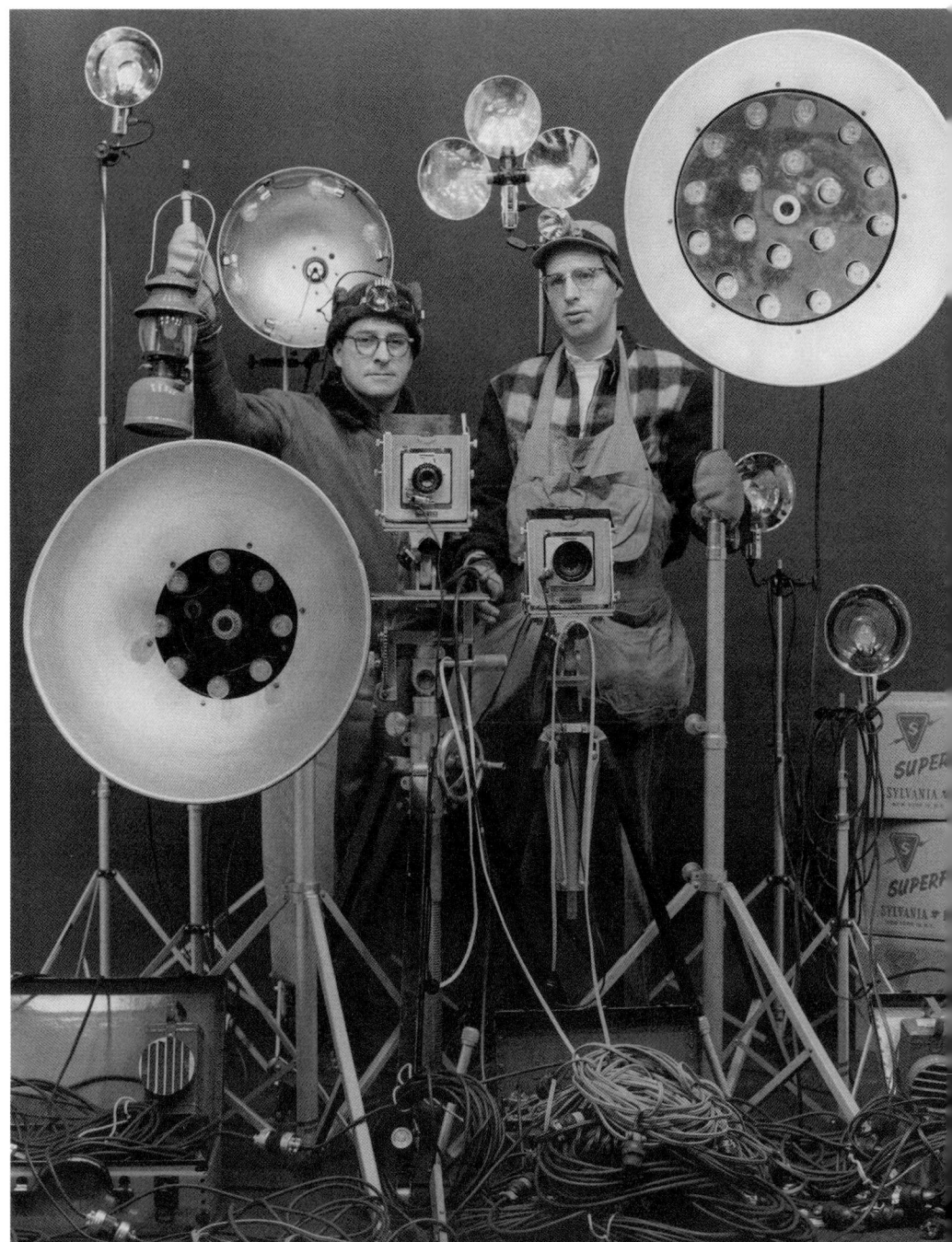

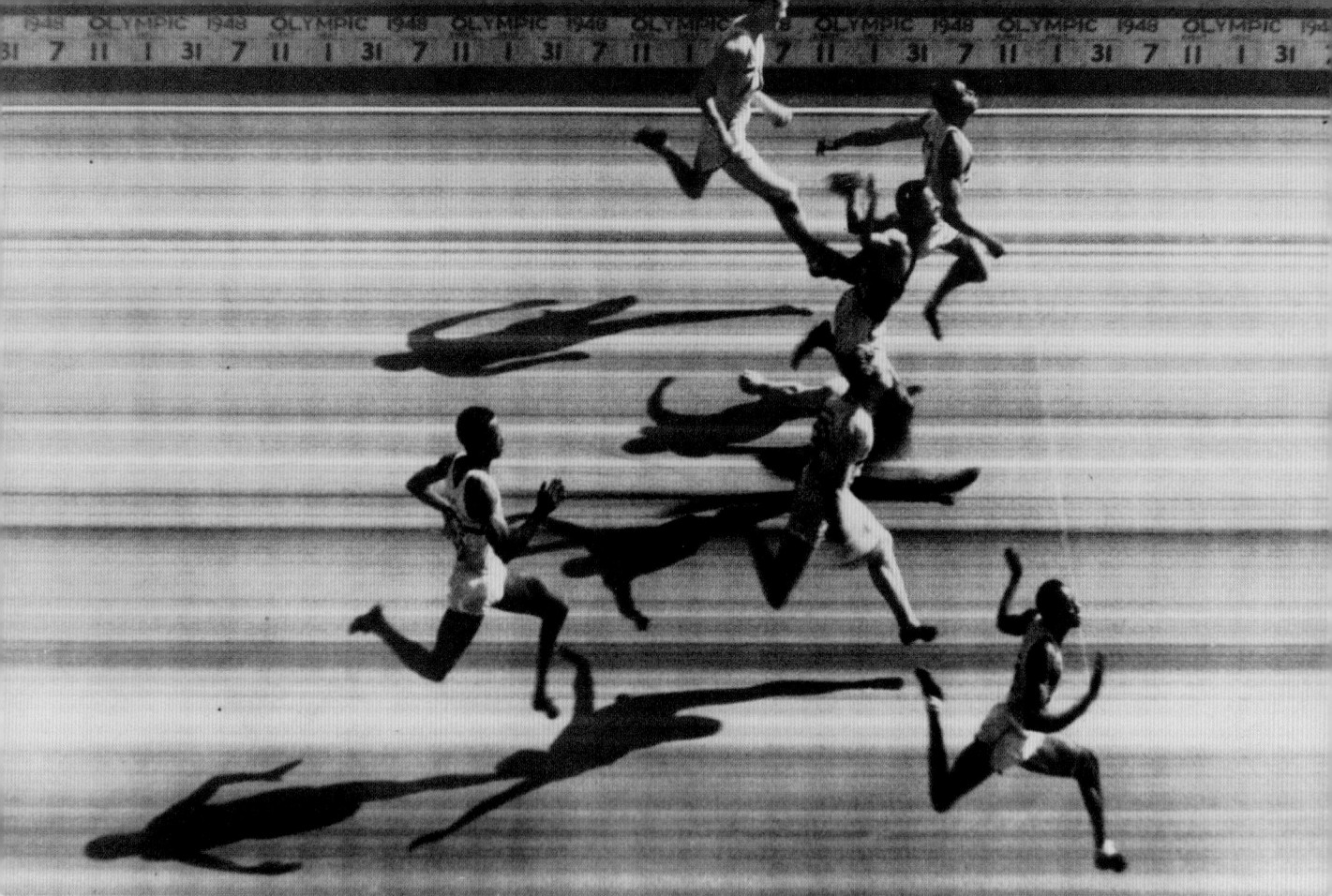

This dramatic photograph caught six of the world's fastest men seemingly in mid-flight, none of their feet touching the ground. In a furious burst of speed, they appear to outrun their own shadows. The photo proved that William Harrison Dillard of the United States won the race.

Photographer unidentified, *Photo Finish of the 100-Meter Dash at the Olympic Games*, London, 1948. Gelatin silver print. Courtesy of PA Images / Alamy Stock Photo.

John Vachon (1914–1975), *Kids at a Ball Game at Briggs Stadium*, Detroit, Michigan, 1942. Gelatin silver print.

Although his job for the Office of War Information called for photographs that documented home front activities during World War II, John Vachon captured a lighter moment in this scene as the crowd cheers with abandon for the Detroit Tigers baseball team.

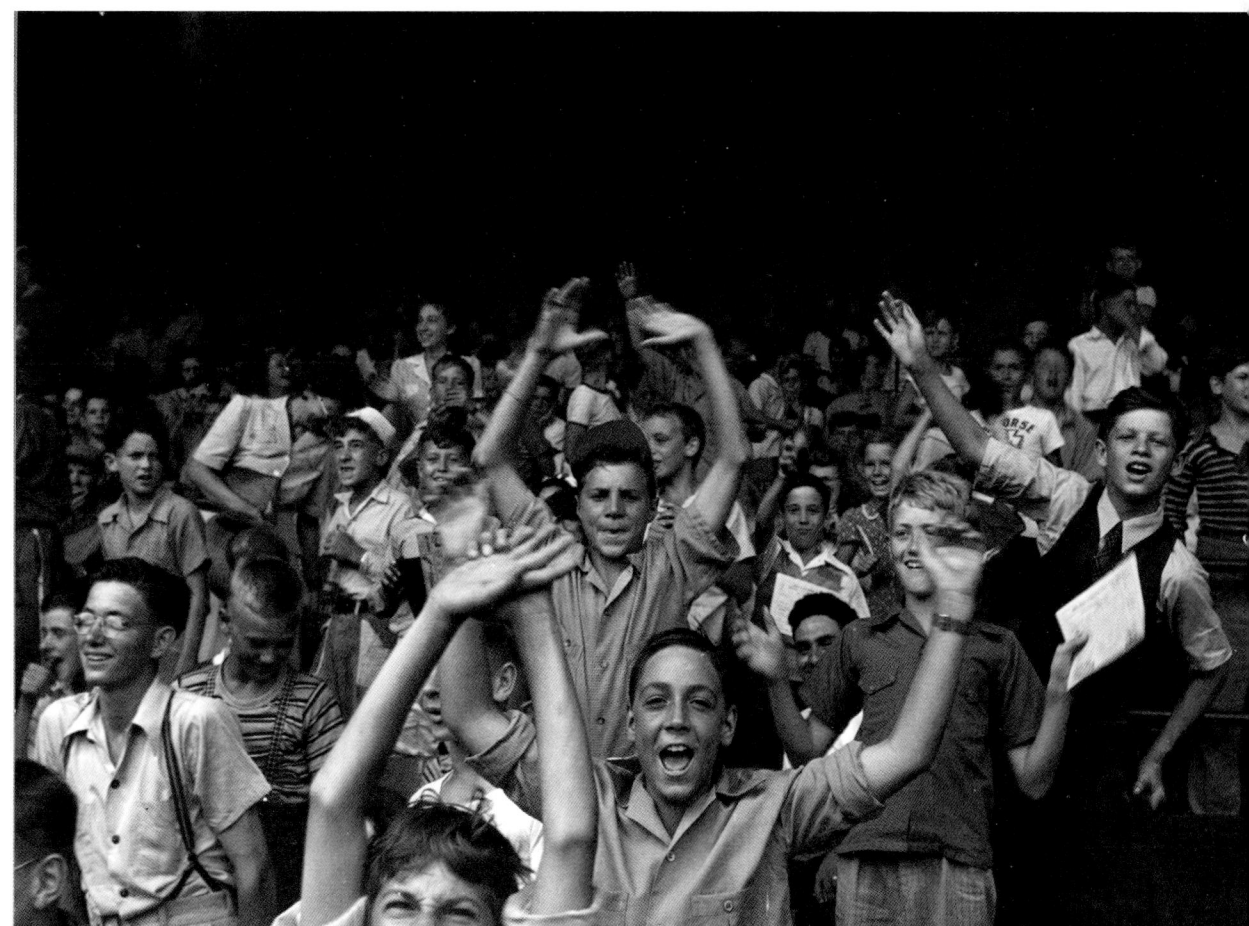

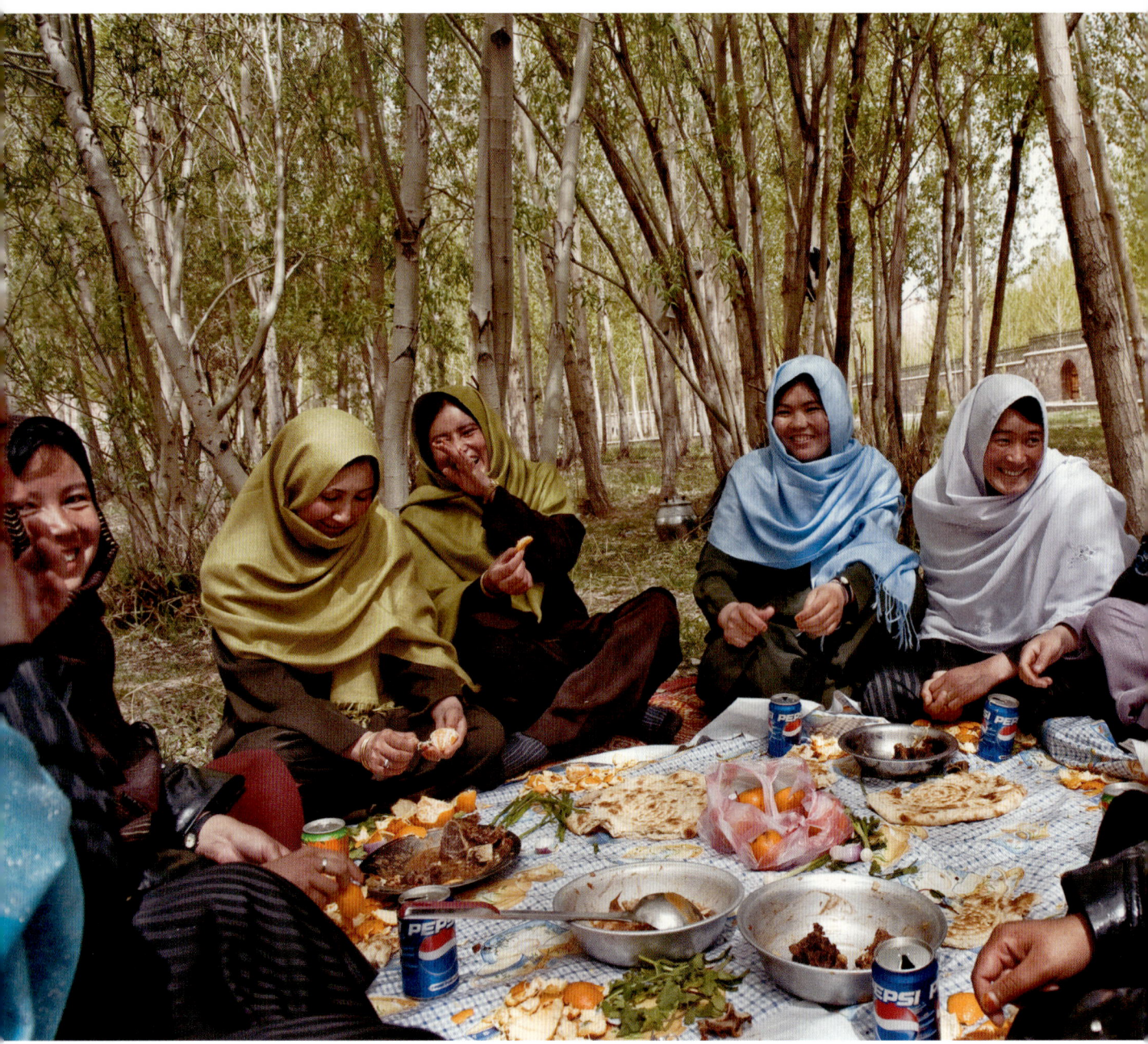

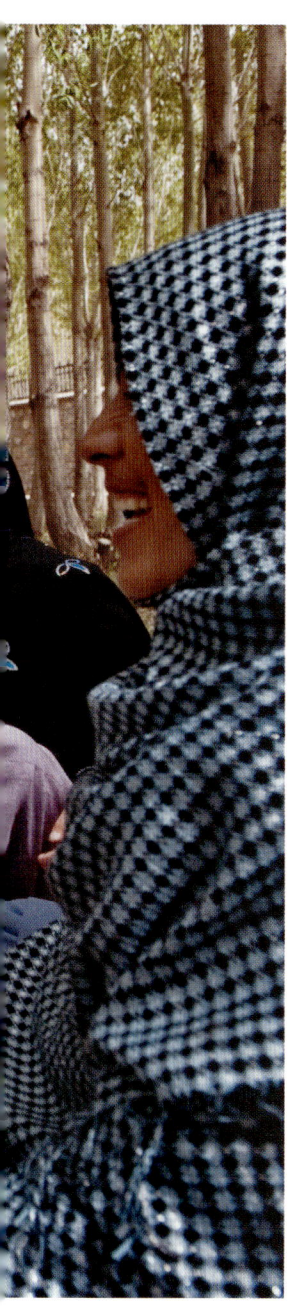

Many of the photographs in Lynsey Addario's *Afghanistan Veiled Rebellion* series reflect the hardships and limitations that Afghan women endure. Here, the mood is celebratory as female students, many of them studying to become teachers, picnic in a women's garden in a park outside of Bamian.

Lynsey Addario (1973–), *Picnic in Women's Garden, a Student's Lunch*, Bamian, Afghanistan, 2010. Inkjet print. *Afghanistan Veiled Rebellion* series. Courtesy of Lynsey Addario.

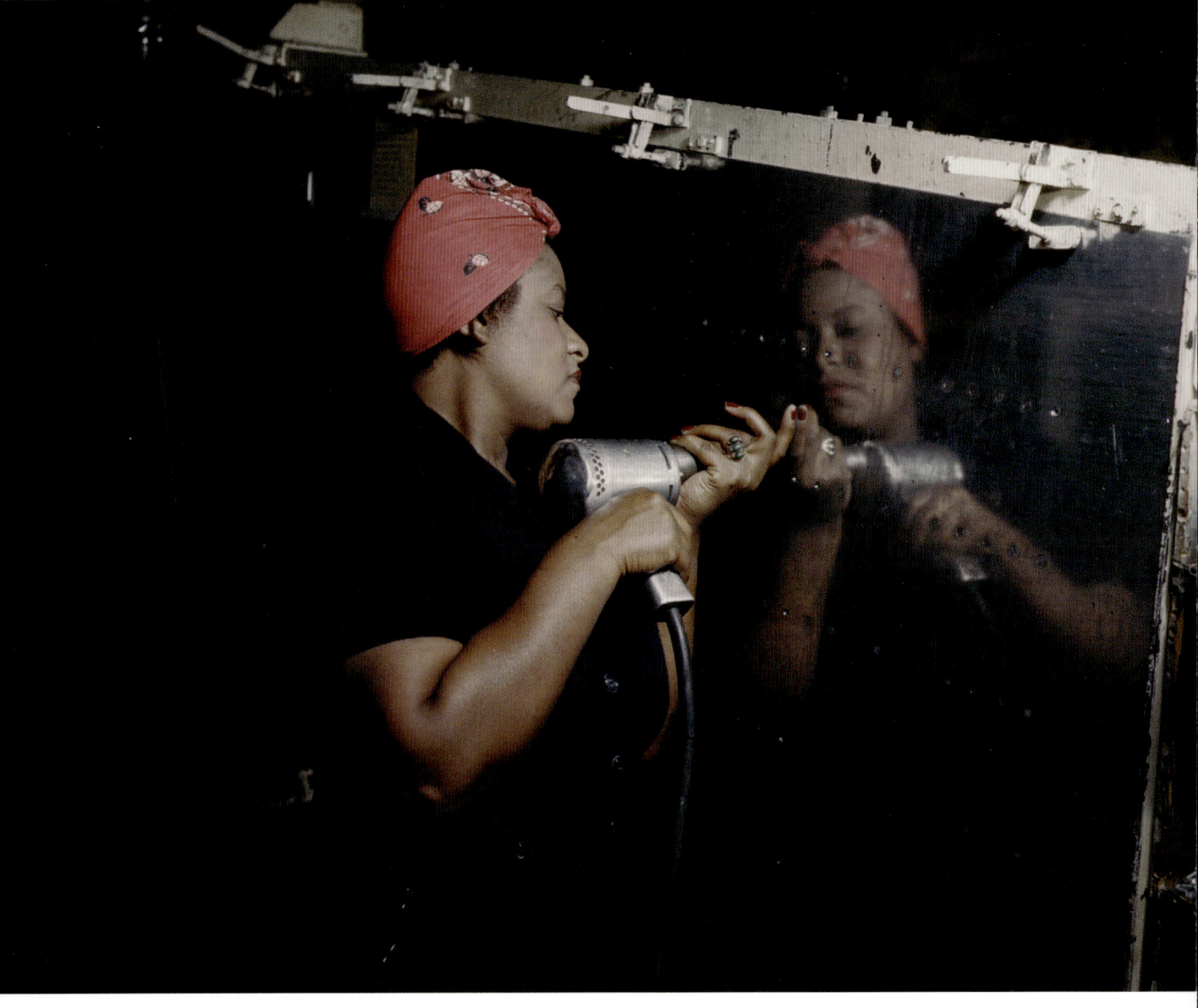

Rosie the Riveter, the defense worker in a red bandana, was an icon of World War II. Here, Alfred T. Palmer offers another view of Rosie—usually portrayed as White—by showing a Black woman at work on a "Vengeance" dive bomber with red painted nails and a green ring, expressing her femininity while she handles her power tool with ease.

Alfred T. Palmer (1906–1993), *Operating a Hand Drill at Vultee Aircraft Inc.*, Nashville, Tennessee, 1943. Color transparency.

The unidentified woman in this daguerreotype sits behind an industrial model Grover and Baker sewing machine. This portrait may have been created as a promotion for the machine's manufacturer, an image of a seamstress displaying the tools of her trade, or a portrait of a woman wealthy enough to have a machine at home.

| Photographer unidentified, *Woman with Sewing Machine*, 1853. Sixth-plate daguerreotype, hand-colored.

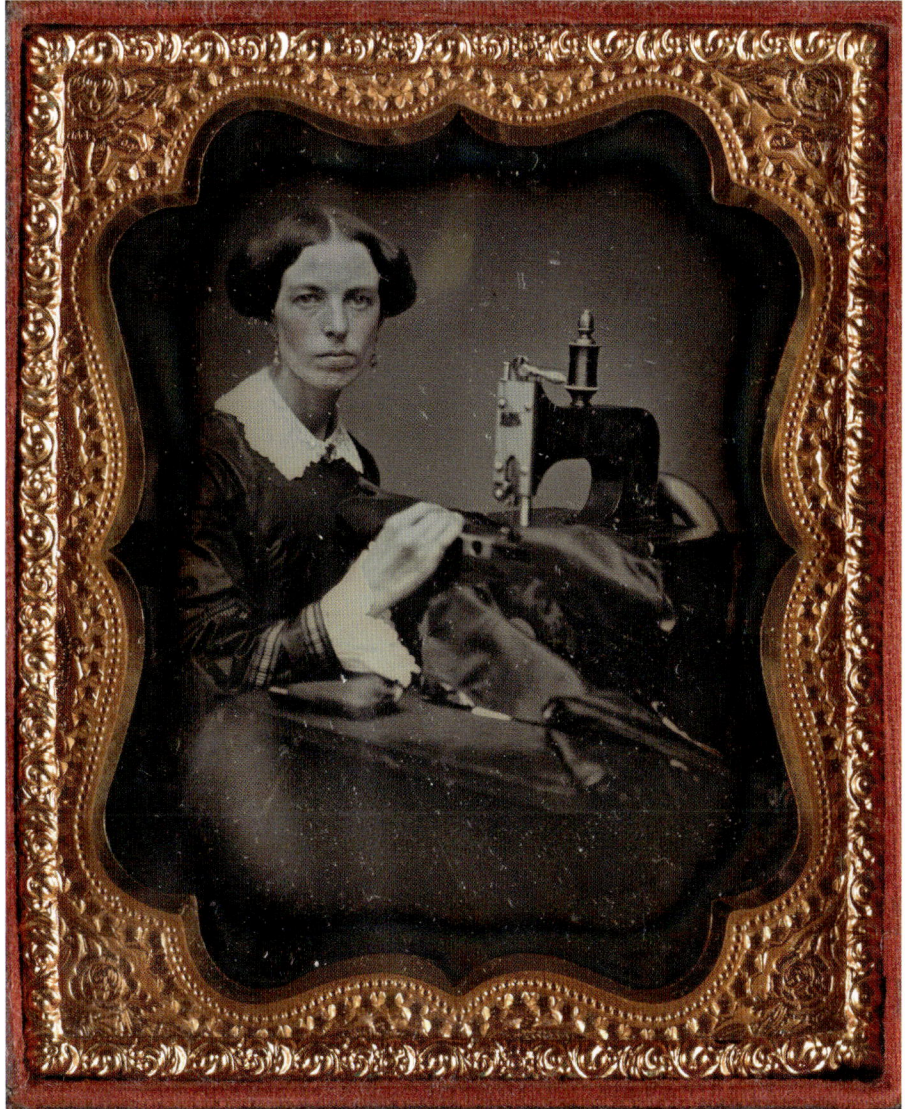

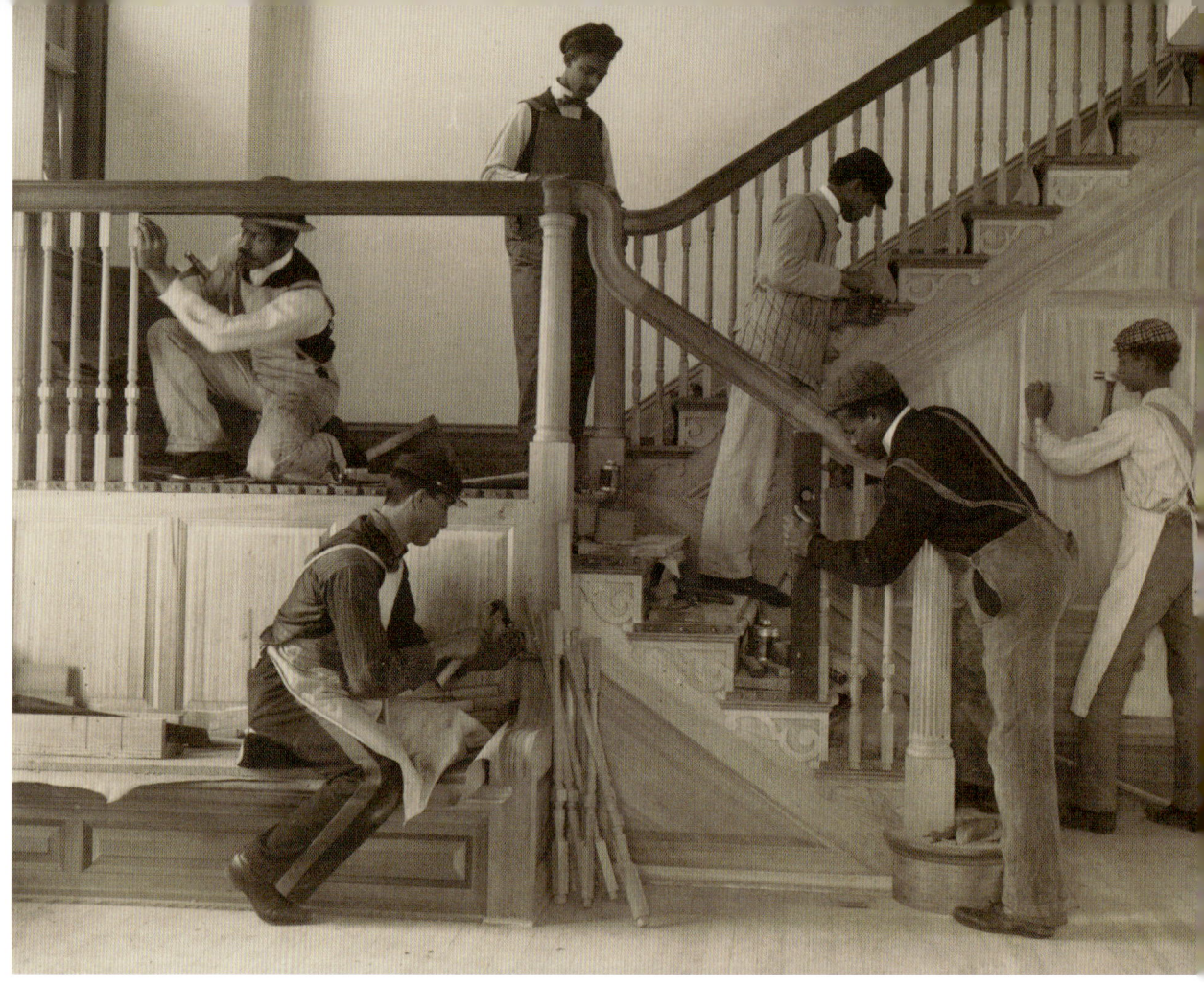

Using glass plate negatives, Frances Benjamin Johnston carefully choreographed the Hampton Institute students constructing a staircase in this photograph. The school, founded in 1868 for newly freed slaves, commissioned Johnston to document its educational philosophies in action. Johnston's photographs were displayed in W. E. B. Du Bois's "American Negro" exhibit at the 1900 Paris Exposition.

Frances Benjamin Johnston (1864–1952), *Students at Work on a House Built Largely by Them*, Hampton, Virginia, 1899–1900. Platinum print.

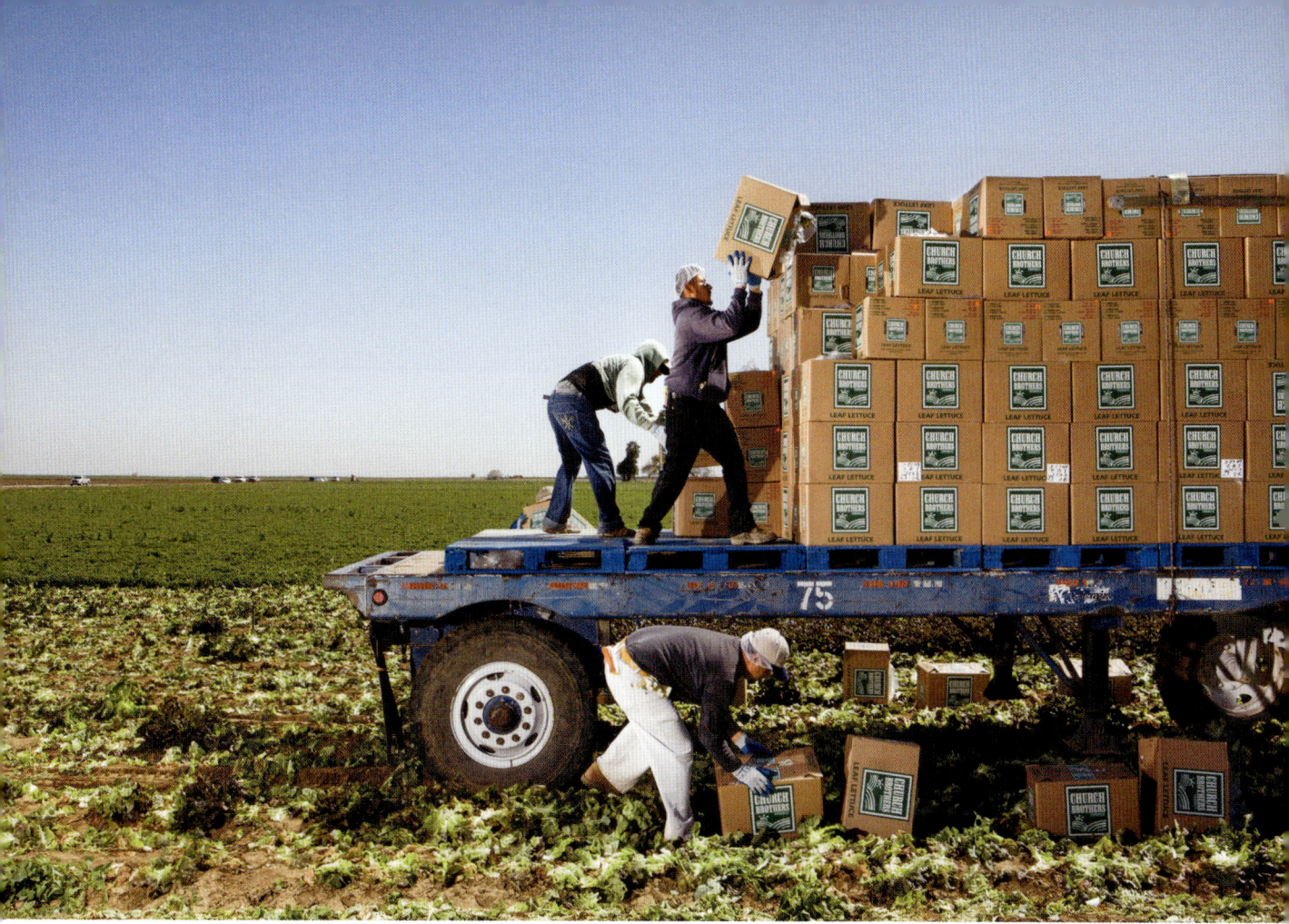

Sam Comen (1980–), *Packing and Loading Red Leaf Lettuce*, near Huron, California, 2009. Inkjet print. *Lost Hills* portfolio. Courtesy of Sam Comen.

Sam Comen was inspired by the Farm Security Administration's photographs of migrant workers during the Great Depression when he set out to photograph the small agricultural town of Lost Hills, California. Using cross-lighting and rich colors more expected in commercial photography, Comen creates a vivid portrait of residents, many of whom are immigrants, undertaking daily tasks at work and home.

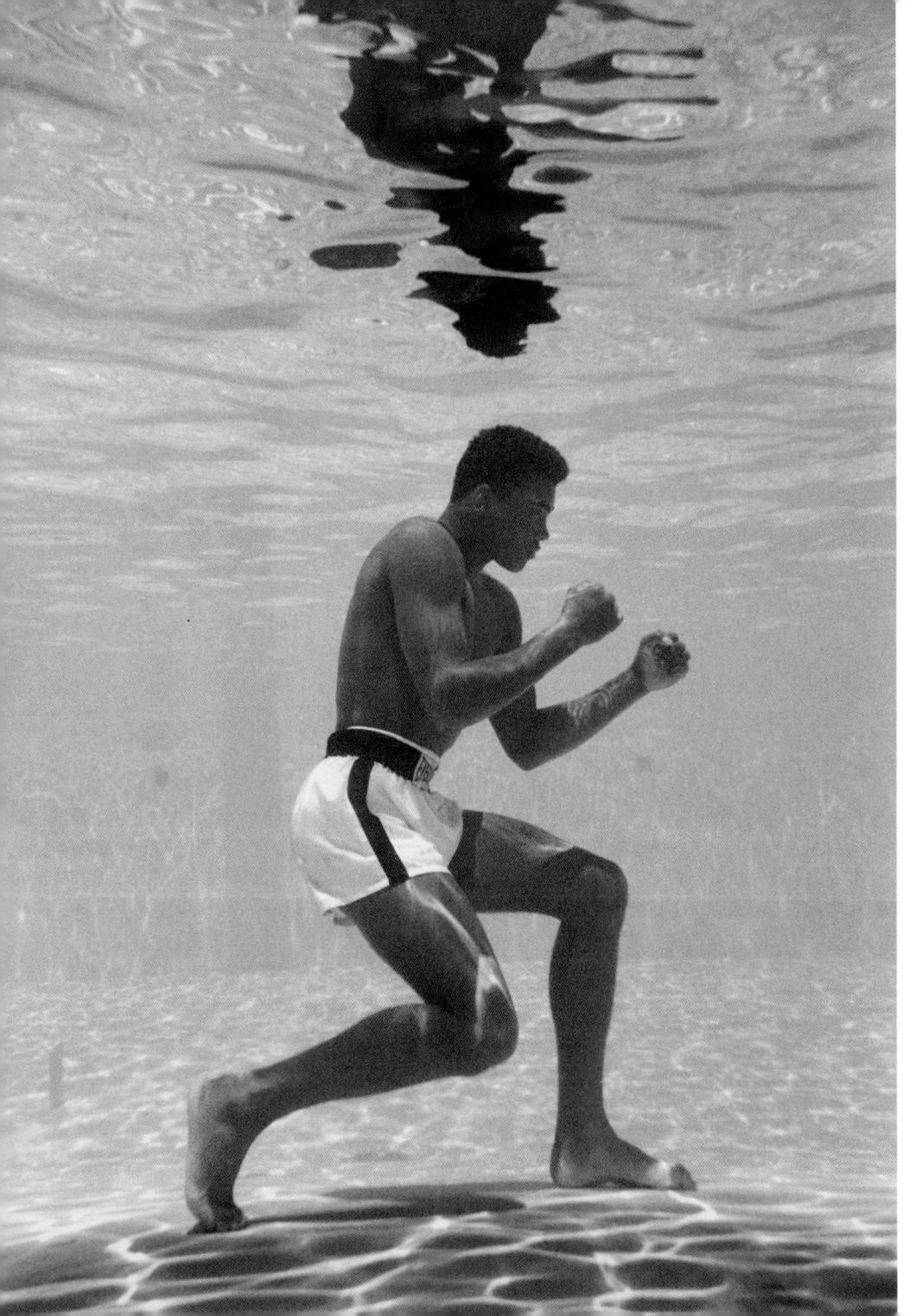

When Flip Schulke arrived at a Miami hotel to photograph a young boxer, then known as Cassius Clay, he found the fighter training in the swimming pool, which he said was his regular practice. Schulke dove in to record the boxer's iconic pose, coiled taut and silhouetted against the rippling light. Years later, Ali revealed the truth: he'd never trained underwater before that day.

| Flip Schulke (1930–2008), *Muhammad Ali Underwater*, Miami, Florida, 1961. Gelatin silver print. © Flip Schulke.

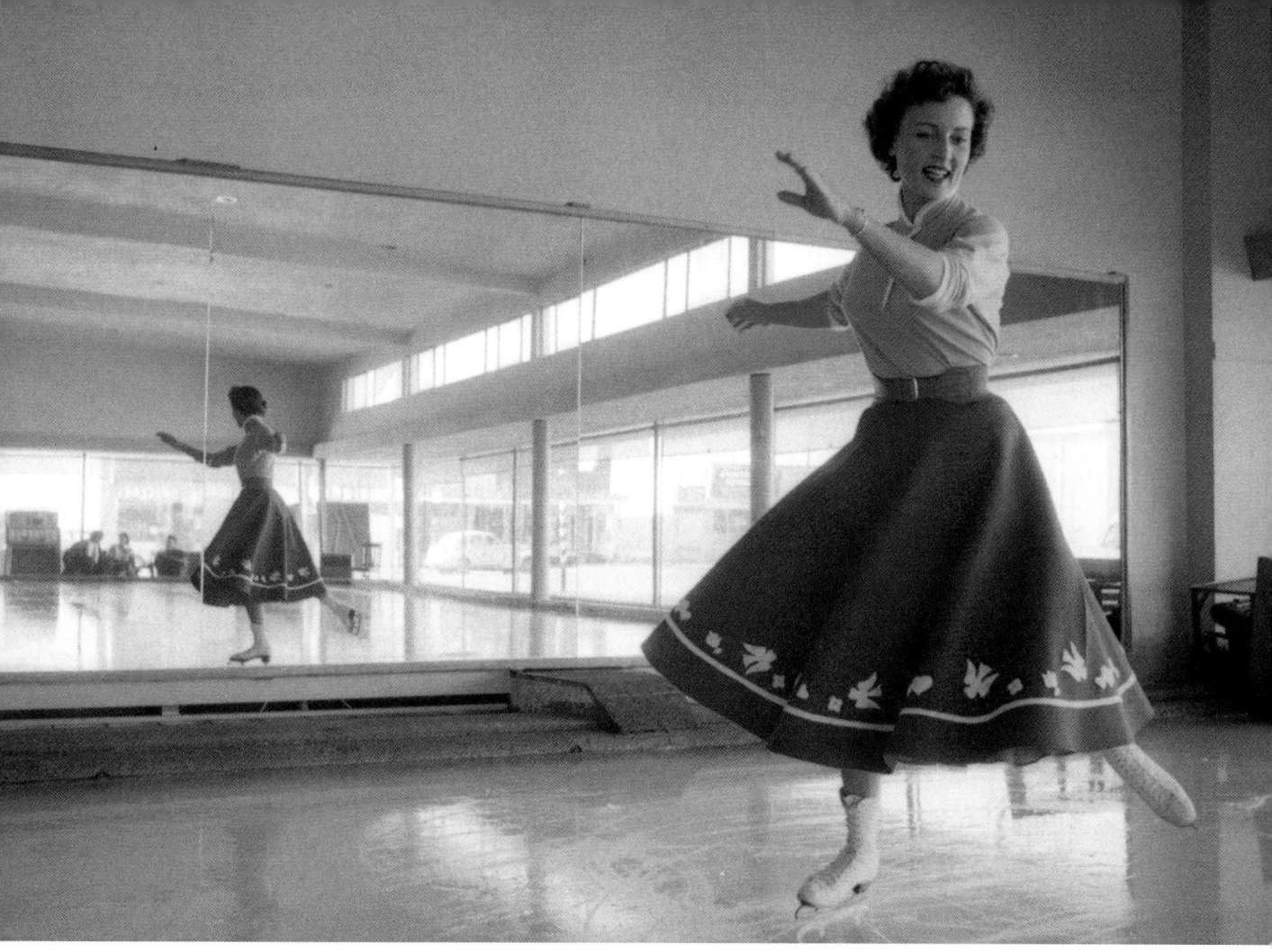

Maurice Terrell photographed actress Betty White looking at home on the ice rink, possibly promoting her eponymous television show, for *Look* magazine. Terrell caught White mid-stride, the long mirror providing a 360-degree view of her twirling skirt, doves dancing along the hemline.

Maurice Terrell (1912–1989), *Betty White, California*, 1954. Film negative.

Best known for his landscape photography, Ansel Adams also photographed daily life at the Manzanar War Relocation Center, one of ten sites where Japanese Americans were incarcerated during World War II. The third baseline draws the eye from the action on the baseball field to the meager barracks housing, set against the majestic mountains in the background.

Ansel Adams (1902–1984), *Baseball Game, Manzanar Relocation Center*, California, 1943. Gelatin silver print.

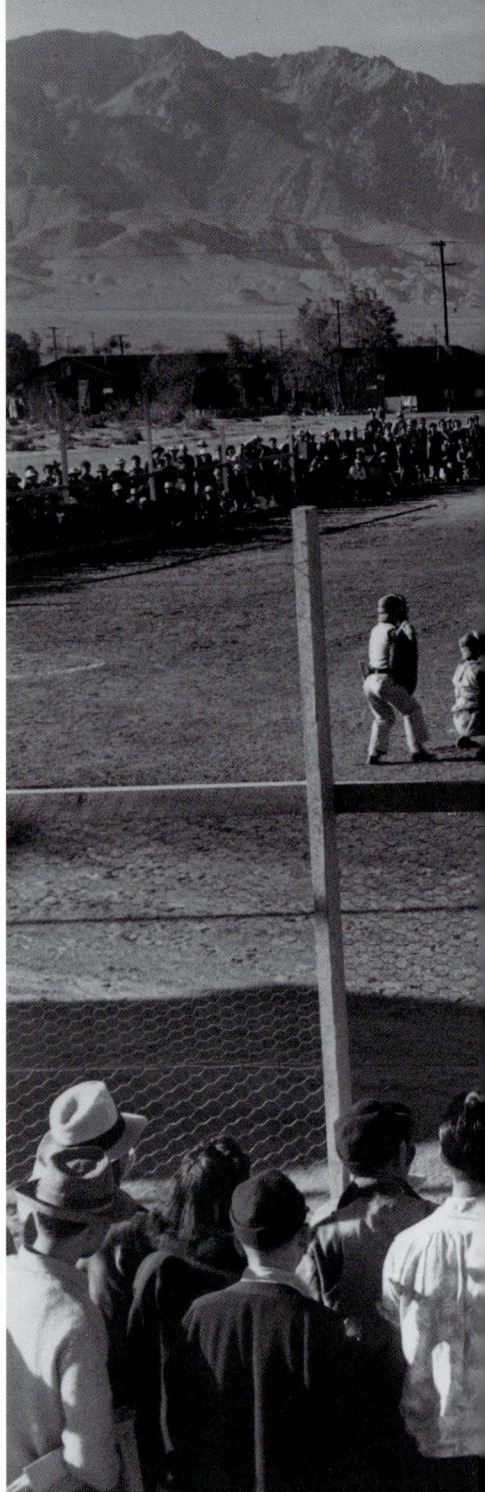

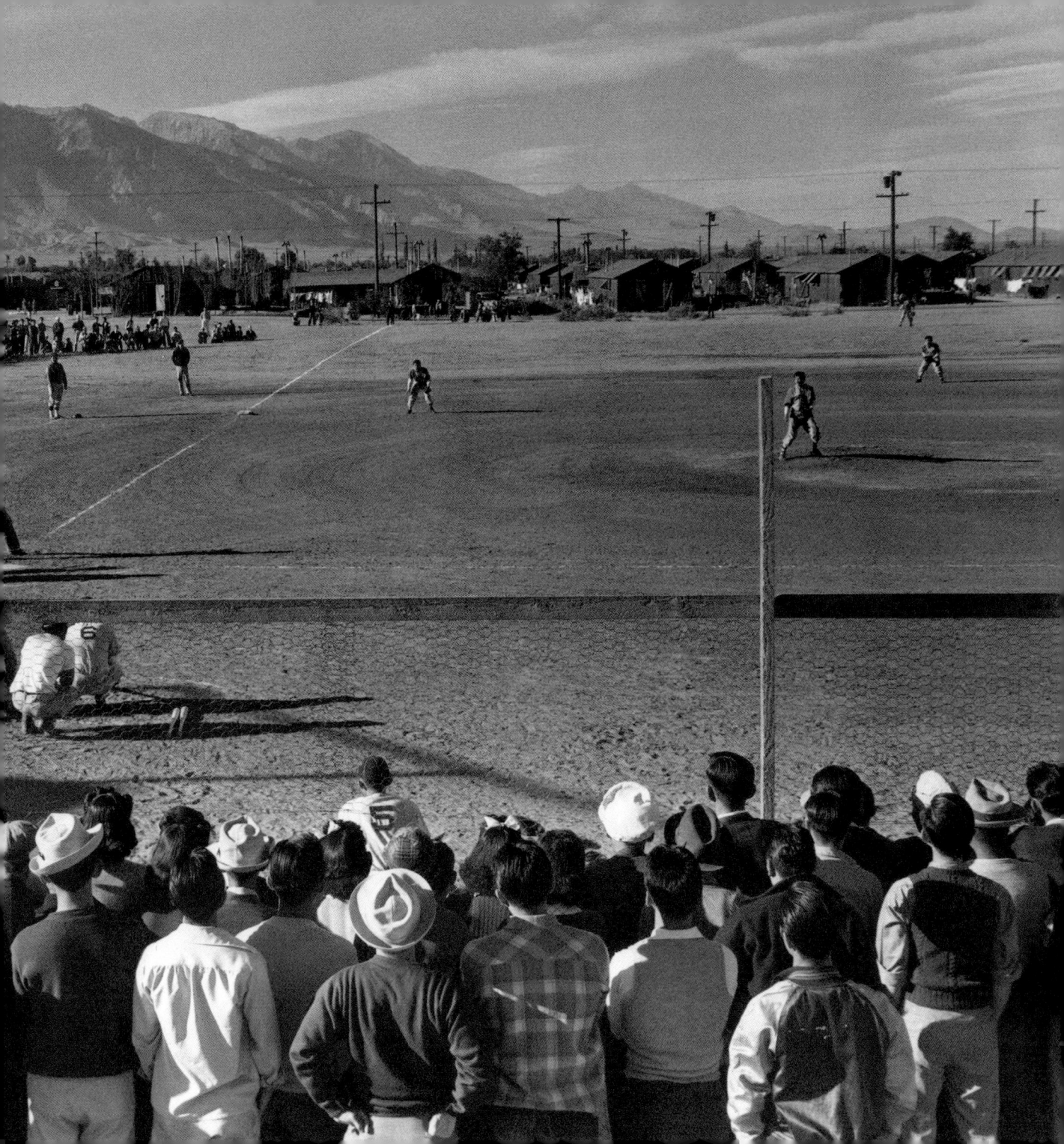

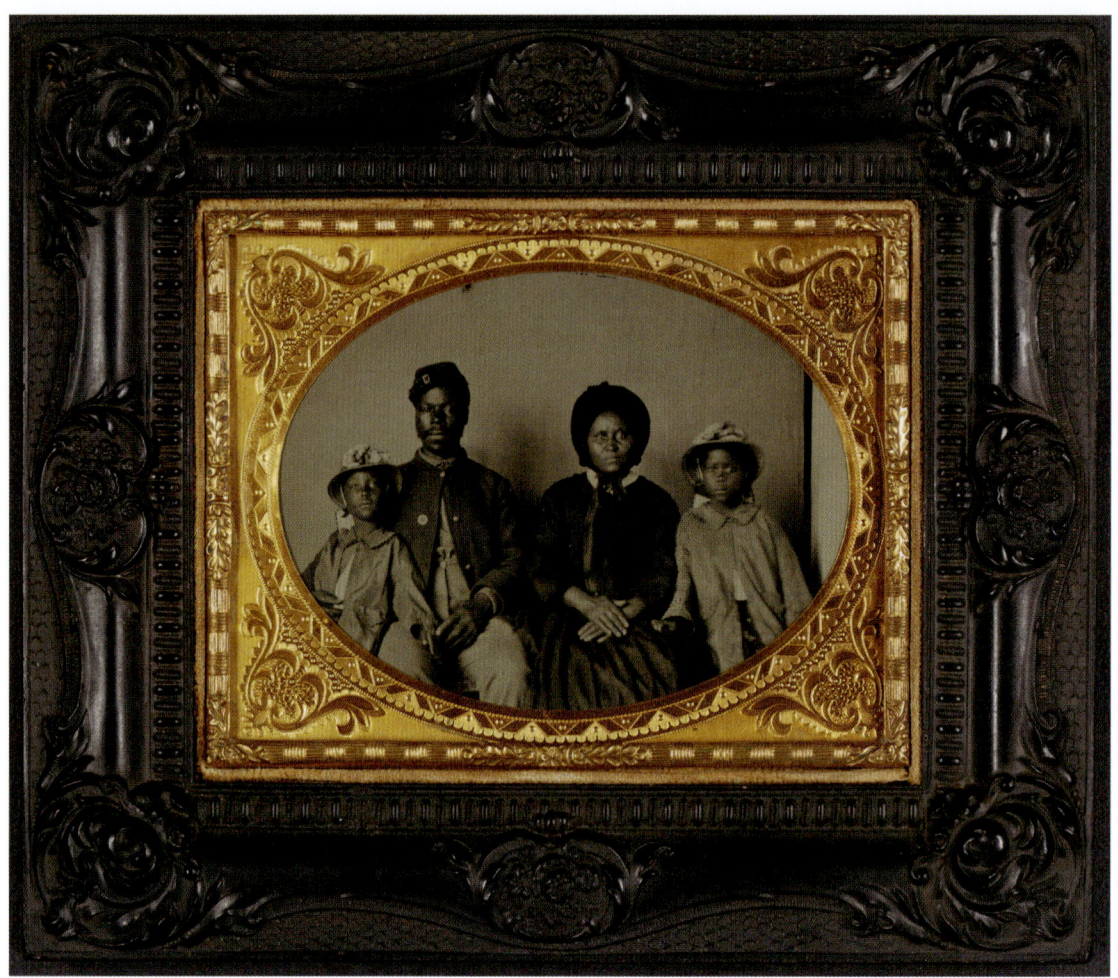

Two girls in matching hats and coats flank their parents, the adults' expressions a mixture of confidence, concern, and defiance, in this anonymous ambrotype. The portrait was found in Cecil County, Maryland, making it likely that the soldier belonged to one of the seven US Colored Troop regiments raised in Maryland during the Civil War.

Photographer unidentified, *African American Soldier in Union Uniform with Wife and Two Daughters*, between 1863 and 1865. Quarter-plate ambrotype.

To create this platinum/palladium print depicting the photographer and his family, Will Wilson began with the nineteenth-century tintype process, then made a digital negative for his luminous, hand-brushed print. With this methodology, Wilson references and challenges historical depictions of Indigenous Americans to forge what he calls "a reimagined vision of who we are as native people."

| Will Wilson (1969–), *Wilson–Kountoupes Clan, CIPX DAM* [Critical Indigenous Photographic Exchange, Denver Art Museum], Denver, Colorado, 2013. Platinum/palladium print. Courtesy of Artist: willwilson. photoshelter.com.

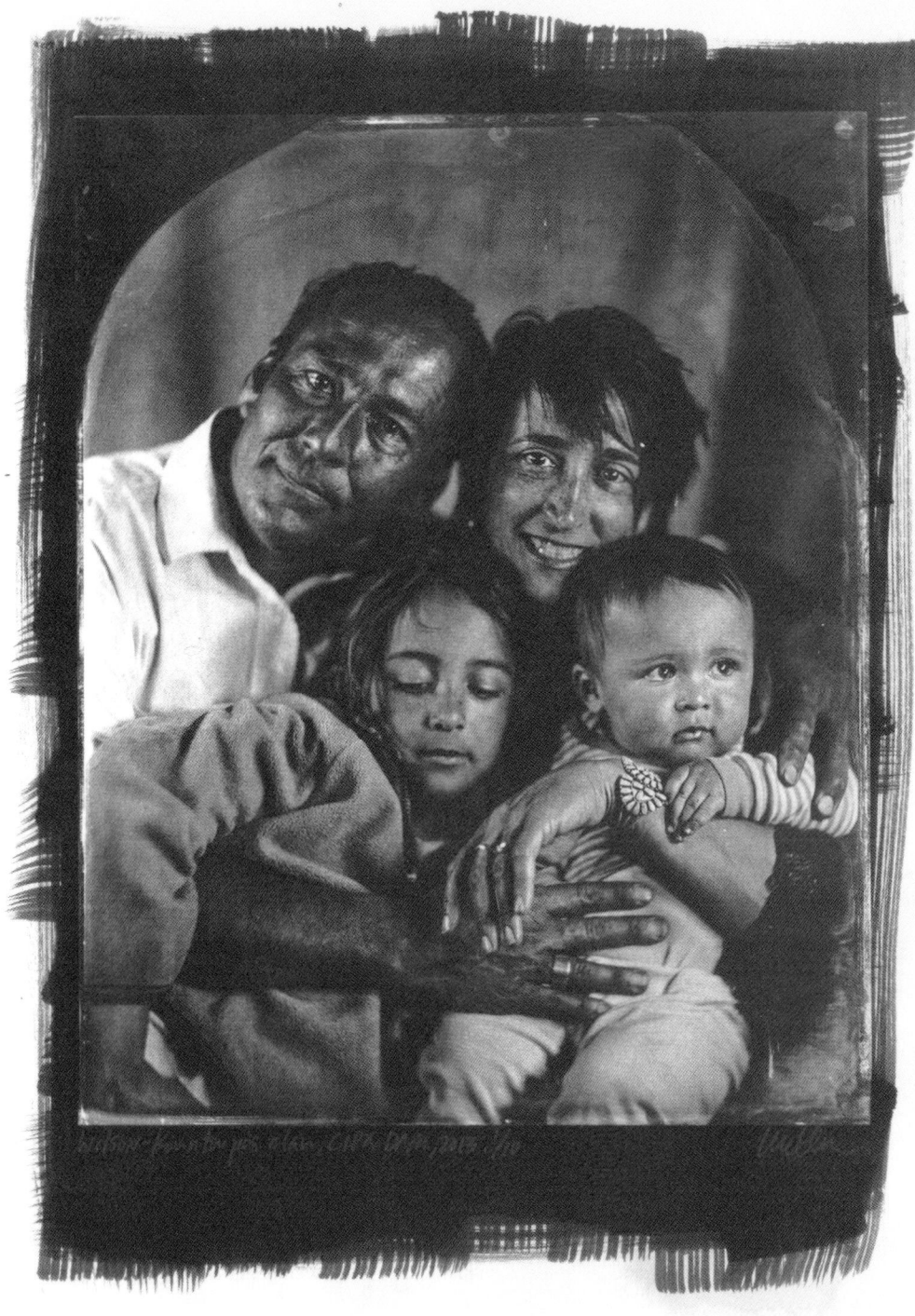

Robert Dawson photographed hundreds of public libraries throughout the United States for his project, *The Public Library: An American Commons.* This library in Death Valley is housed in a remote, dusty trailer, protected from the heat by a shade roof under the relentlessly sunny skies.

Robert Dawson (1950–), *Public Library, Death Valley National Park*, California, 2009. Inkjet print. *The Public Library: An American Commons* project. Courtesy of Robert Dawson.

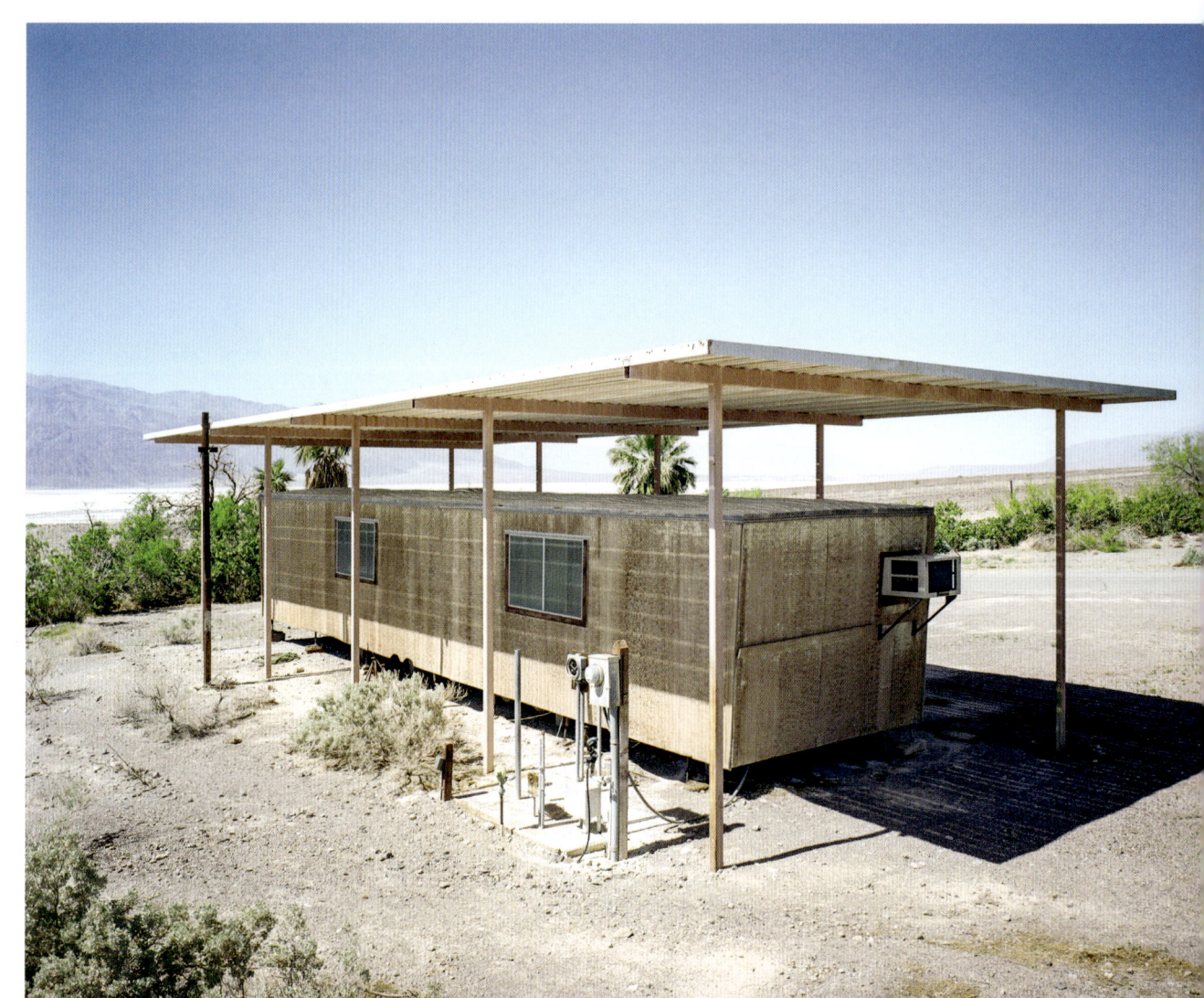

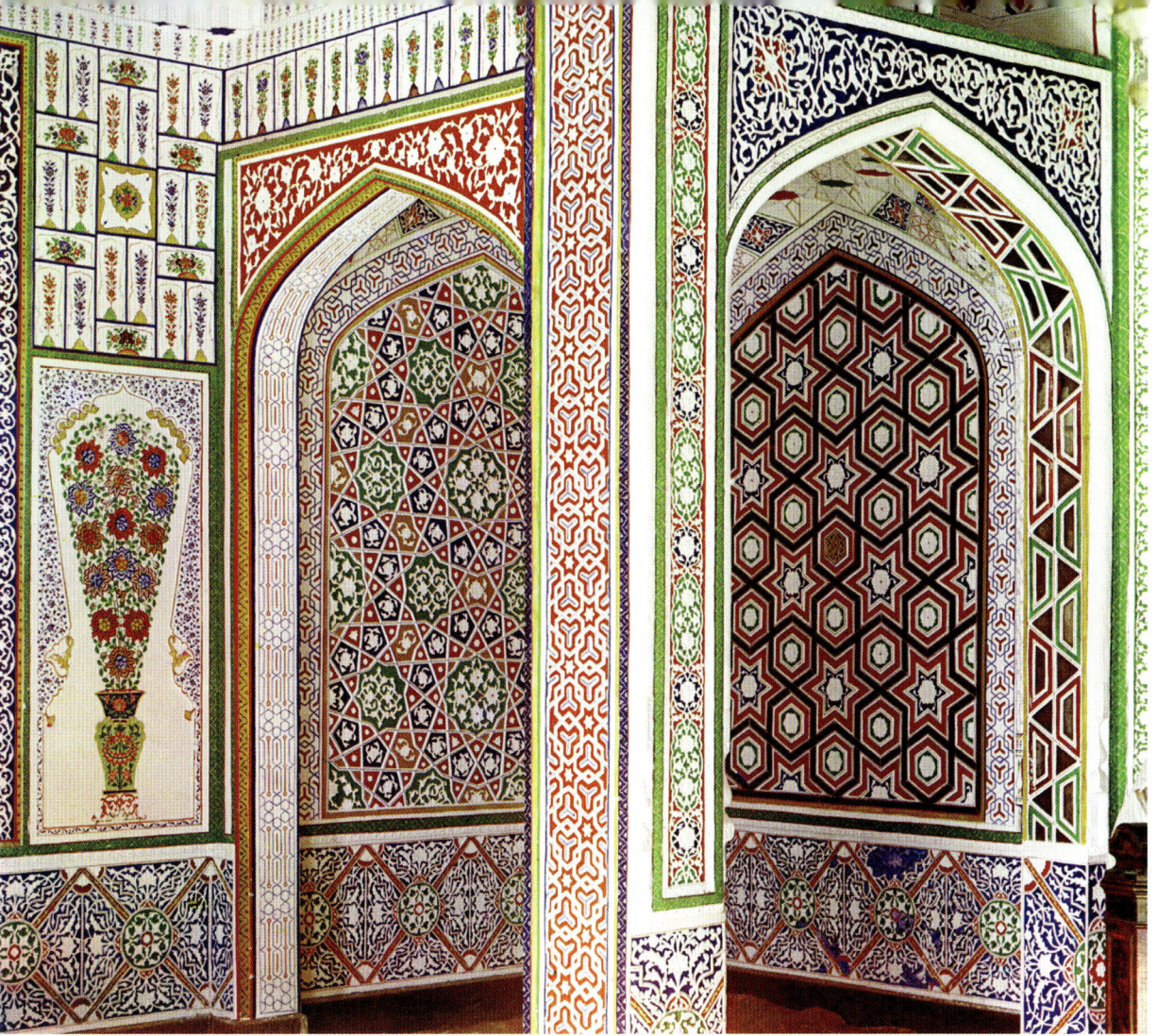

Sergeĭ Mikhaĭlovich Prokudin-Gorskiĭ documented the vast Russian Empire on glass plate negatives with red, blue, and green filters, using a camera of his own design. When layered and viewed through transmitted light, the negatives produce images in dazzling full color, such as this one of the kaleidoscopic tiles at the Emir of Bukhara's country palace.

Sergeĭ Mikhaĭlovich Prokudin-Gorskiĭ (1863–1944), *Mosaics on the Walls in the Country Palace of the Bukhara Emir*, near Bukhara, Russia (now Uzbekistan), between 1905 and 1915. Glass negatives. Digital color rendering and retouching by Walt Frankhauser, WalterStudio, 2005–2020.

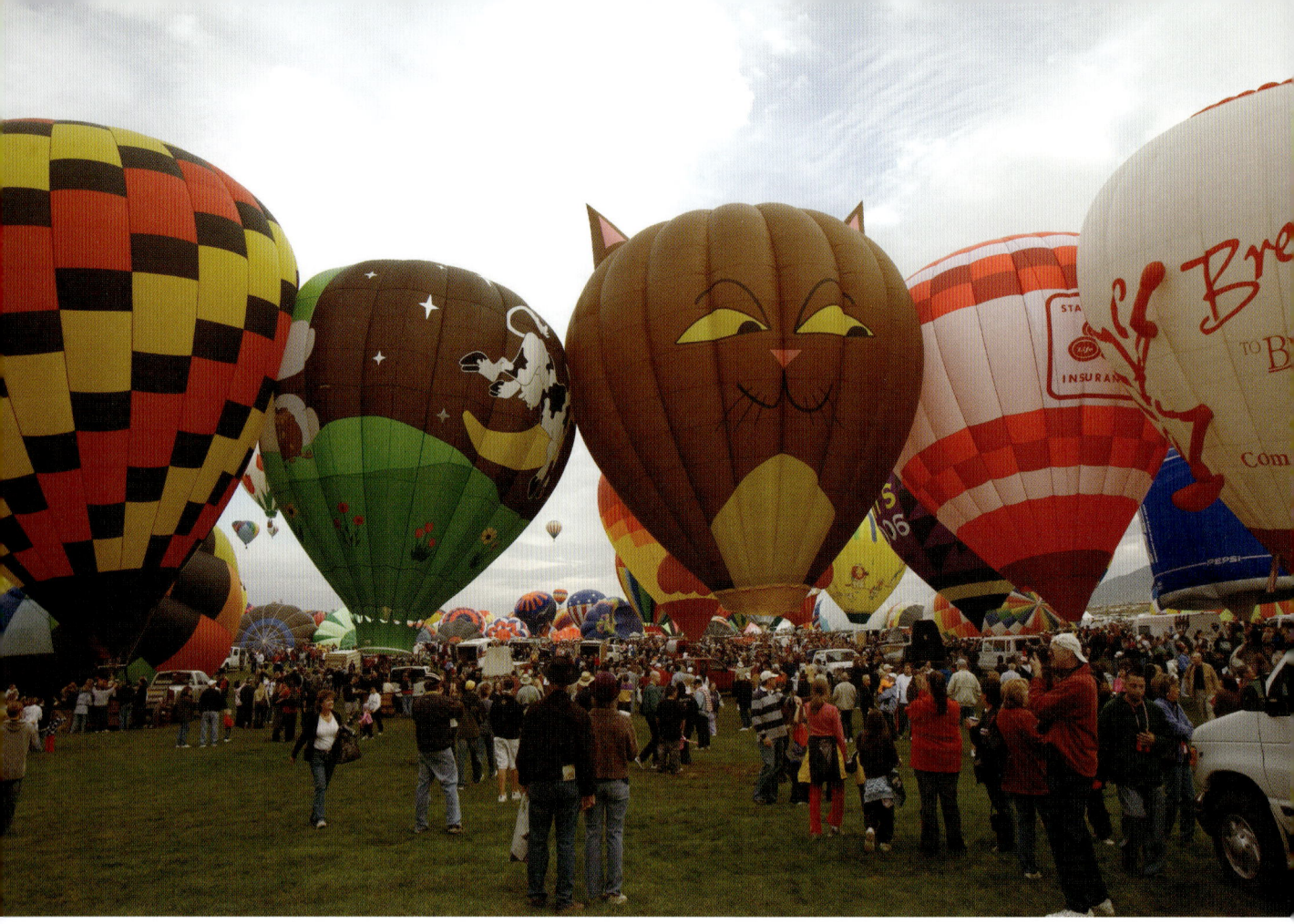

As part of her ongoing journey to document activity and architecture in each state, Carol M. Highsmith captures landmark buildings, breathtaking landscapes, and community events. Here, an enormous cat balloon giving a sideways glance to its competition infuses her shot of the annual Albuquerque International Balloon Fiesta with a little humor.

Carol M. Highsmith (1946–), *Annual Balloon Festival*, Albuquerque, New Mexico, 2006. Digital photograph.

John T. Daniels (1873–1948), *First Flight*, Kitty Hawk, North Carolina, 1903. Glass negative.

This photograph, taken by John T. Daniels with equipment set up by the Wright brothers, captures on a glass plate the exhilarating moment when Orville (piloting) and Wilbur's (running alongside) dreams of flight were realized. After several years of experimentation, on December 17, 1903, they achieved the first powered, controlled, and sustained flight, which spanned 120 feet and lasted twelve seconds.

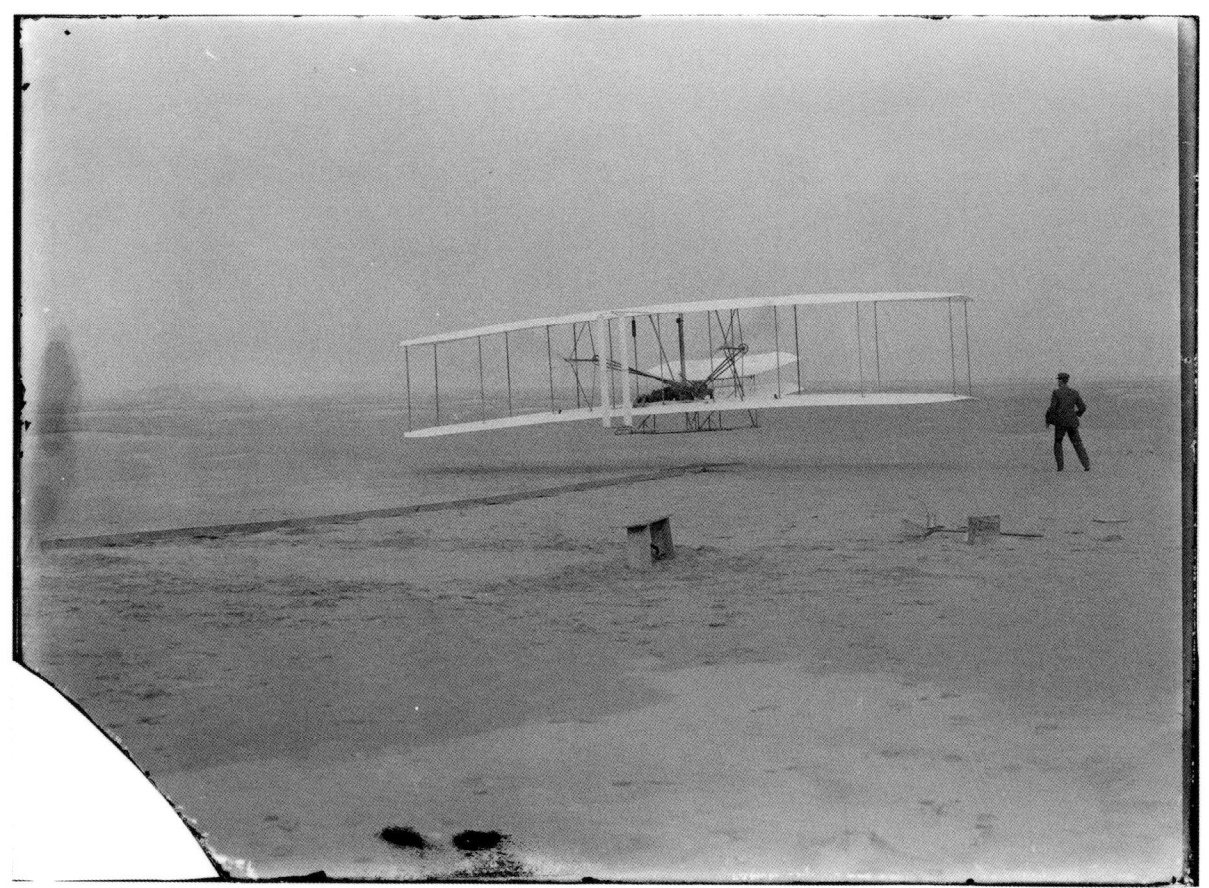

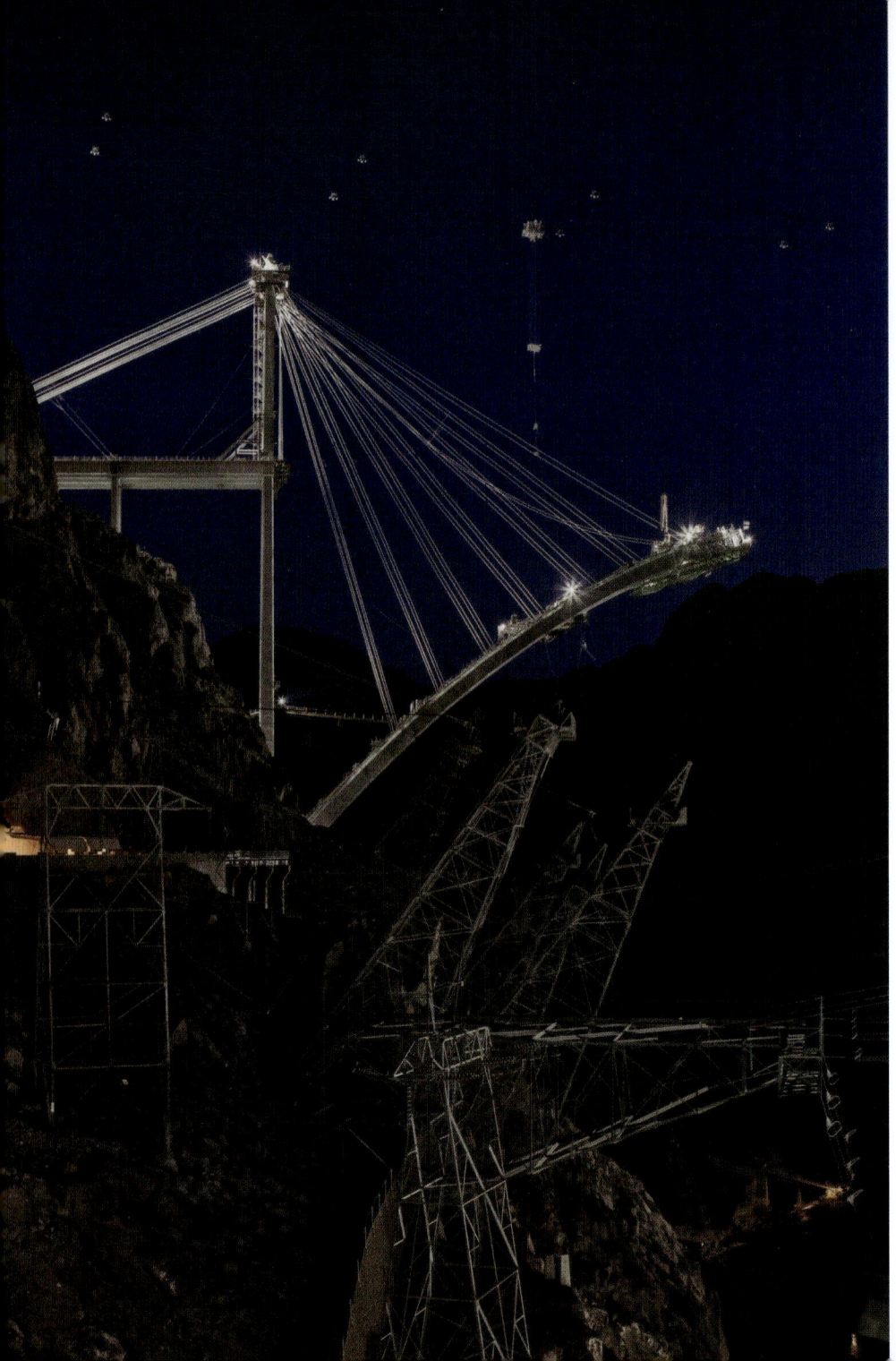

For two years, Jamey Stillings documented the construction of the Mike O'Callaghan–Pat Tillman Memorial Bridge, which spans the Colorado River between Arizona and Nevada. This stunning twilight photograph invites viewers to contemplate what Stillings describes as "the juncture of nature and technology on a scale that is both grand and human."

Jamey Stillings (1955–), *Arizona Arch Segment. #1282*, 2009. Inkjet print. © 2009 Jamey Stillings.

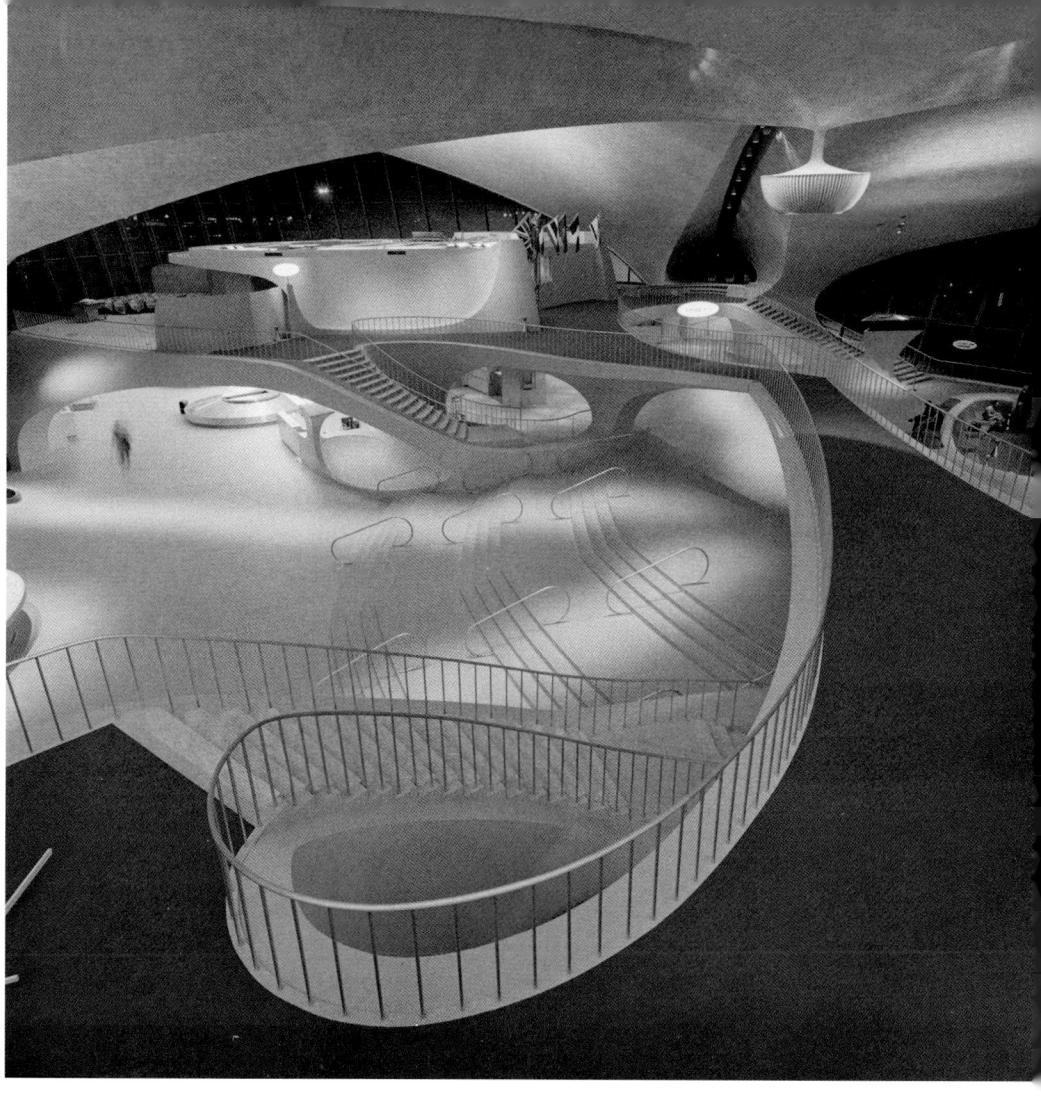

Balthazar Korab
(1926–2013), *Interior,
Trans World Airlines
Terminal, John F.
Kennedy Airport*, New
York City, 1956. Film
negative.

Celebrated architectural photographer Balthazar Korab
took some of his most iconic photographs while working
for architect Eero Saarinen. Here, Korab uses a disorienting
perspective reminiscent of the interlocking patterns of
an M. C. Escher illustration to highlight the unlikely curved
concrete lines of the former TWA terminal in New York.

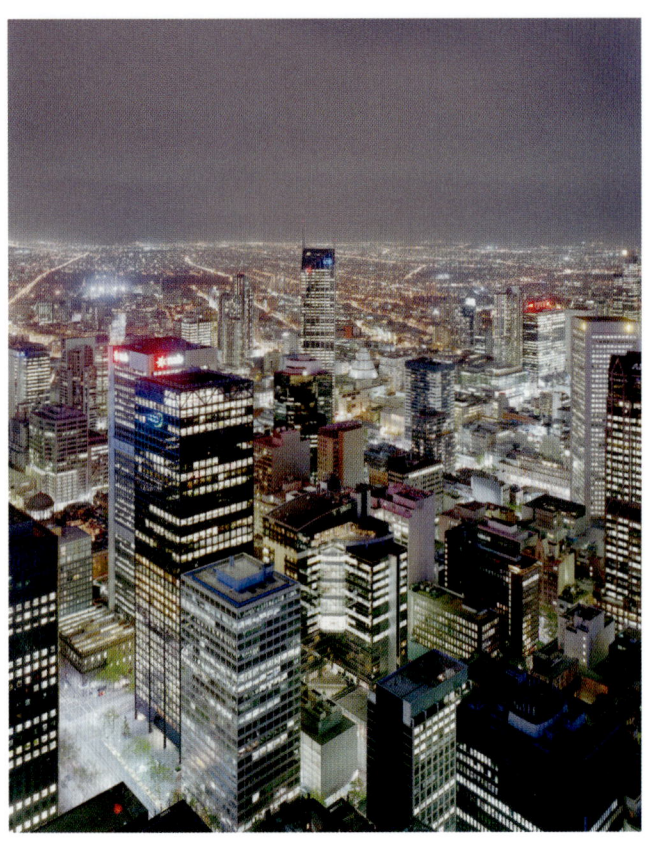
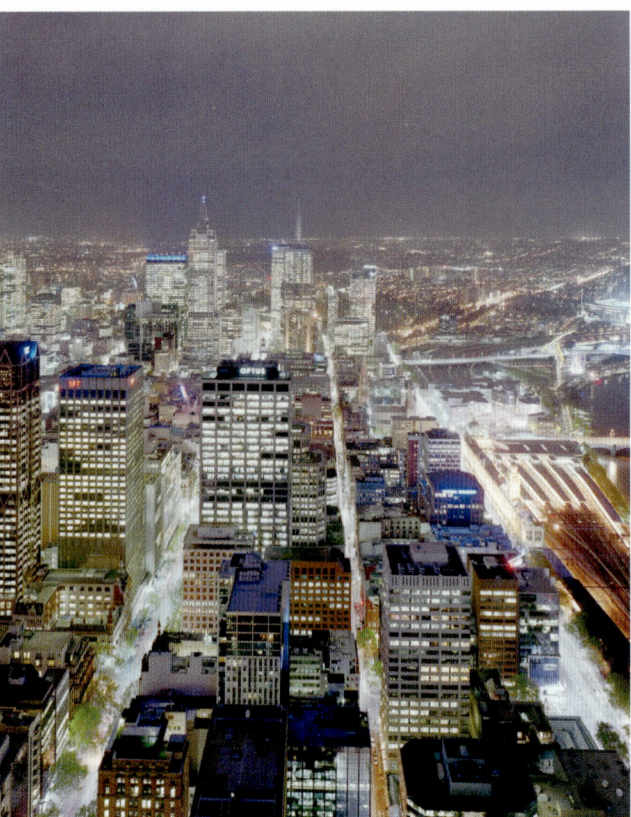

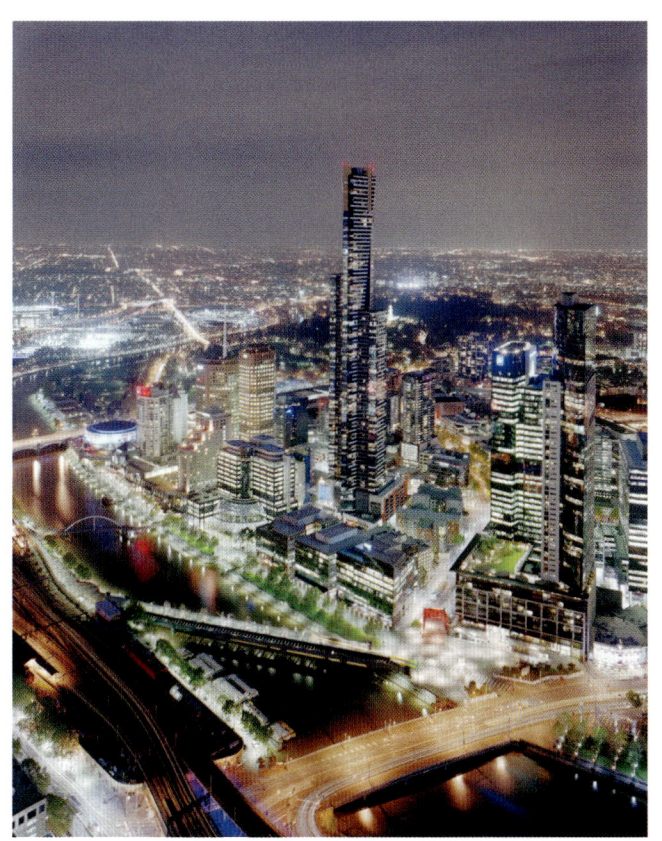

This Australian cityscape glows beautiful and bright thanks to David Stephenson's mastery of long exposure. At the same time, the electric hum of the sprawling metropolis—which Stephenson calls "energy flow"—hints at the eventual repercussions of humanity's monumental altering of the environment.

David Stephenson (1955–), *Melbourne Looking East from Rialto Tower 1, 2, and 3*, 2005. Inkjet print. *Light Cities* portfolio. Courtesy of the artist and Julie Saul Projects, New York.

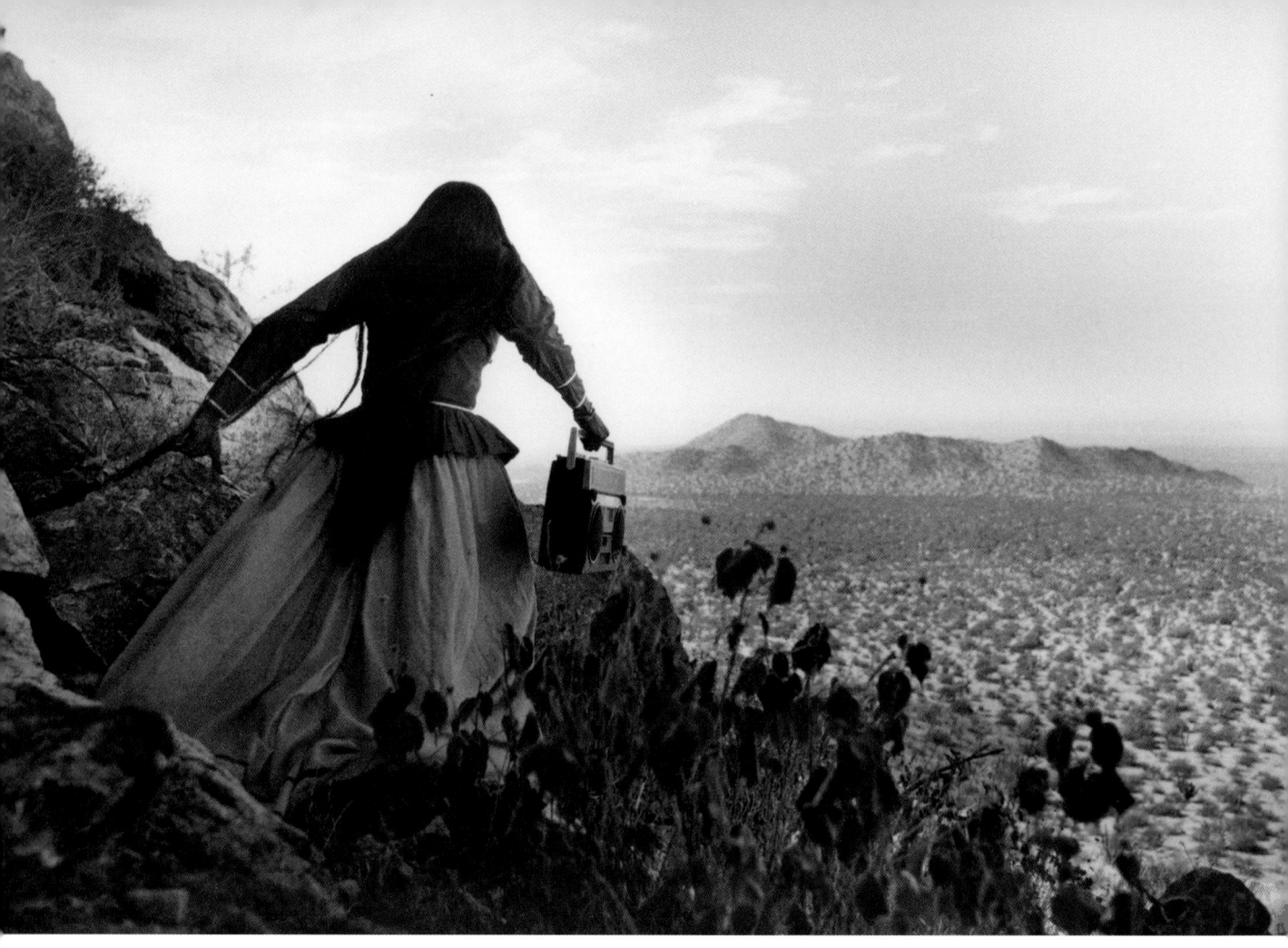

A mysterious figure, her back to the camera, appears to walk between worlds as she is poised over an expansive desert, boom box in hand. Graciela Iturbide took this photograph while documenting the indigenous Seri people in the Sonoran Desert, witnessing the blending of traditional and modern ways of life.

Graciela Iturbide (1942–), *Mujer Ángel (Angel Woman)*, Sonoran Desert, Mexico, 1979. Gelatin silver print. Courtesy of Graciela Iturbide.

Brian Adams (1985–), *Marie Rexford Outside of Her Home in Kaktovik, Alaska, Surrounded by Bowhead Whale That She is Helping to Prepare for the Village's Thanksgiving Day Feast*, 2015. Inkjet print. *I Am Inuit* series. Courtesy of Brian Adams.

Pink and black whale meat stands out against white snow in Iñupiat photographer Brian Adams's portrait of Marie Rexford. Adorned in a blue floral coat, Rexford is readying the community's Thanksgiving meal, maintaining tradition amidst a changing climate.

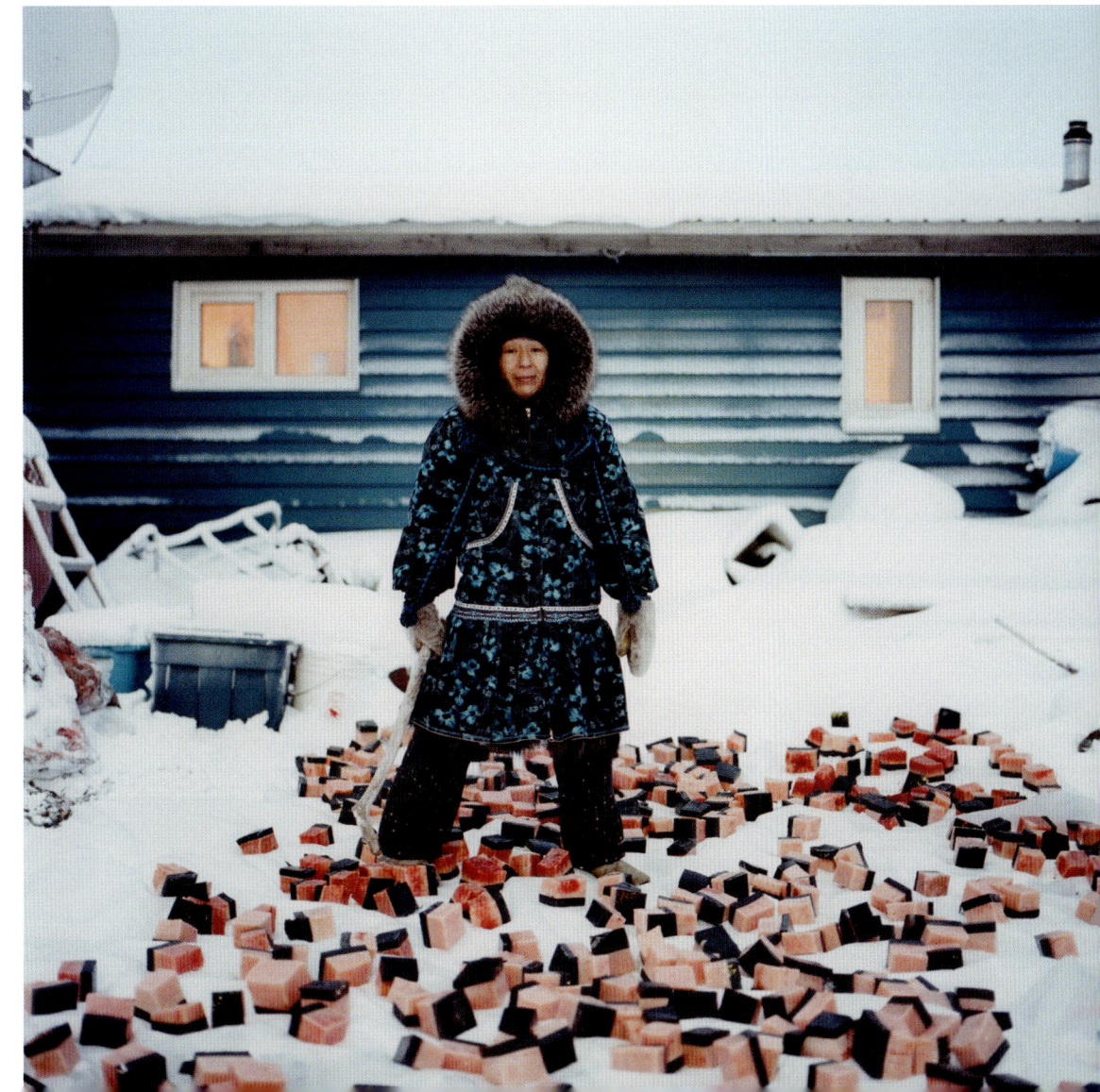

Black sanitation workers in Memphis bore signs declaring "I AM A MAN" during their strike for safer working conditions after two garbage collectors died on the job. Ernest C. Withers captured both the collective—the seemingly infinite signs, the men standing together as a wall—and the individual—each person's dress, pose, and expression—in his photograph of a momentous civil rights protest.

Ernest C. Withers (1922–2007), *Sanitation Workers Assemble in Front of Clayborn Temple for a Solidarity March*, Memphis, Tennessee, 1968. Gelatin silver print. © Dr. Ernest C. Withers Sr., courtesy of the Withers Family Trust.

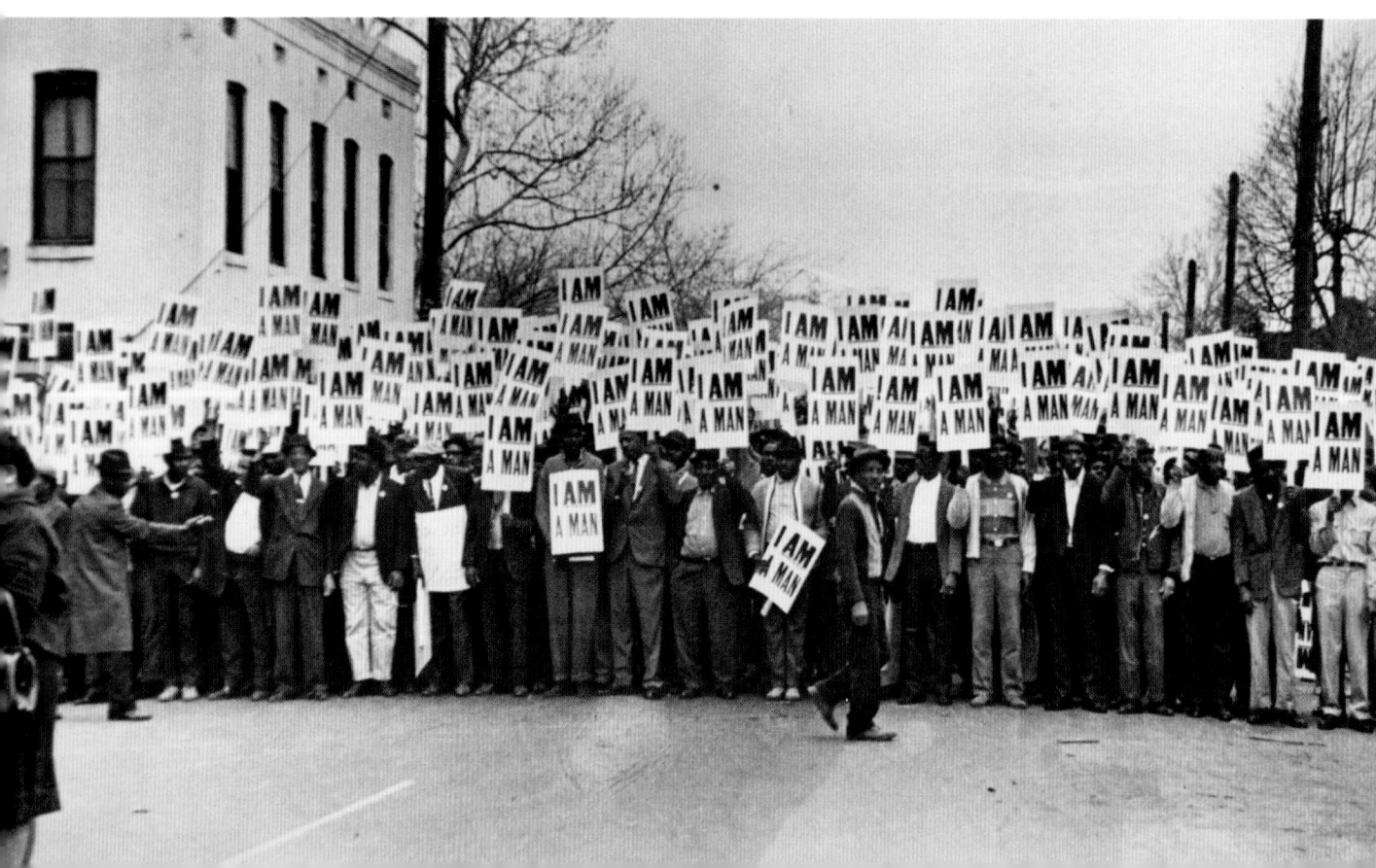

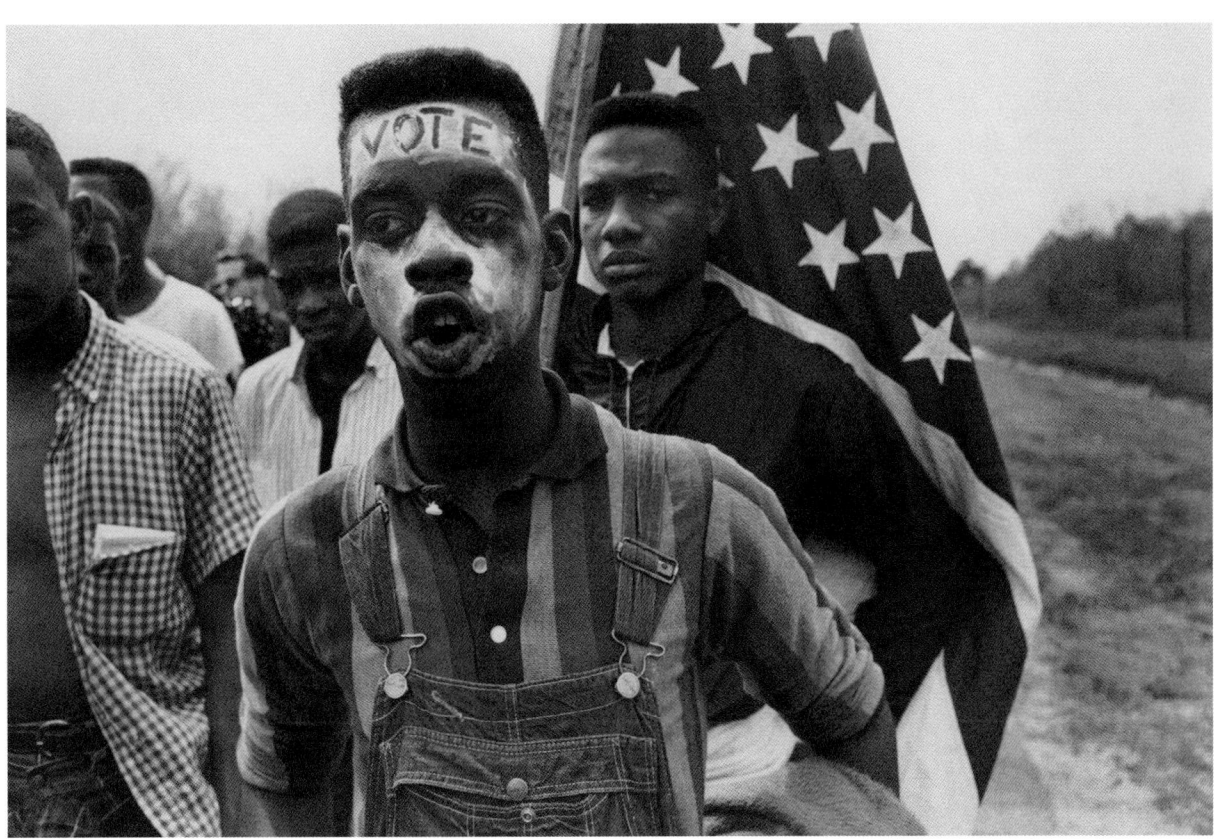

In Bruce Davidson's photograph of voting rights protestors marching from Selma to Montgomery, Alabama, Bobby Simmons exhorts bystanders to "VOTE," the letters written in sunscreen on his forehead. The unidentified man behind him looks directly at Davidson's camera with purpose and, perhaps, some trepidation.

Bruce Davidson (1933–), *Civil Rights Demonstrators March from Selma to Montgomery*, Alabama, 1965. Gelatin silver print. Courtesy of Bruce Davidson / Magnum Photos.

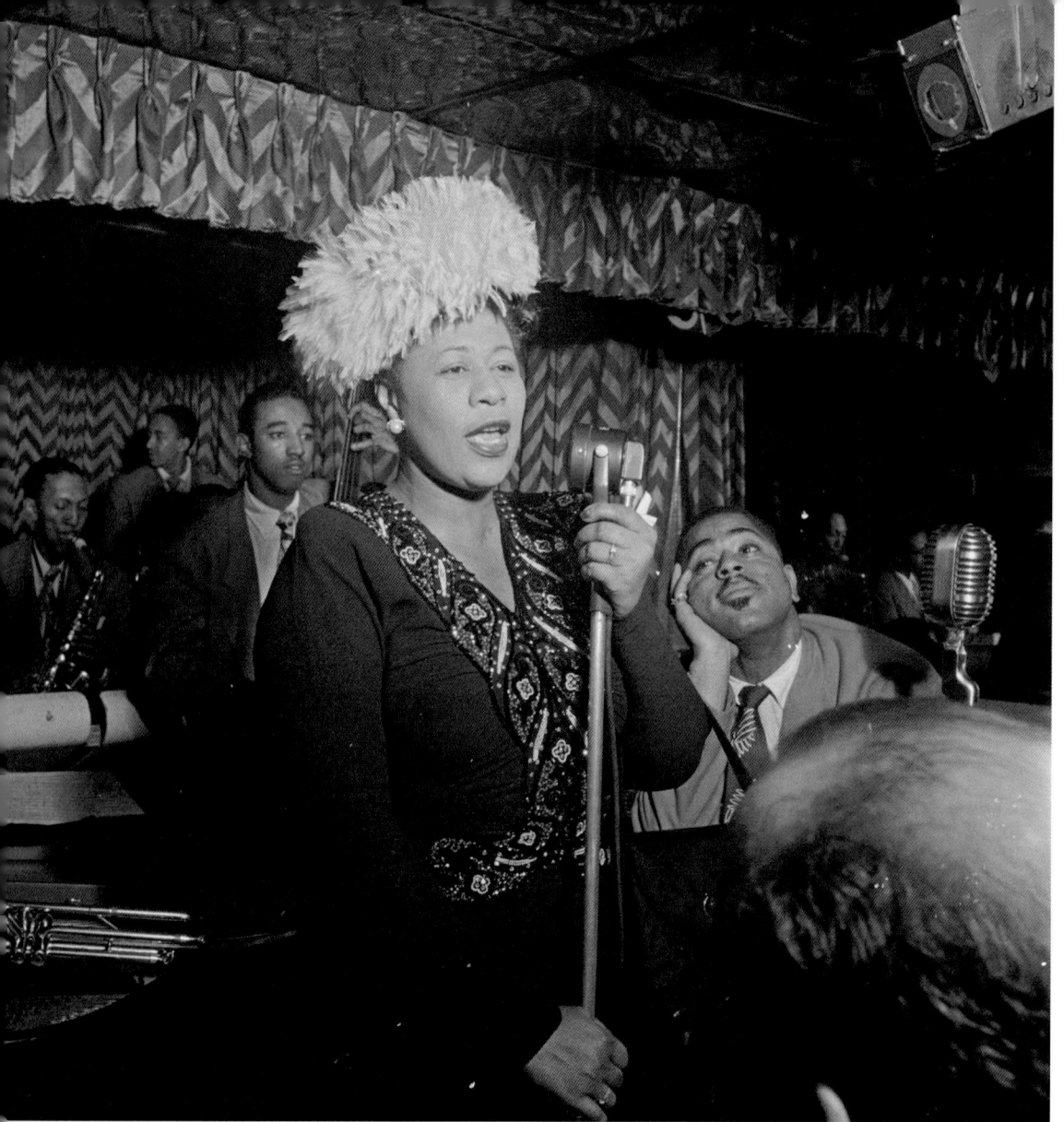

William P. Gottlieb, who interviewed and photographed numerous jazz musicians and singers for the *Washington Post*, *DownBeat*, and *Record Changer*, had a talent for capturing his subjects' unique personalities. In this photograph, master trumpeter Dizzy Gillespie gazes adoringly as "First Lady of Song" Ella Fitzgerald sings at Club Downbeat on Fifty-second Street in Manhattan.

William P. Gottlieb (1917–2006), *Ella Fitzgerald and Dizzy Gillespie*, New York City, 1947. Film negative.

Called the "First Lady of Radio," Mary Margaret McBride's radio career spanned more than four decades and her exceptionally popular shows, aimed at American housewives, reached between six and eight million listeners daily. This candid shot captures the emotional moment after McBride's final sign off for ABC.

Photographer unidentified, *Mary Margaret McBride at the End of Her Final Broadcast*, New York City, 1954. Photographic print. Courtesy of Michel P. Haggerty, Esq.

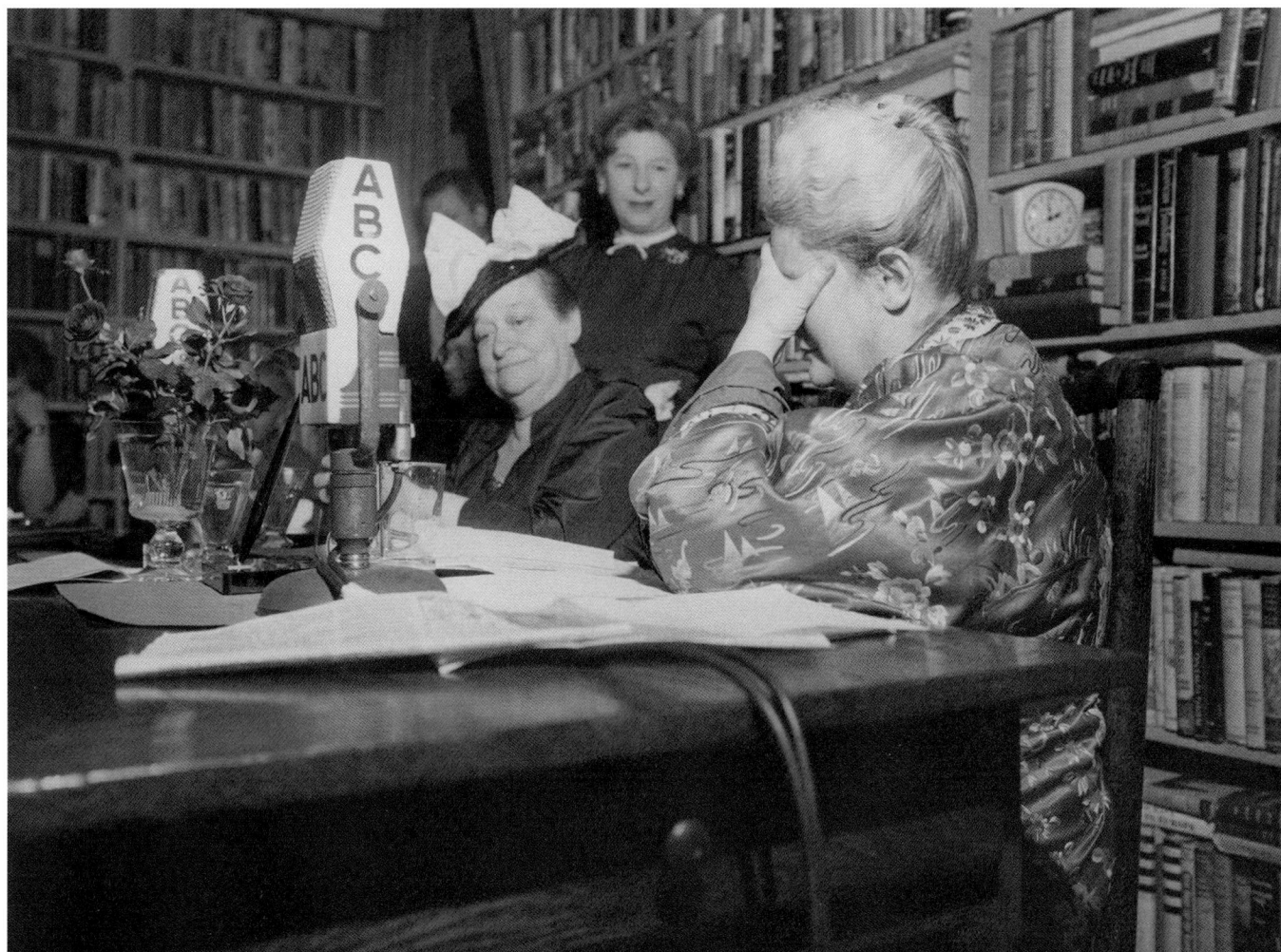

Introduced by the Mexican government to ease tensions among the indigenous Mixe in the Sierra Norte of Oaxaca, basketball is an important part of community life. This photo, taken by Alicia Vera in Santa María Tlahuitoltepec, depicts young Mixe women playing in the pouring rain, gracefully lofting the ball toward the net.

Alicia Vera (1986–), *Team Gubby Plays Against Las Combinadas de Tlahui During a Patron Saint Festival in Santa María Tlahuitoltepec*, Oaxaca, Mexico, 2018. Inkjet print. Courtesy of Alicia Vera.

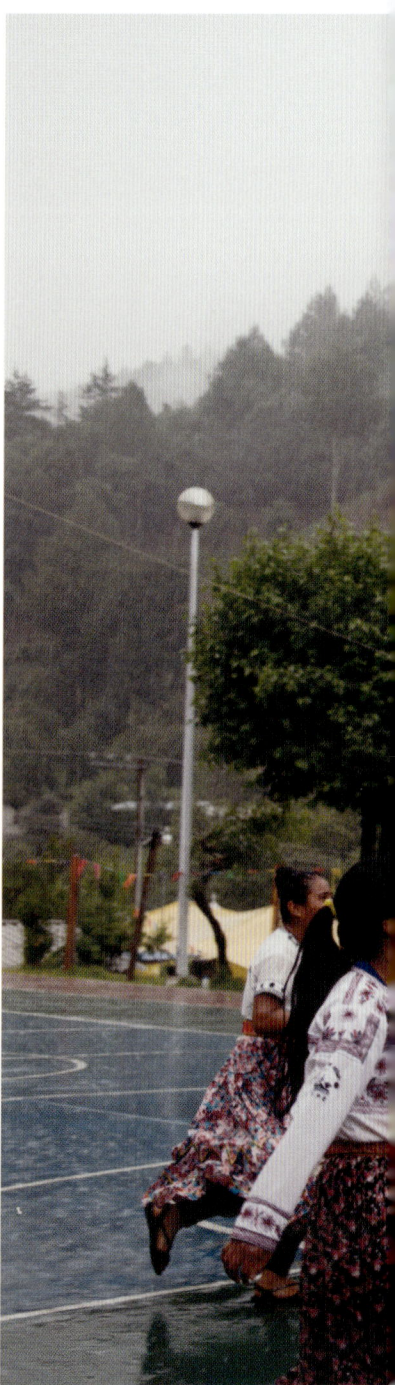

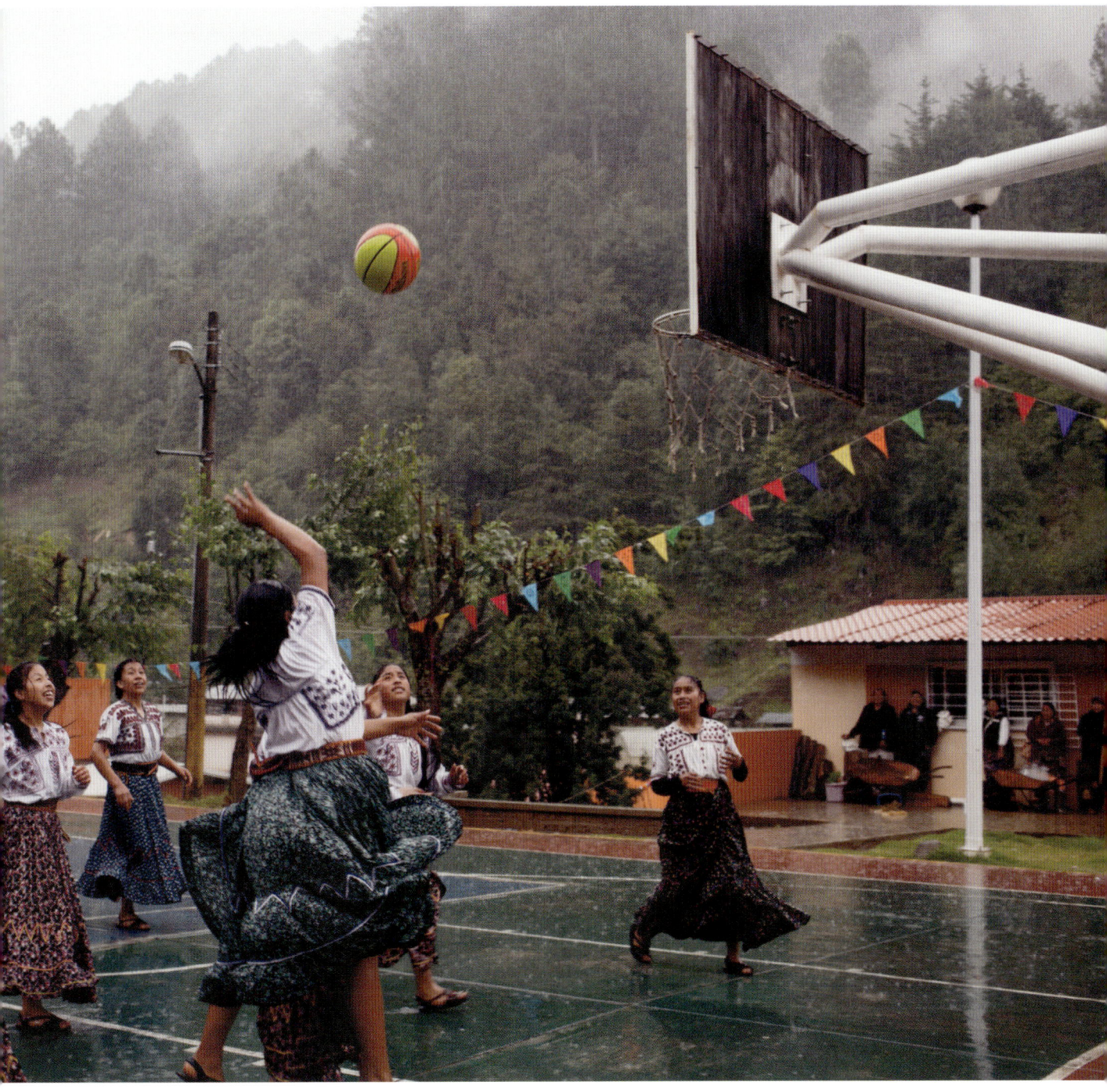

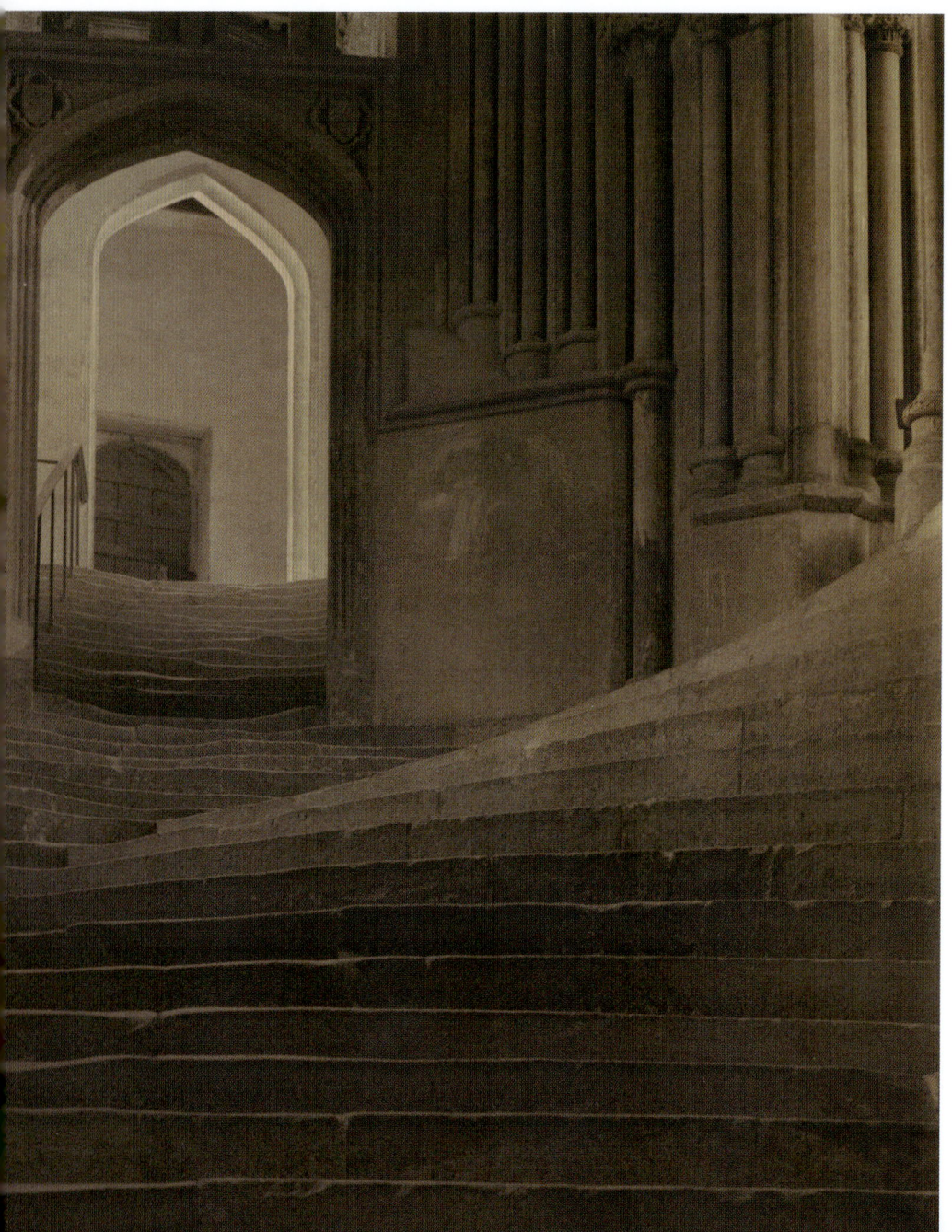

A celebrated photographer of medieval cathedrals, Frederick H. Evans preferred the rich tonal range of platinum prints and used them to expertly capture the light, textures, and spiritual air of each structure. He was particularly drawn to "this superb mounting of the steps" at the thirteenth-century Wells Cathedral in Somerset.

Frederick H. Evans (1853–1943), "A Sea of Steps," Wells Cathedral, Stairs to Chapter House and Bridge to Vicar's Close, Somerset, England, 1902. Platinum print.

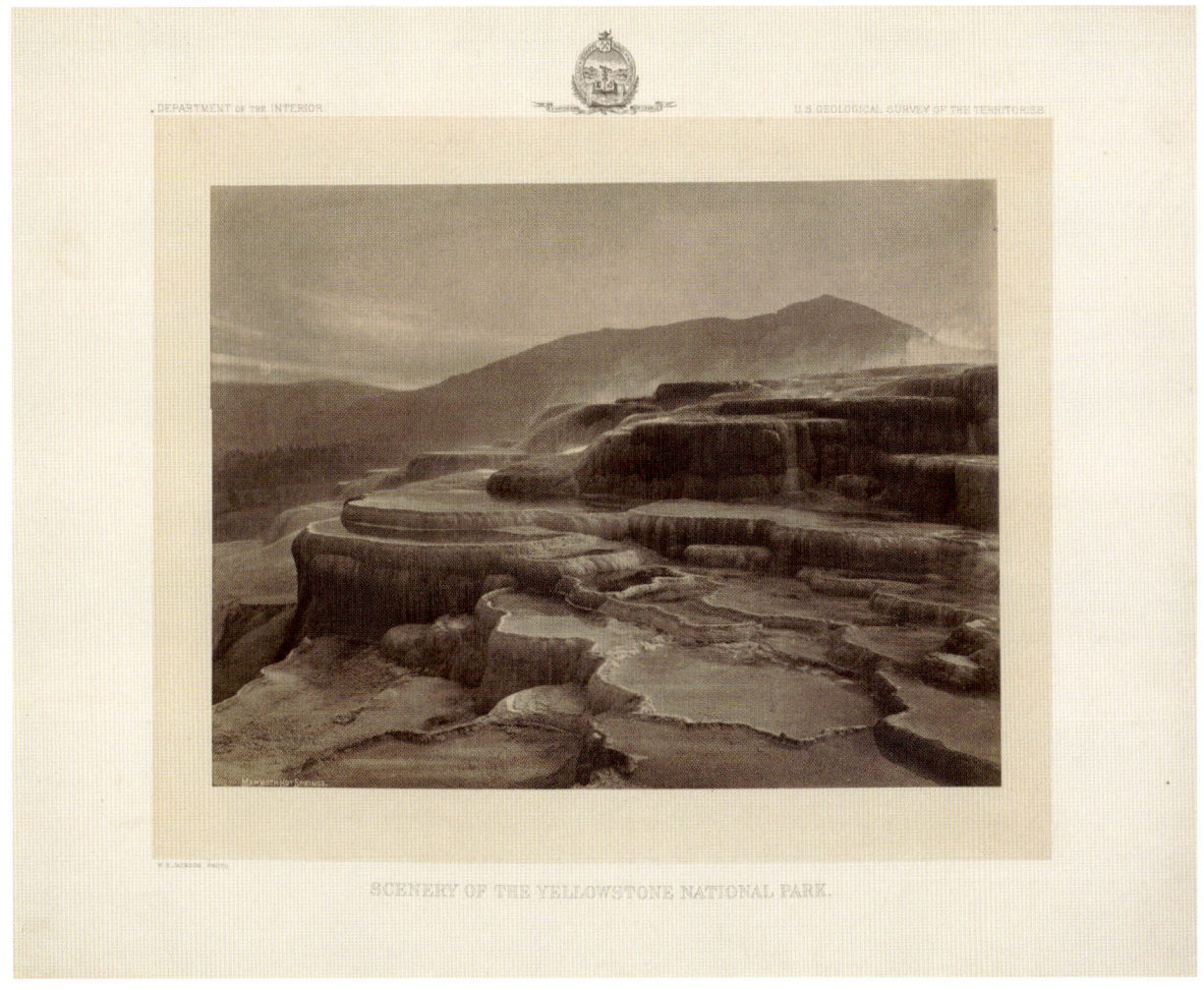

DEPARTMENT OF THE INTERIOR.

U.S. GEOLOGICAL SURVEY OF THE TERRITORIES.

SCENERY OF THE YELLOWSTONE NATIONAL PARK.

William Henry Jackson (1843–1942), *Mammoth Hot Springs*, Wyoming, 1872. Albumen silver print. On Department of the Interior's US Geological Survey of the Territories, Scenery of the Yellowstone National Park mount.

William Henry Jackson shot this atmospheric photograph of the steam-shrouded terraces of Yellowstone's Mammoth Hot Springs while part of an 1871–1872 survey of the western territories directed by geologist Ferdinand V. Hayden. This government survey was one of many that integrated visual and scientific documentation.

When government photographer Marion Post Wolcott pointed out that she had worked for two years with hardly a break, her boss sent her to his vacation house in Vermont. During that snowy visit to New England, she made some of her signature images, including this magical nighttime scene of snow blanketing a street in the center of town.

Marion Post Wolcott (1910–1990), *Snowy Night*, Woodstock, Vermont, 1940. Safety film negative.

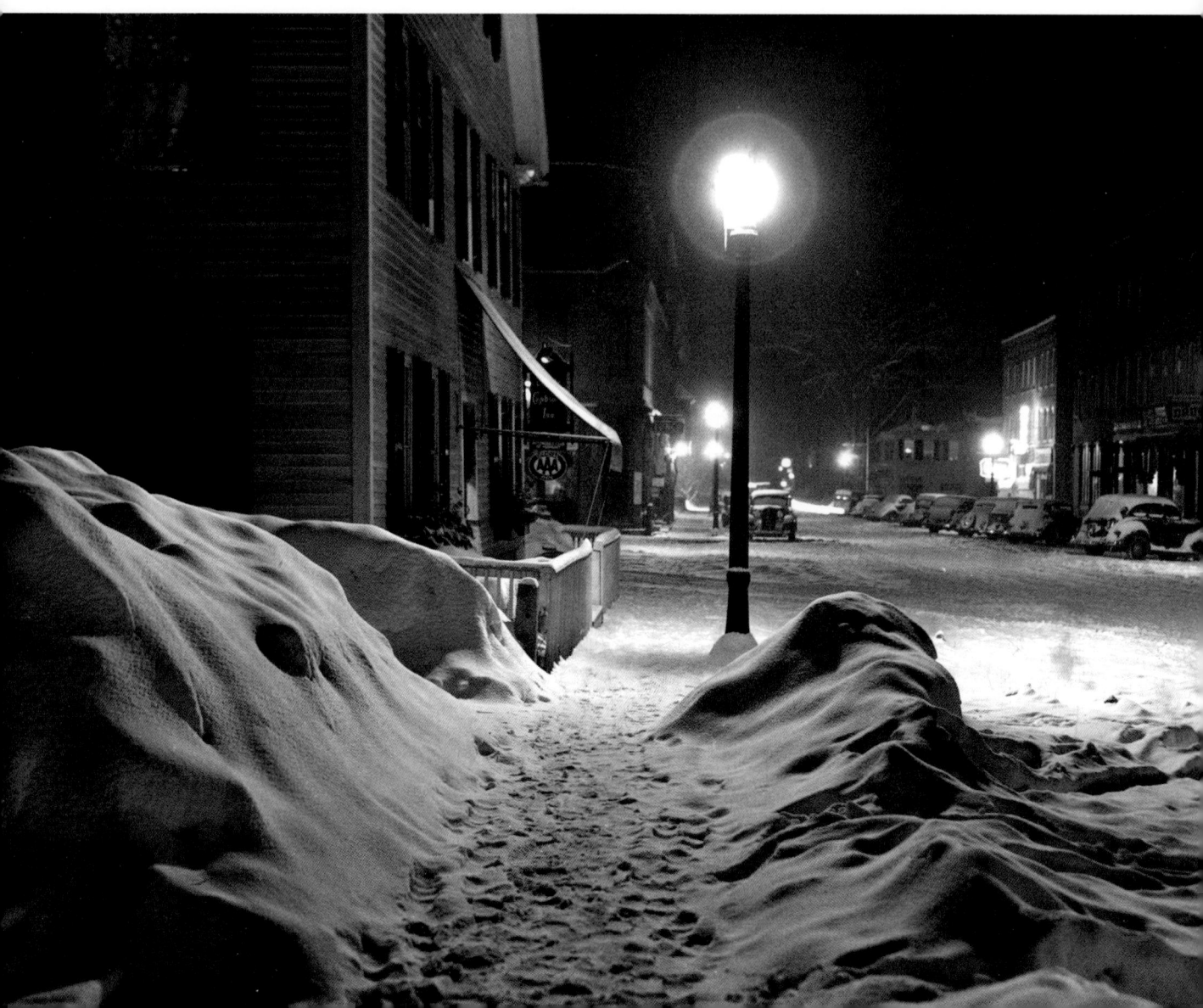

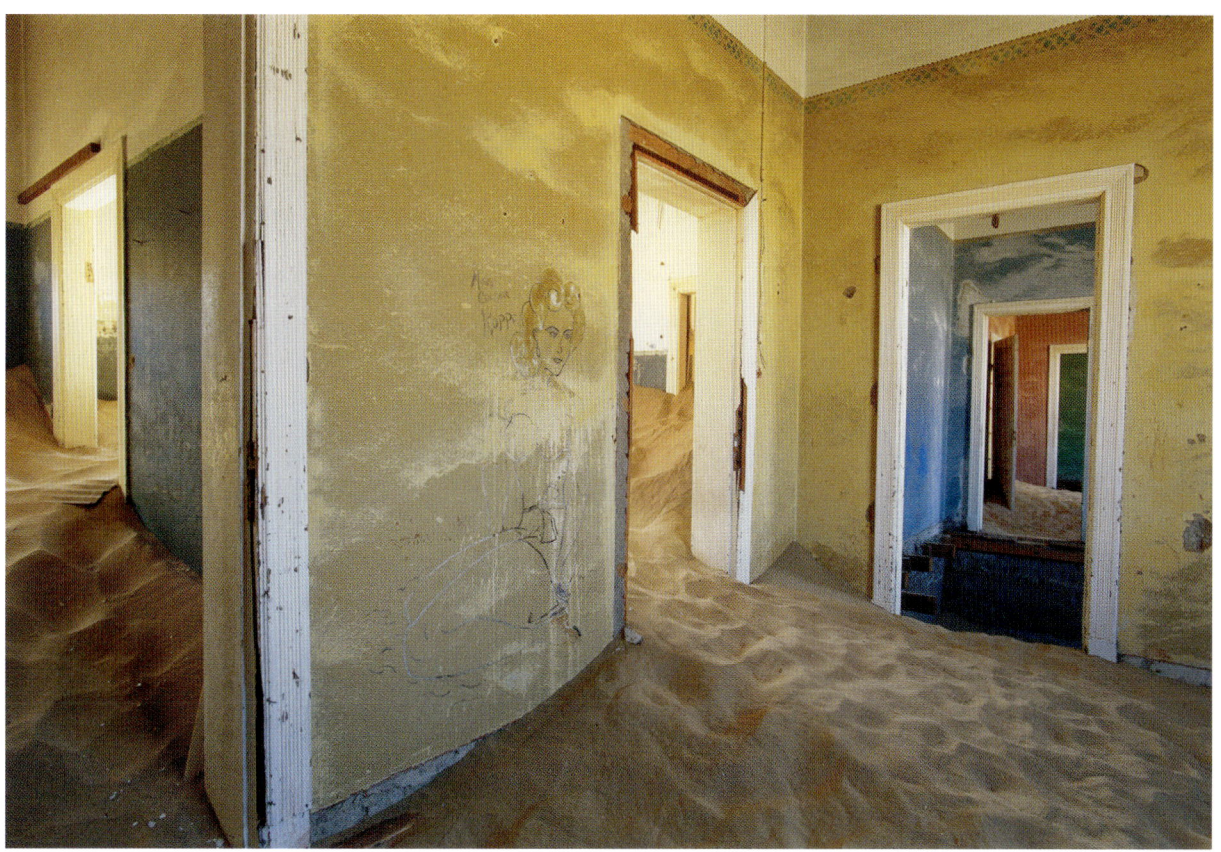

Known especially for his aerial photography, George Steinmetz stayed on the ground for this shot of sand dunes encroaching on the interior of an abandoned building in the long-deserted diamond mining town of Kolmanskop in the Namib Desert. Steinmetz's eerie photograph captures the futility of imposing European architecture on a desert environment.

George Steinmetz (1957–), *Abandoned Building*, Kolmanskop, Namibia, 2002. Inkjet print. Courtesy of George Steinmetz.

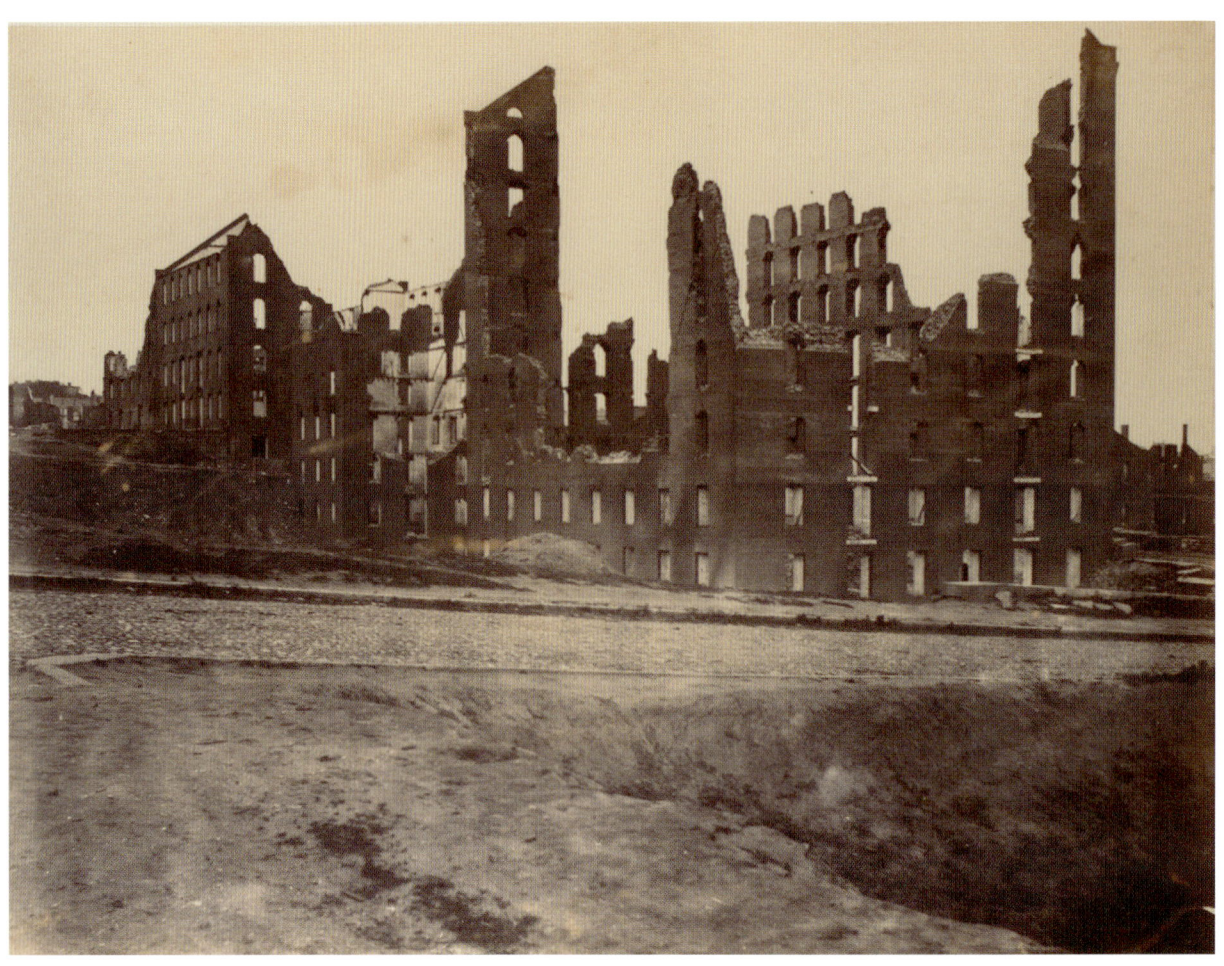

Andrew J. Russell (1830–1902), *Ruins of Large Flouring Mill*, Richmond, Virginia, May 1865. Albumen silver print. United States Military Railroad Photographic Album.

Captain Andrew J. Russell was one of the rare officers who also served as a photographer during the Civil War. His stark photograph of the shell of a Richmond flour mill, taken after Confederates burned the city to keep supplies out of Union hands, appears in an album he made memorializing the war for General Winfield Scott Hancock.

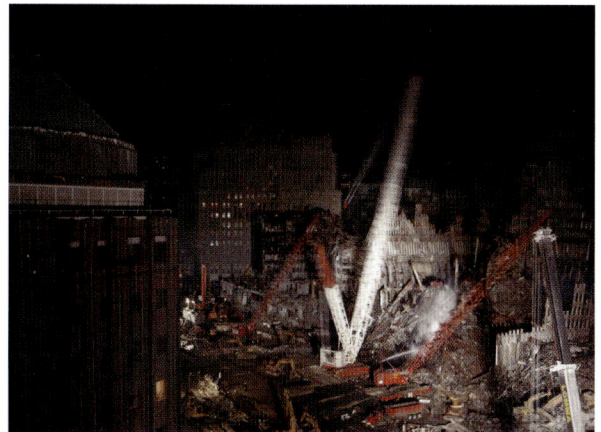 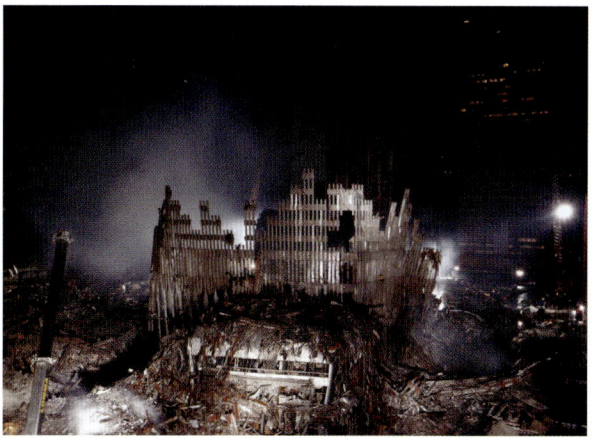

The only photographer permitted access to Ground Zero after the terrorist attacks on the World Trade Center on September 11, 2001, Joel Meyerowitz took thousands of shots documenting the recovery efforts. In this haunting nighttime diptych, work lights catch twisted beams while also illuminating the persistent dust in the sky, cranes a blur of motion.

Joel Meyerowitz (1938–), *Looking Northeast from the World Financial Center, across West Street to the World Trade Center Site*, New York City, 2001. Dye coupler print. © Joel Meyerowitz.

Polish-American photographer Theodor Horydczak made his living documenting the architecture and social life of the Washington metropolitan area from the 1920s to the 1940s. His technically sophisticated photographs include views of neighborhoods, such as the seemingly endless zig-zags of this new development in Northwest DC.

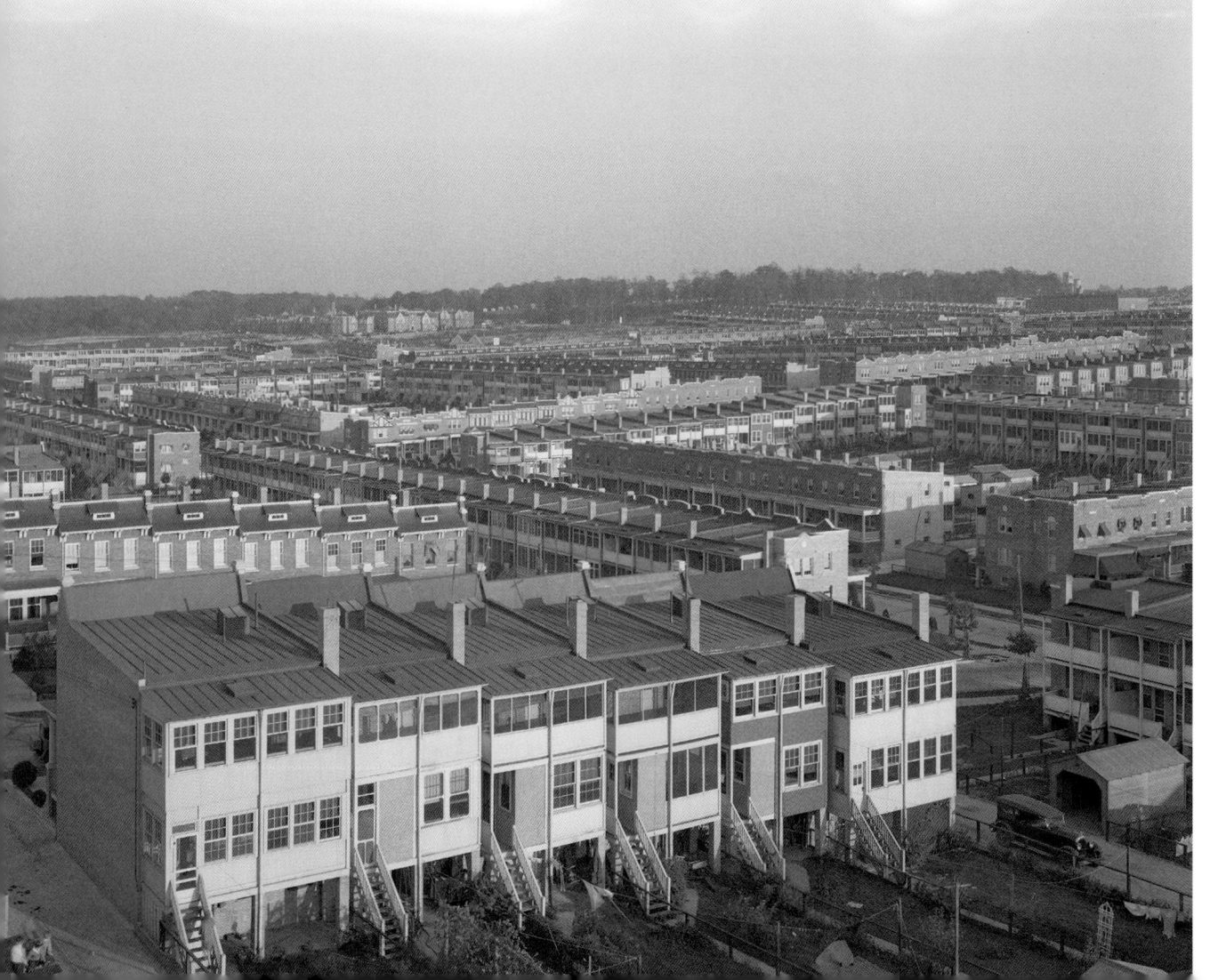

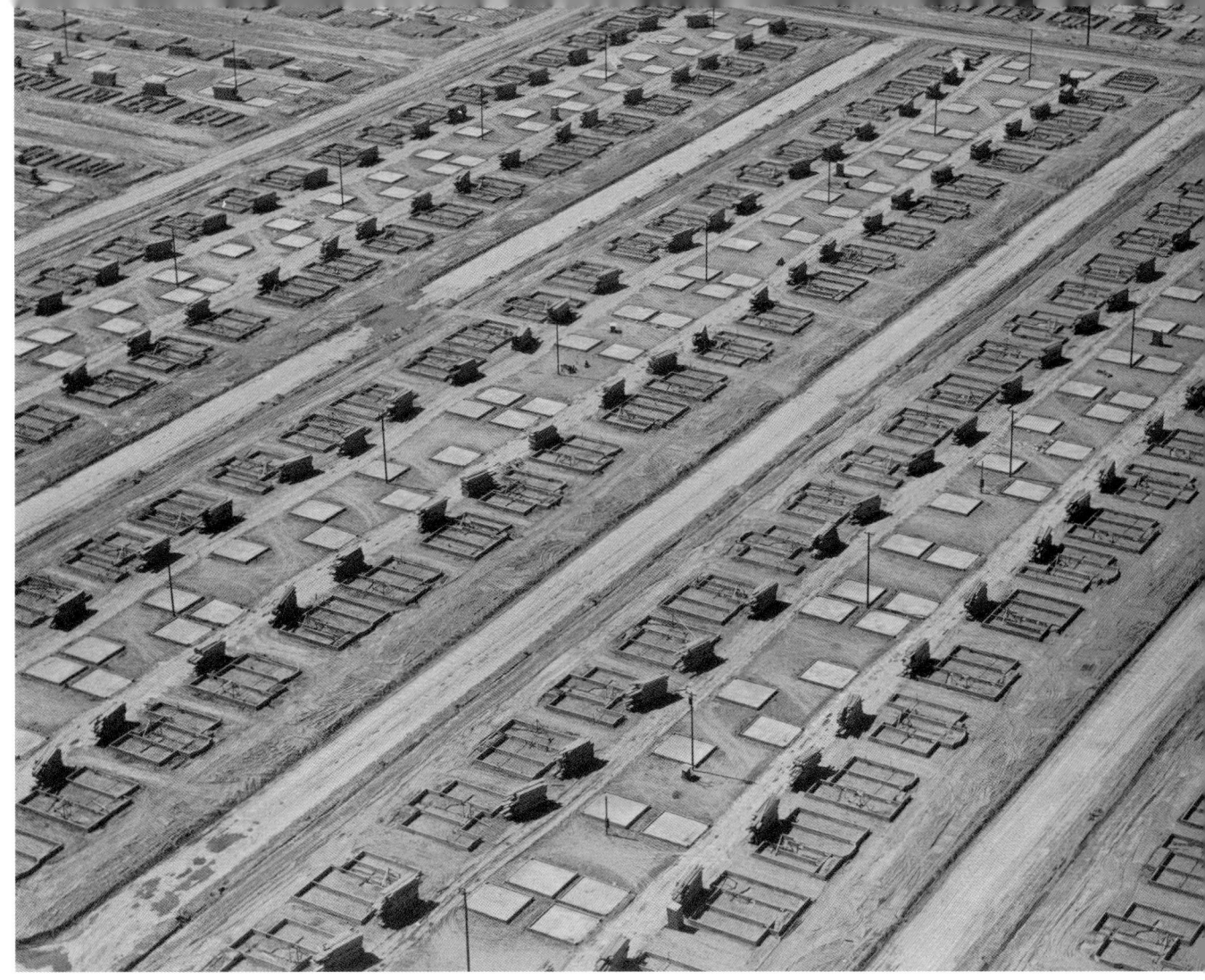

| William Garnett (1916–2006), *Mass Production Housing*, Lakewood, California, 1950. Gelatin silver print. Courtesy of Jay M. Garnett and Nancy J. Garnett Trust.

As a photographer for the United States Army Signal Corps, William Garnett became enamored with the way the landscape looked from above. He earned his pilot's license and spent his career capturing the patterns of the earth from the air, such as the repeating shapes made by the prefabricated materials of this new housing development.

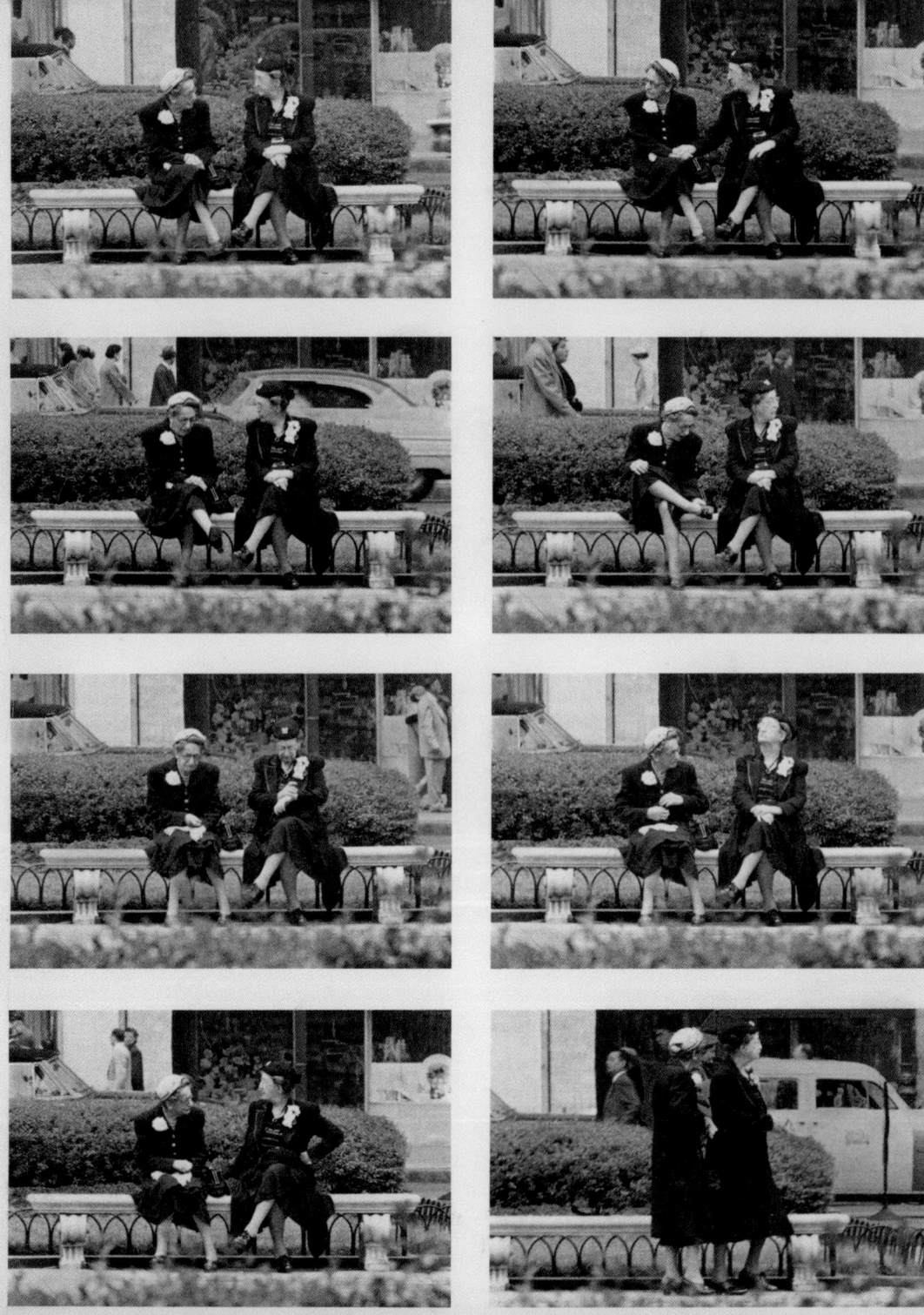

Essentially unknown during his lifetime, Anthony Angel created a sweeping visual record of New York City during the mid-twentieth century. Many of his photographs depict candid moments, like this series of two women on a park bench. An entire story can be imagined in their gestures: from clasping hands to checking a shoe, a watch, and then getting up and going on their way.

Anthony Angel (born Angelo A. Rizzuto, 1906–1967), *Composite Photograph of Eight Images Showing Two Women on Park Bench*, New York City, 1952. Gelatin silver print.

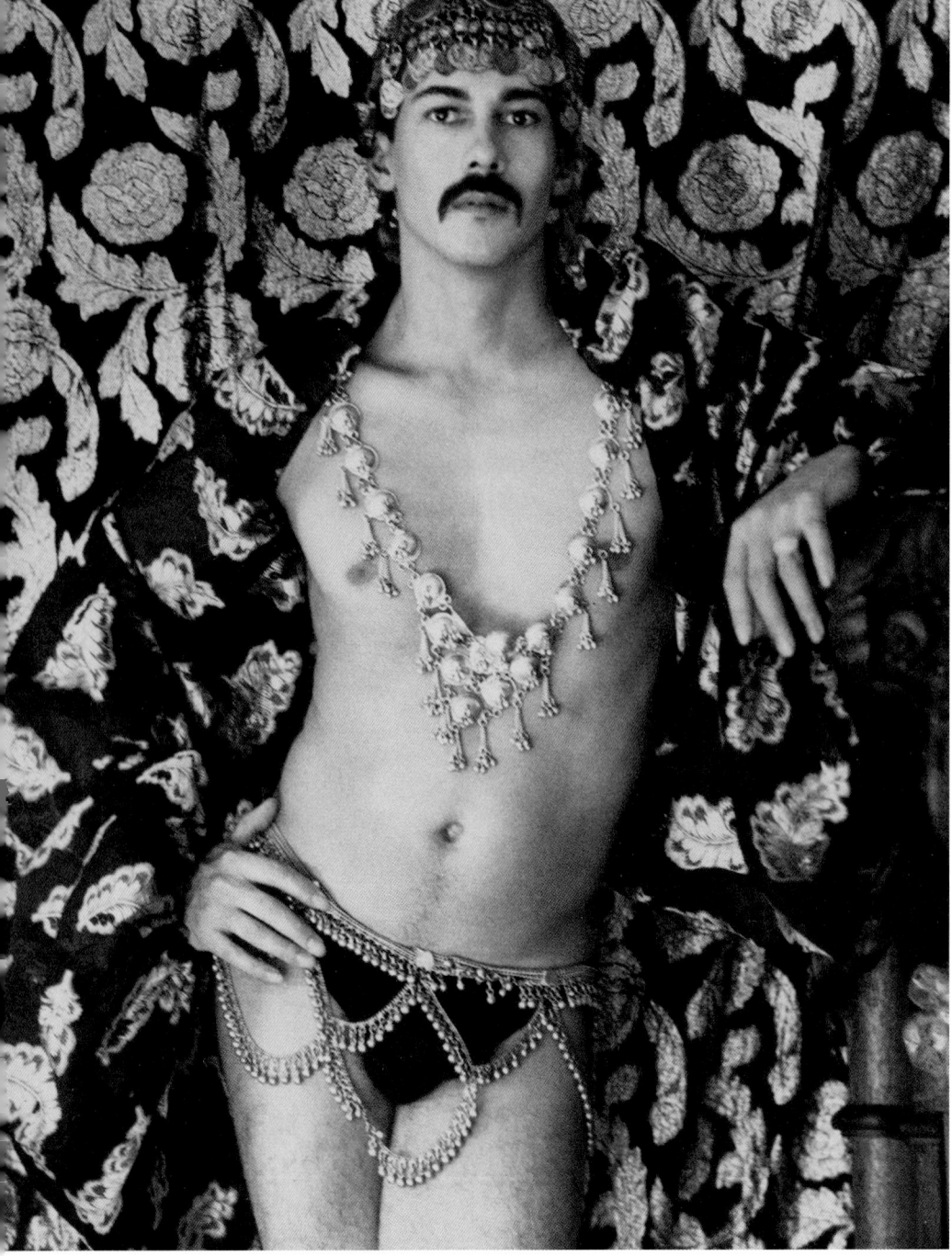

Stathis Orphanos co-founded the LGBT publishing firm Sylvester & Orphanos, known for high-end publications by major writers such as Gore Vidal, John Updike, and Tennessee Williams. He also photographed literary figures, athletes, and activists. Here, Orphanos plays with sumptuous fabrics, body adornments, and the male form to create an arresting portrait of art curator Tony Clark.

| Stathis Orphanos (1940–2018), *Tony Clark*, 1976. Gelatin silver print. Courtesy of James Garfinkel.

Annie Leibovitz (1949–), *Jessye Norman (Singing)*, New York City, 1988. Platinum print. © Annie Leibovitz.

Annie Leibovitz's portrait of opera singer Jessye Norman represents two artists at the peak of their professions uniting to create an image of rapture. Norman's hair fans out behind her, evoking the electricity of her performance, while her closed eyes, clasped hands, and draped cloak suggest her inward focus.

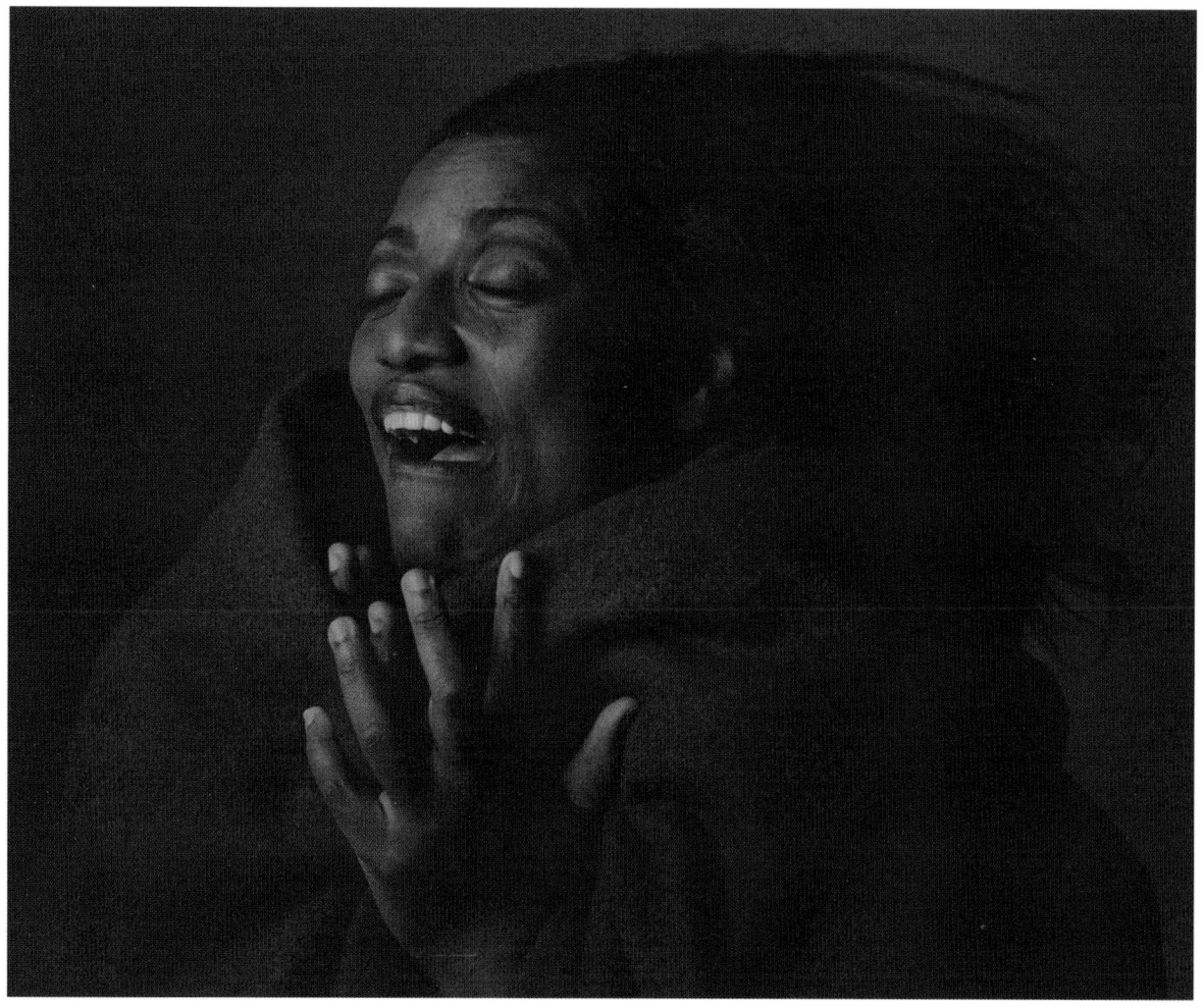

Salwan Georges captures a young Syrian girl's tentative yet hopeful smile in this portrait, one of many he has taken of refugees in Michigan, where Georges's own family settled after fleeing political violence in Iraq.

Salwan Georges (1990–), *Syrian Dream: Starting Again in the New World*, Bloomfield Hills, Michigan, 2015. Inkjet print. Courtesy of Salwan Georges.

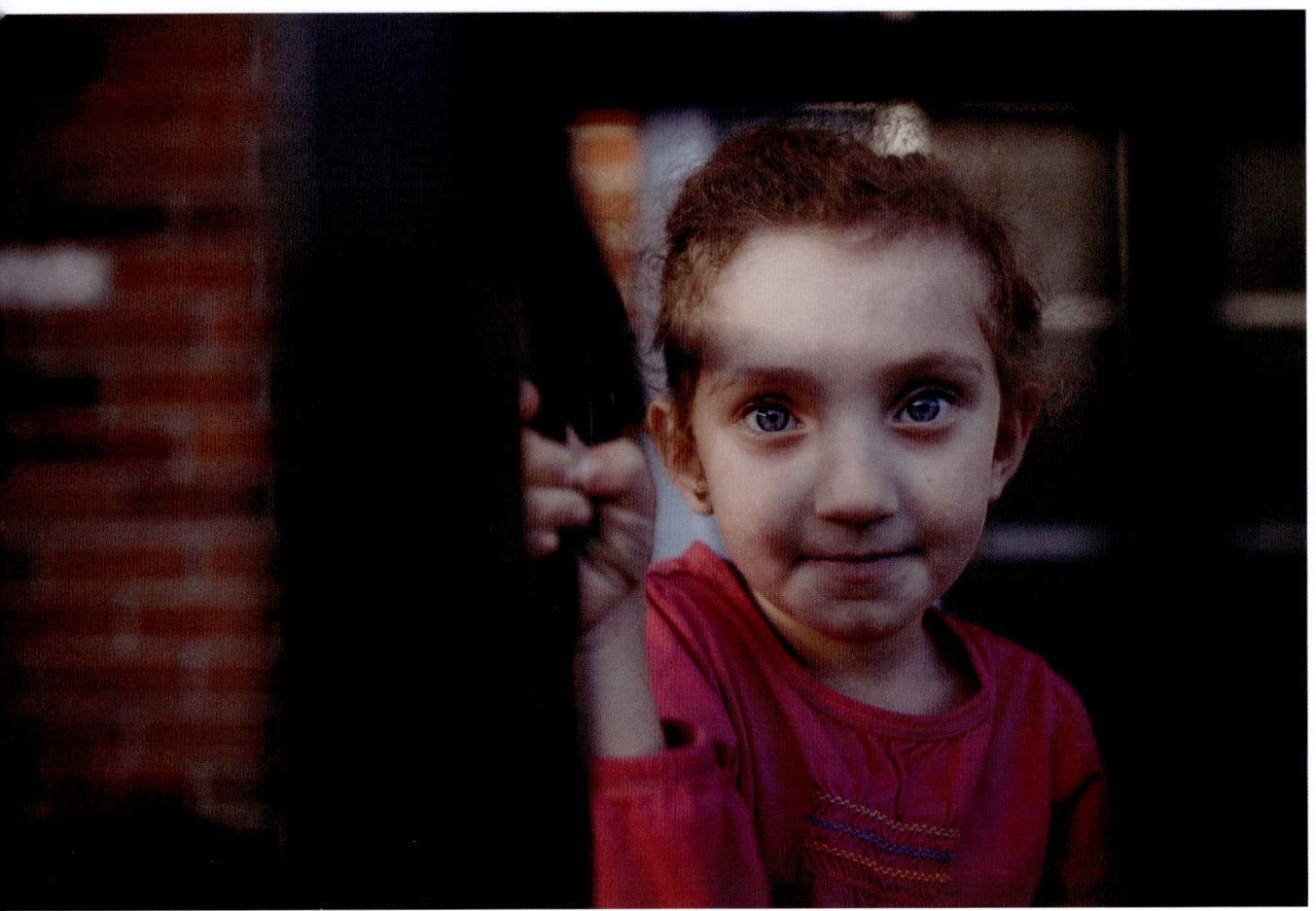

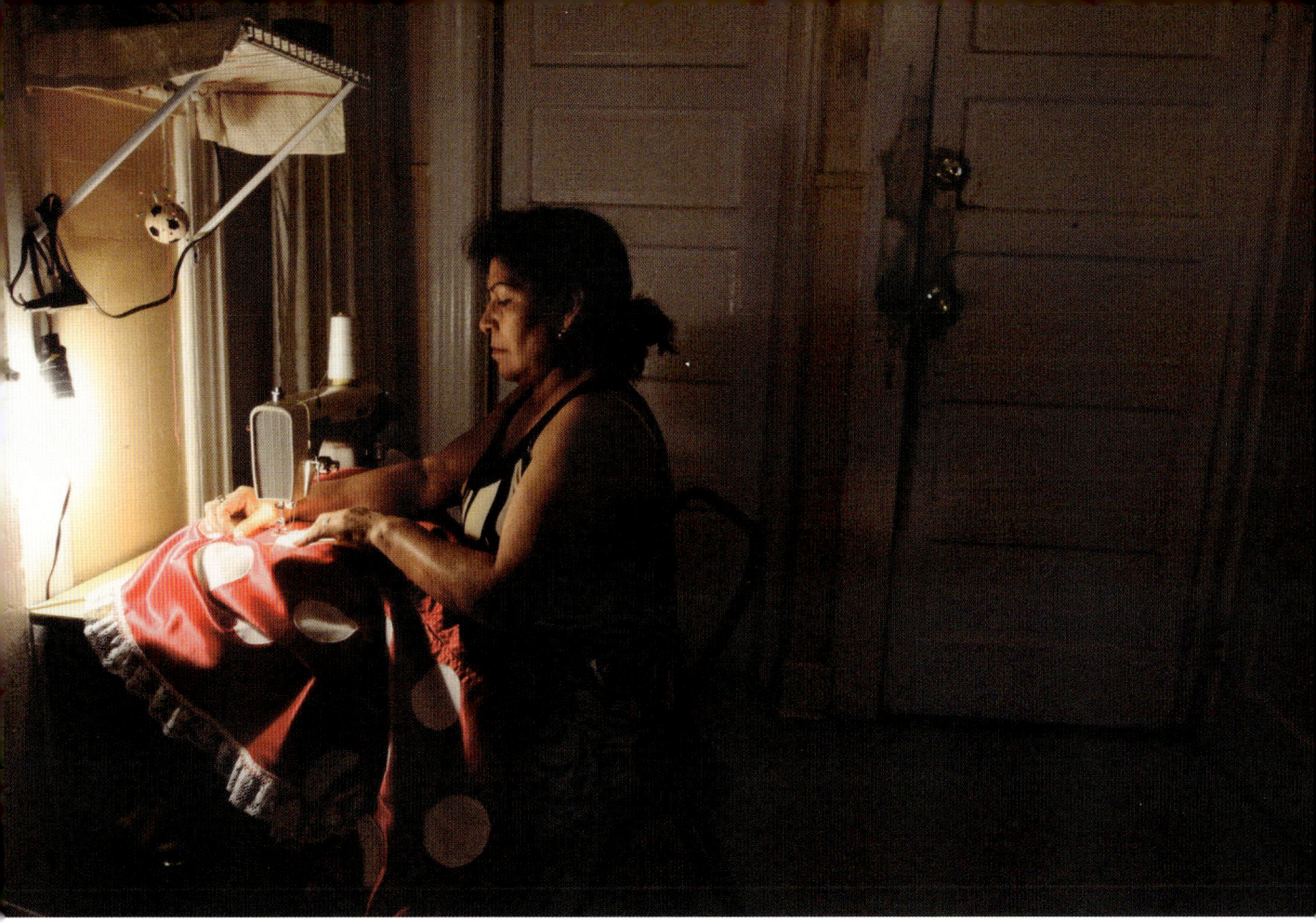

Joana Toro (1976–),
*Doña Berta Guerra, 55,
from Mexico, Repairs
Her Minnie Mouse
Costume at Her House,*
New Jersey, 2013.
Inkjet print. *Hello, I Am
Kitty* series. Courtesy
of Joana Toro.

Colombian photographer Joana Toro put herself
through school by donning a Hello Kitty costume
and posing for photographs in Times Square. Here,
she depicts fellow performer Doña Berta Guerra
mending her Minnie Mouse costume, part of a
series exploring the everyday lives of costumed
performers, many of whom are immigrants, invisible
behind their masks.

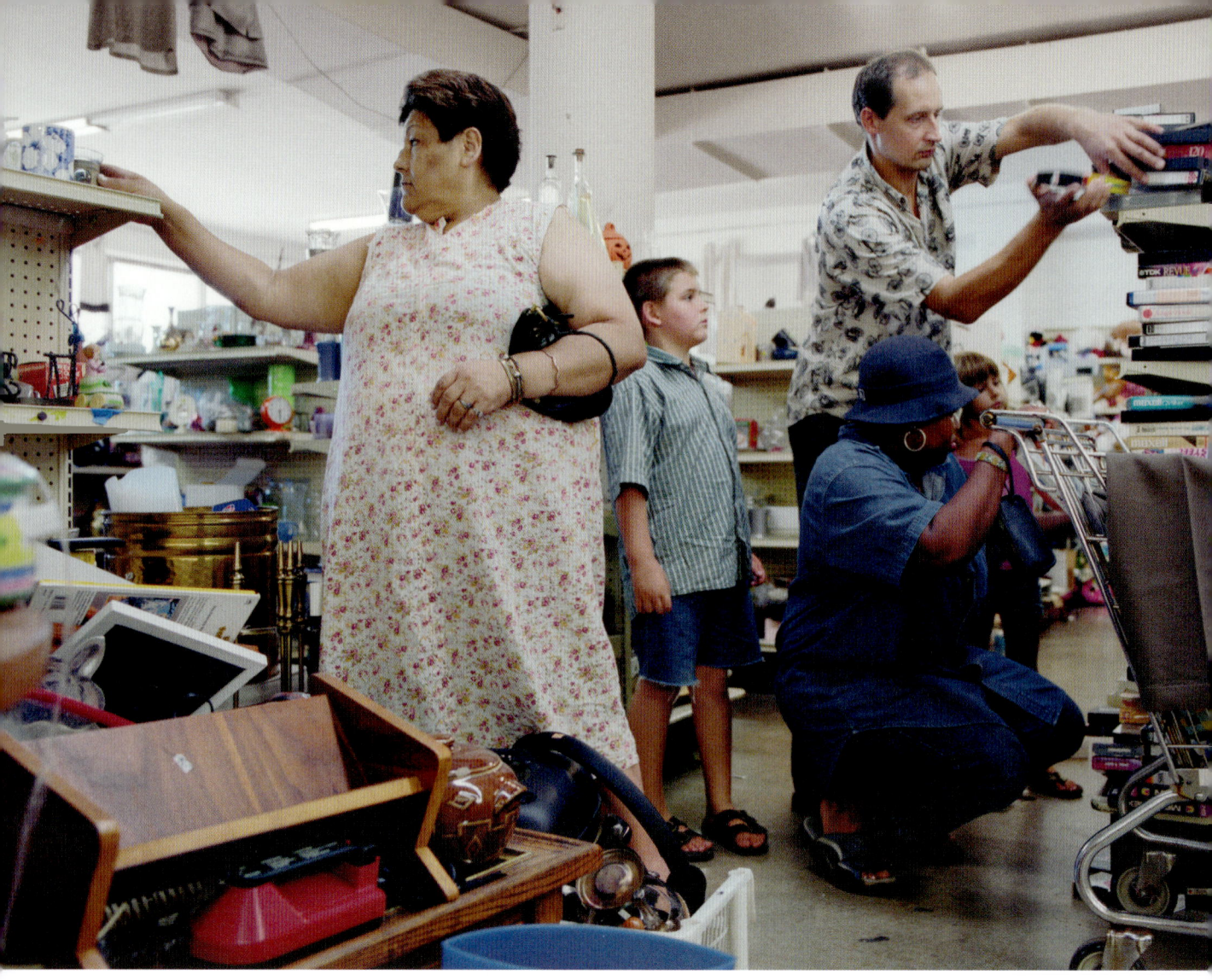

In his series *Retail, Thrift, Dark Stores, Ghost Boxes and Dead Malls*, Brian Ulrich documents American consumer culture and the evolution of retail. This photograph features shoppers sifting through goods on the shelves of a Salvation Army store in search of a bargain. It conveys a common scene that nonetheless has rarely been recorded for contemplation.

Brian Ulrich (1971–), *Untitled*, Chicago, 2005. Inkjet print. *Retail, Thrift, Dark Stores, Ghost Boxes and Dead Malls* series. Courtesy of the artist and Robert Koch Gallery.

Milton Rogovin (1909–2011), *Untitled*, Buffalo, New York, 1973. Gelatin silver print. Courtesy of the Rogovin family.

A champion of the working class, Milton Rogovin made photographs in the diverse Lower West Side of Buffalo for decades, creating a deeply moving and expansive picture of people's lives over the course of thirty years. His dignified portraits, such as this one of a shopkeeper and child, speak of the community's dreams and aspirations.

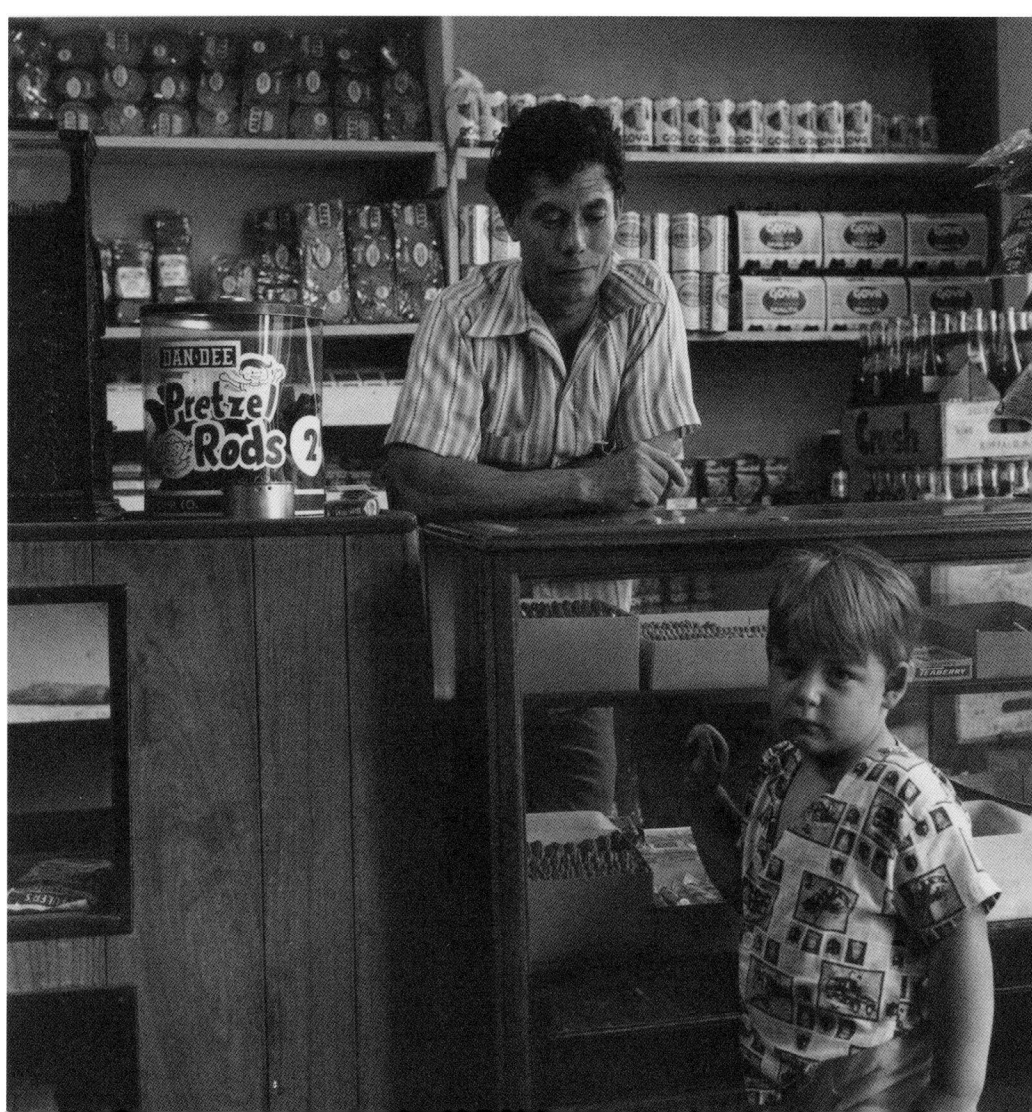

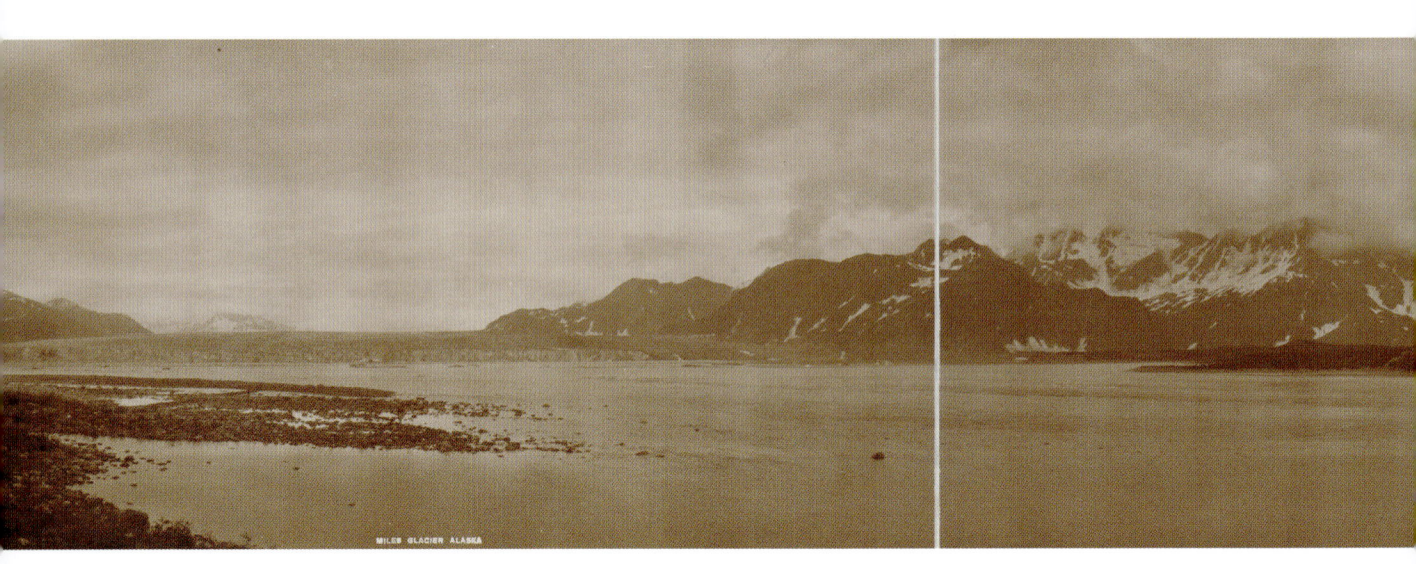

MILES GLACIER ALASKA

Reaching the height of its popularity at the start of the twentieth century, the panoramic photo format allowed photographers to fully capture various scenes—large groups, engineering feats, landscapes, and sports—like never before. This panorama of the newly completed Miles Glacier Bridge has an unexpected composition: rather than emphasizing the length of the bridge, the camera stares directly down it, enabling the viewer to see through to the other side.

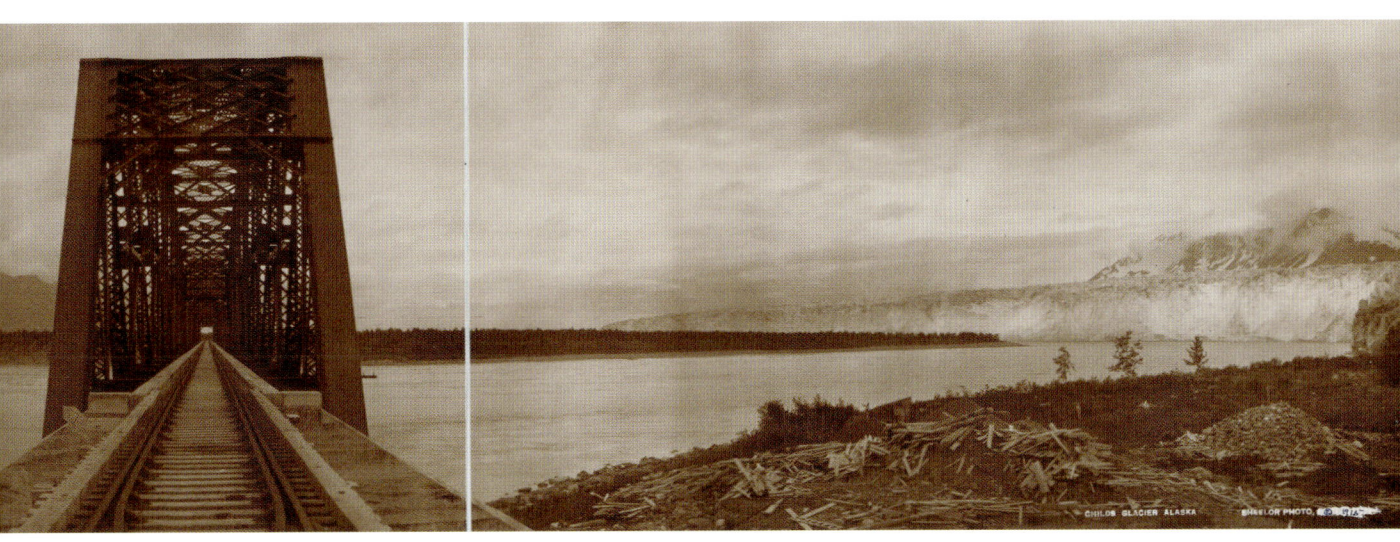

F. W. Sheelor, *Bridge Connecting Miles Glacier and Childs Glacier*, Alaska, 1915. Gelatin silver print.

Edward S. Curtis took this photo while serving as official photographer on a scientific expedition along the Alaskan coast. The expedition included a host of luminaries, including famed naturalist John Muir, after whom this glacier was named. Curtis's softly rendered photograph serves as a record of a glacier that has undergone enormous change and is still changing today.

Edward S. Curtis (1868–1952), *Muir Glacier*, Alaska, 1899. Gelatin silver print. Harriman Alaska Expedition Album.

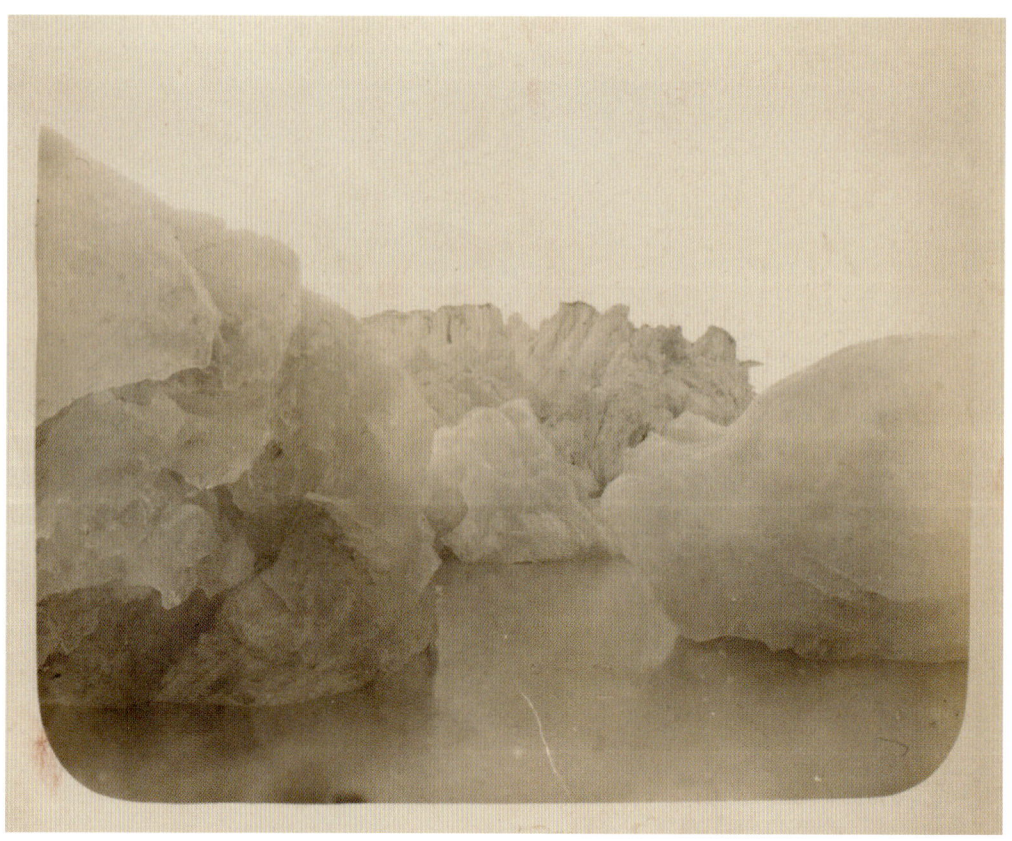

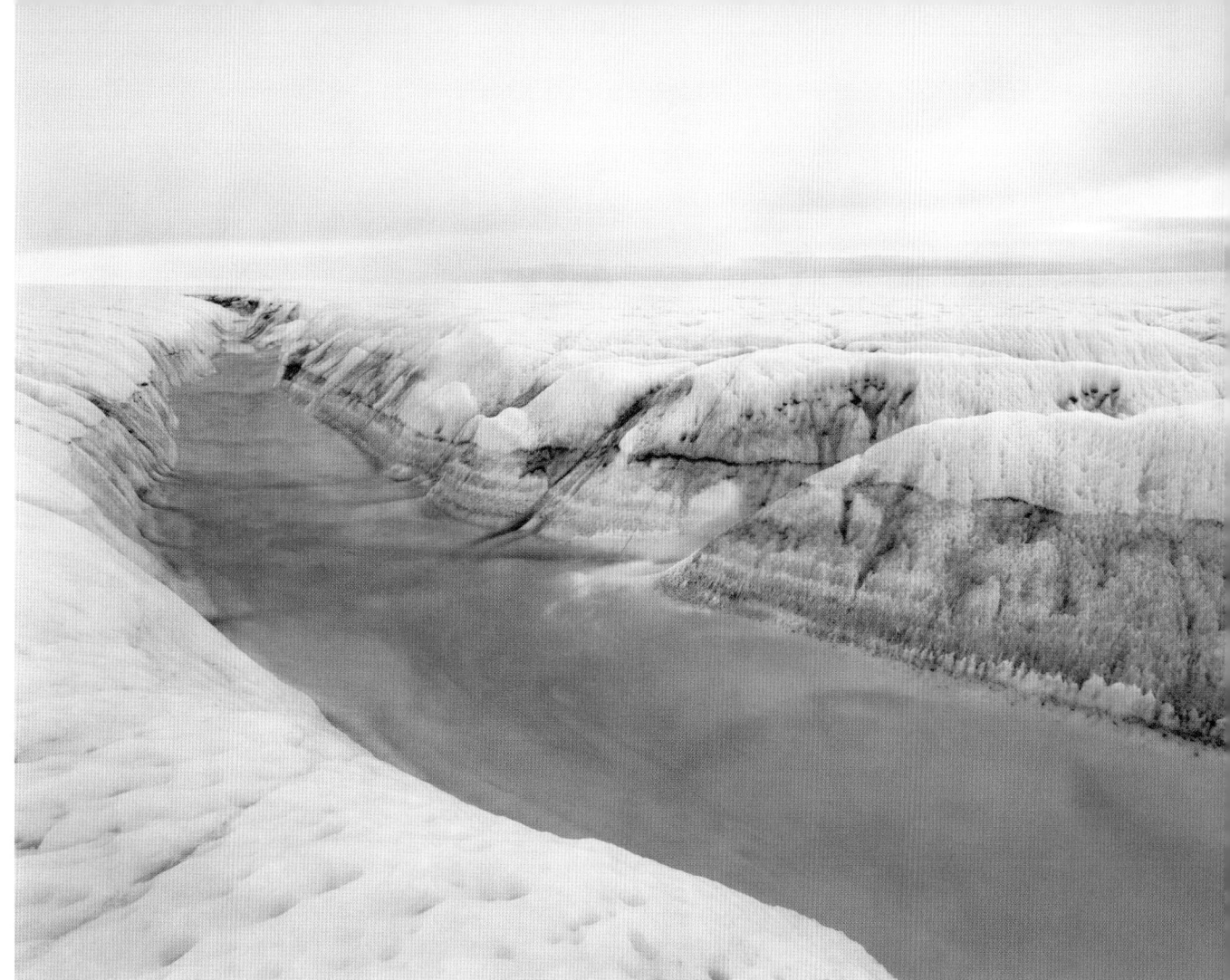

Olaf Otto Becker (1959–), *River 1, Position 16, Altitude 707 m, Greenland Ice Cap Melting Area*, 2007. Inkjet print. *Above Zero* series. Courtesy of Olaf Otto Becker.

German landscape photographer Olaf Otto Becker strives to document humanity's impact on the planet. Here, he captured a river formed by melting ice in Greenland. Becker recorded the precise location of each photograph in the series to help track alterations to the ice as the climate continues to change.

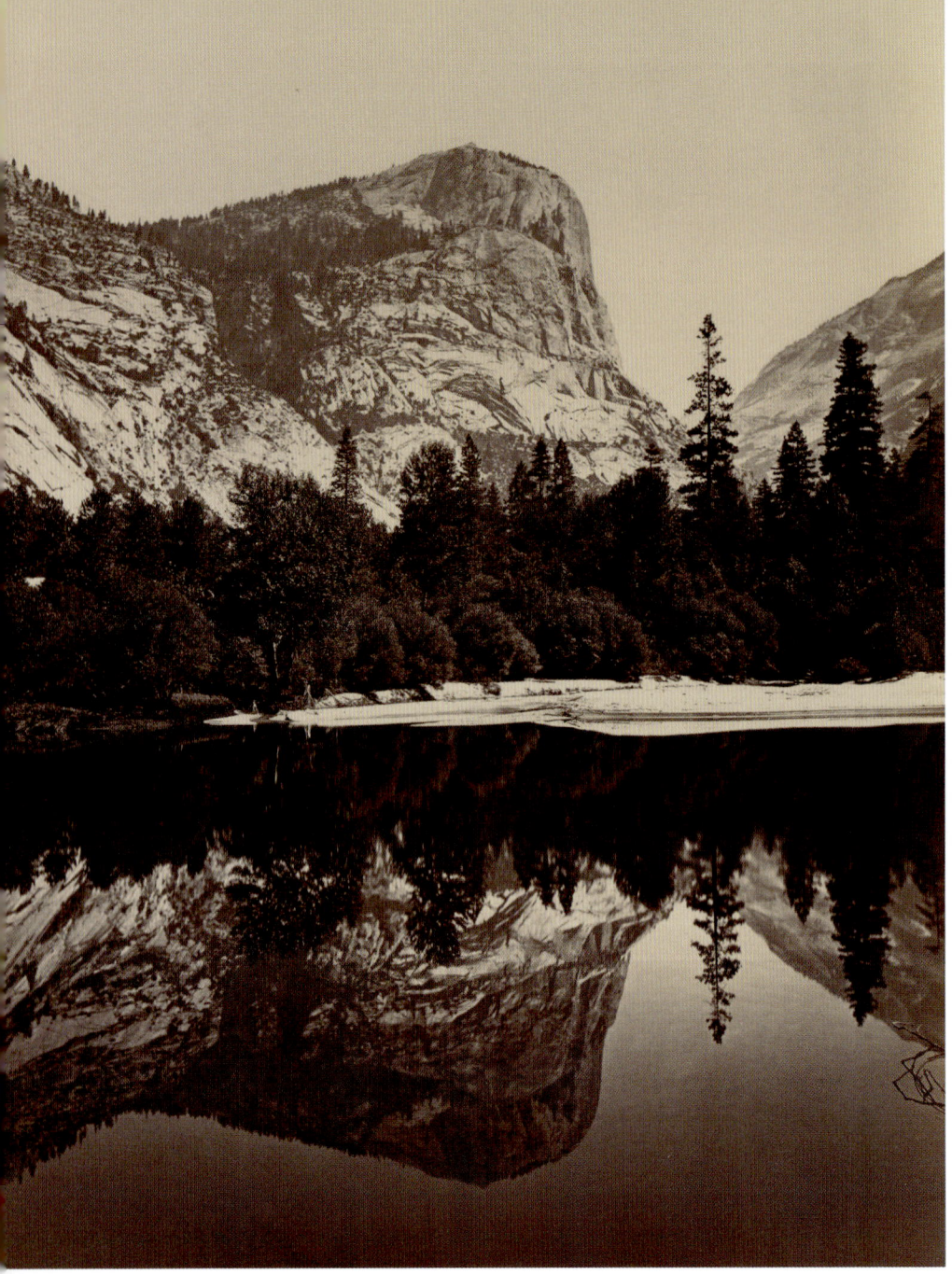

Carleton E. Watkins captured this pristine view of the aptly named Mirror Lake, using cumbersome glass wet plate negatives to produce stunning views of Yosemite's extraordinary wilderness. Watkins's photographs are credited with persuading Congress to protect the area from development, eventually leading to it becoming a national park in 1890.

| Carleton E. Watkins (1829–1916), *Mirror Lake*, Yosemite, California, ca. 1865. Albumen silver print.

The San Francisco de Asís Church has inspired many artists to depict its massive eighteenth-century adobe architecture. Philip Trager's photograph highlights the church's monolithic shape, while the absence of any environmental context makes it feel both timeless and other-worldly.

| Philip Trager (1935–), *Church, Ranchos de Taos 1*, New Mexico, 1970. Platinum print. Courtesy of Philip Trager.

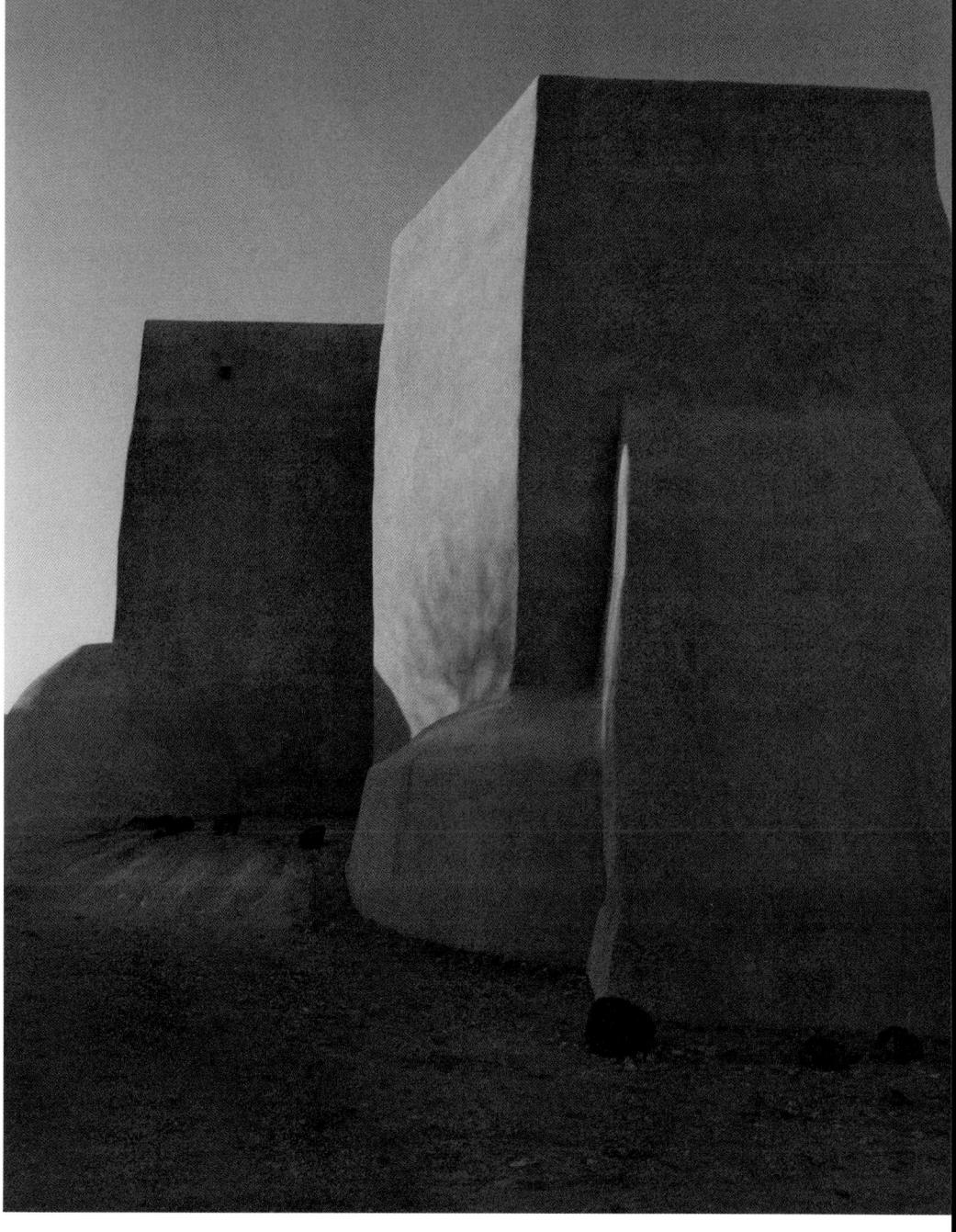

Around the turn of the twentieth century, a new photomechanical process called photochrom made mass production of vivid color prints possible. These pictures were sold at tourist sites and through mail order catalogs. This shot depicts the mesmerizing arches of a winter gallery, or avalanche gallery, constructed to keep the road open even in severe weather conditions, on a vertigo-inducing cliffside in the Swiss Alps.

Photographer unidentified, *Simplon Pass, Winter Gallery*, Valais, Switzerland, ca. 1890–1900. Photochrom print.

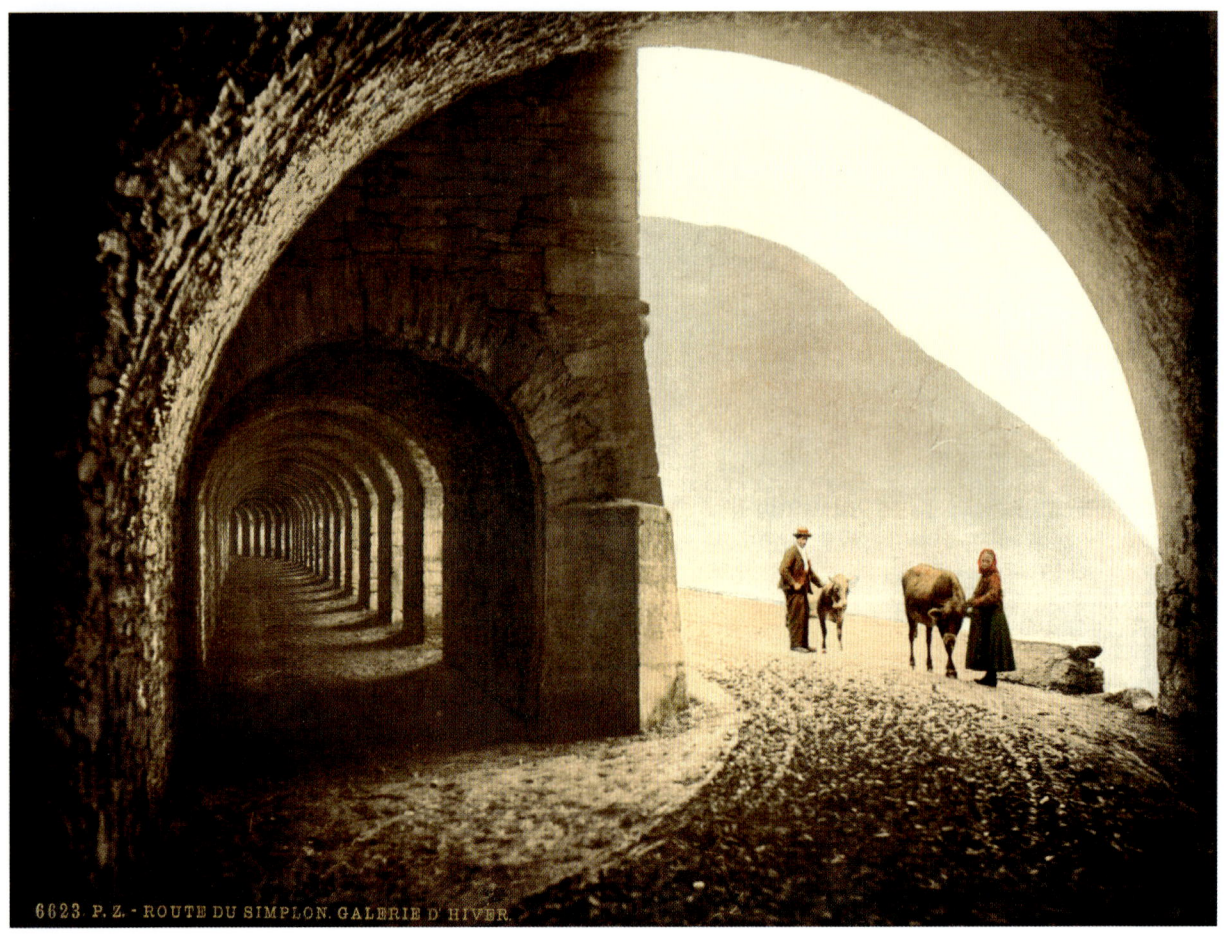

6623 P. Z. - ROUTE DU SIMPLON. GALERIE D'HIVER.

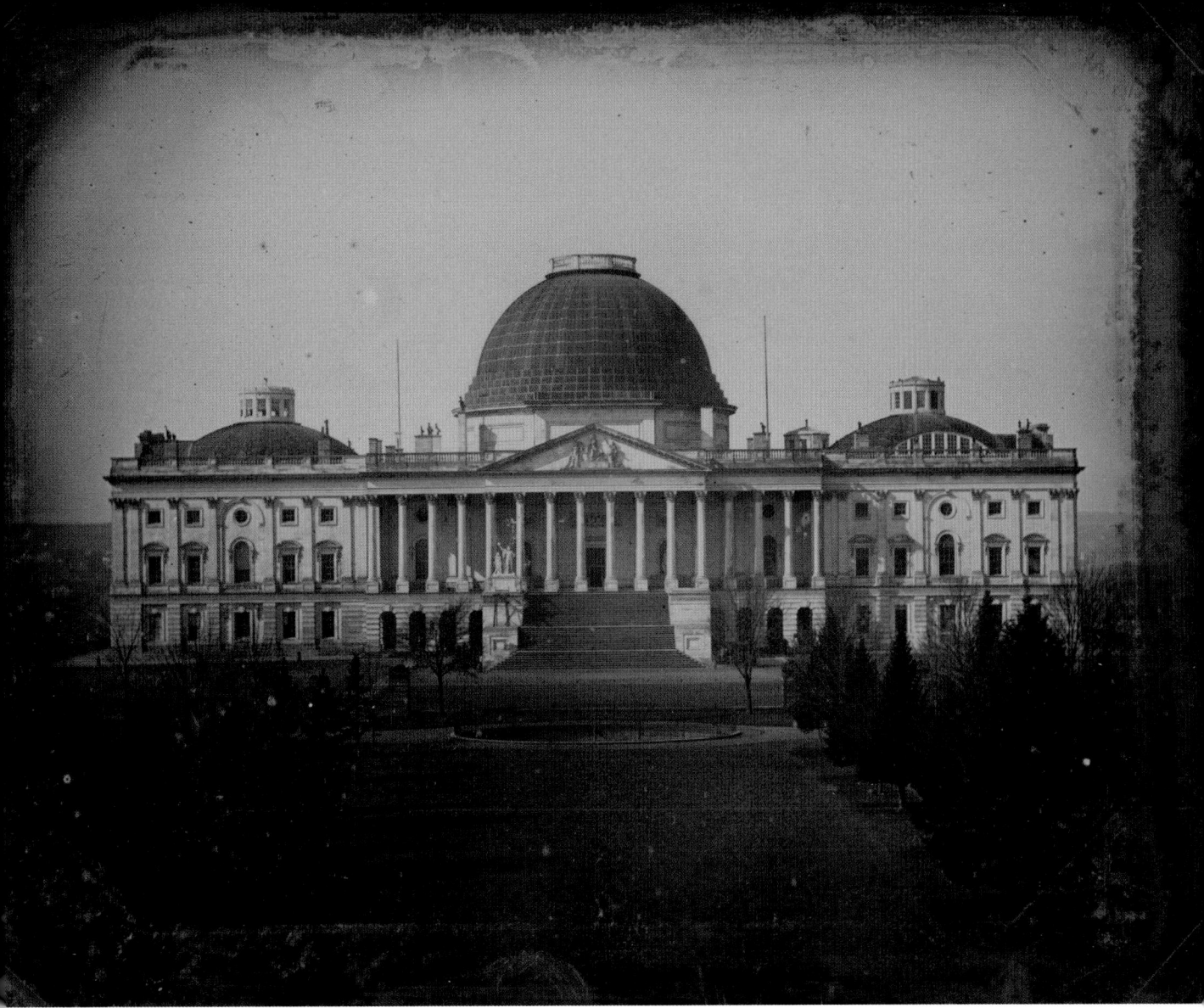

John Plumbe Jr. opened one of the first professional photography studios in Washington, DC, in the mid-1840s. Plumbe's image of the Capitol, with its former copper-sheathed wooden dome, is the earliest surviving photograph of the building. Near the end of the Civil War, this dome was replaced by a fireproof, cast-iron dome capped by the Statue of Freedom.

John Plumbe Jr. (1809–1857), *United States Capitol, East Front Elevation*, Washington, DC, 1846. Half-plate daguerreotype.

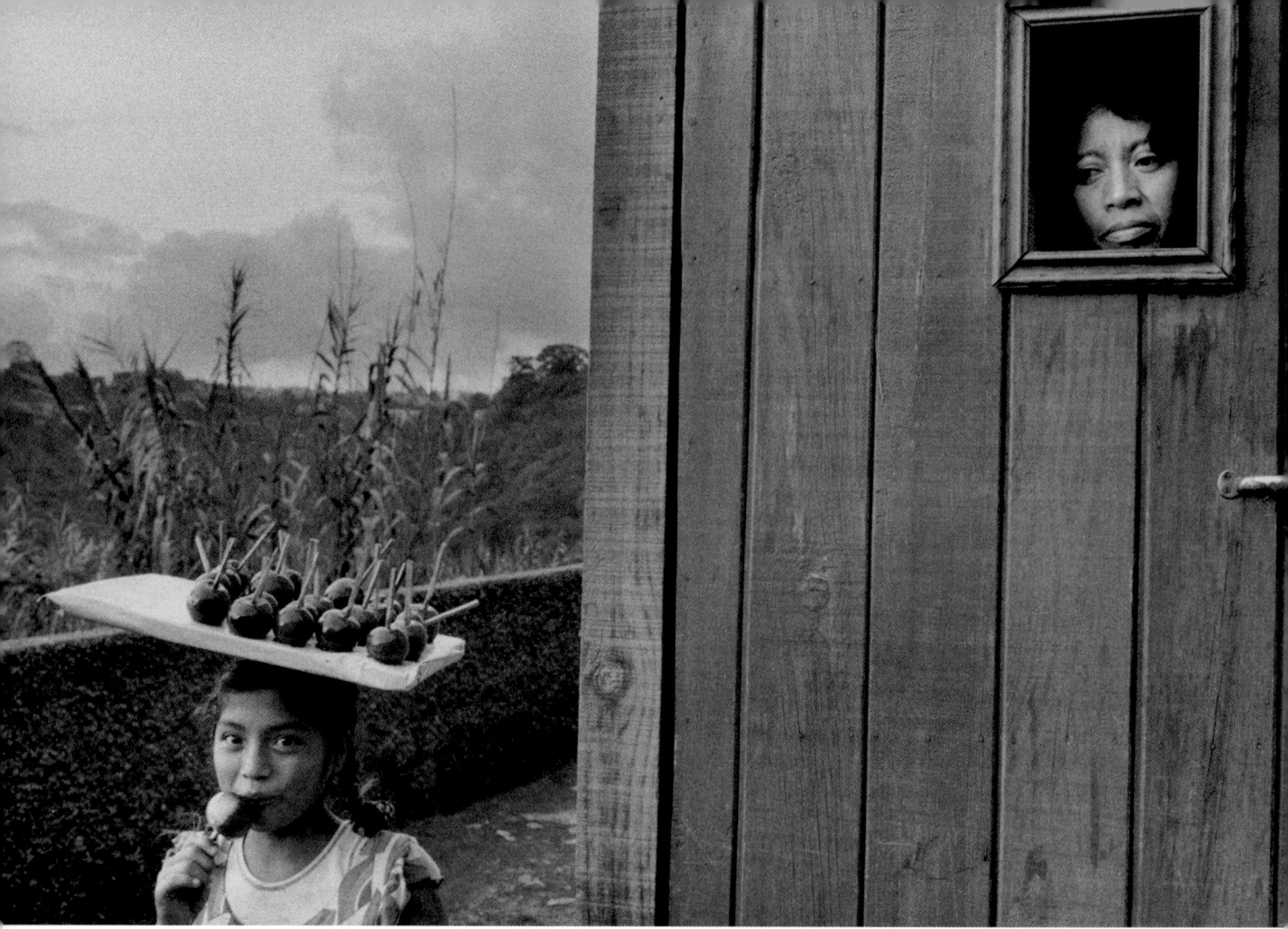

Brazilian photojournalist Sebastião Salgado has created a stunning body of work in black and white, specializing in capturing the majesty of the earth and the dignity of people living and working in harsh conditions. In this charming scene on the outskirts of Guatemala City, a young candy apple vendor tastes her wares while a woman peers out of a nearby window.

Sebastião Salgado (1944–), *Guatemalan Candied Apple Vendor*, Guatemala City, 1978. Gelatin silver print. Courtesy of Sebastião Salgado.

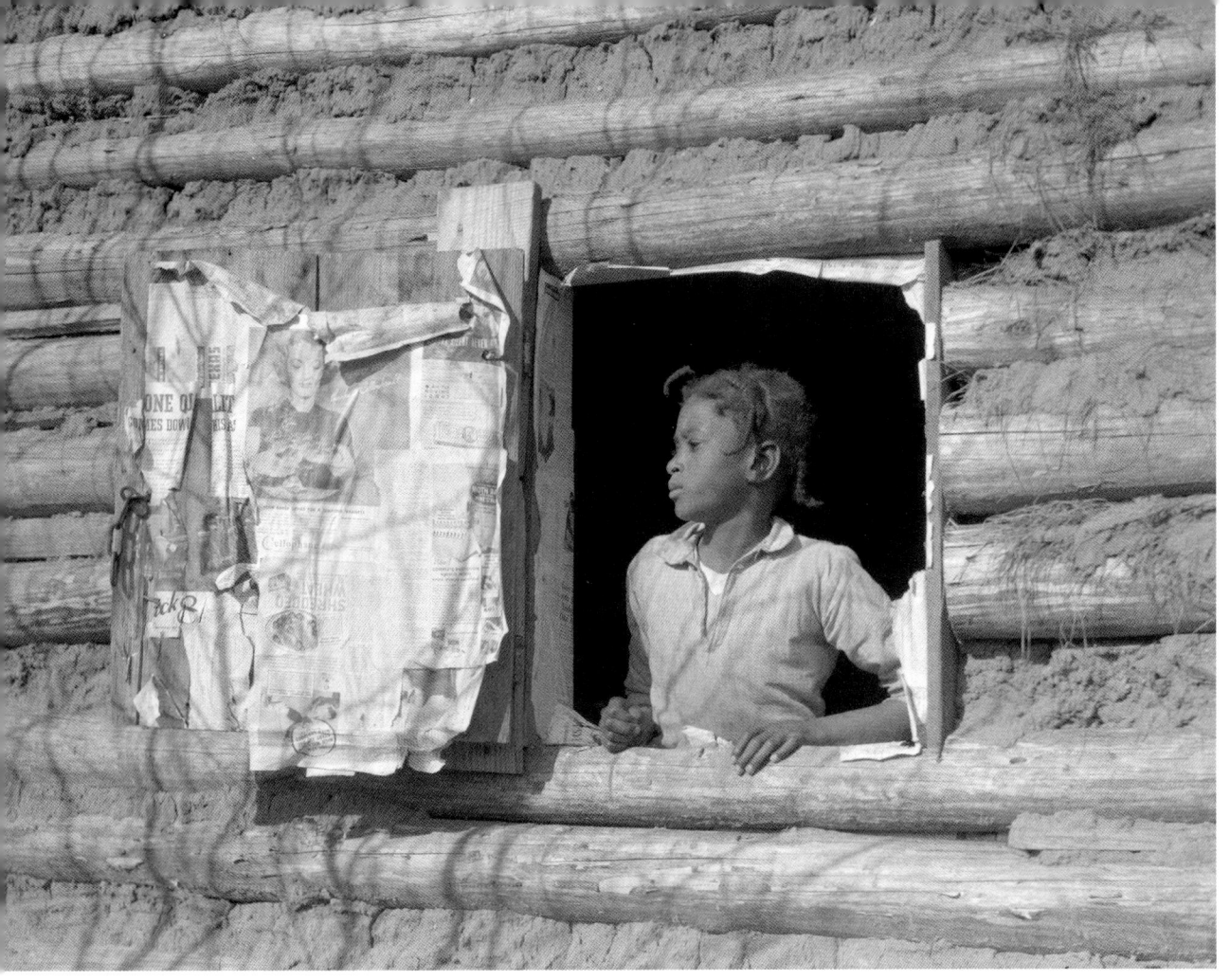

Arthur Rothstein (1915–1985), *Girl at Gee's Bend*, Alabama, 1937. Nitrate negative.

In 1937, the Resettlement Administration directed Arthur Rothstein to take pictures of the tenant community, mostly descendants of enslaved people, at Gee's Bend, Alabama, to generate support for new farm tenant legislation in Congress. In this striking portrait, Artelia Bendolph's expression of maturity and resilience belies her ten years of age.

Since the early 1970s, Chilean-born documentarian Camilo J. Vergara has photographed low-income, minority communities in postindustrial cities. This shot, taken in the Brush Park neighborhood of Detroit—once called "Little Paris" because of its elegant buildings—reveals a block particularly devastated by the city's economic decline in the late twentieth century and early 2000s.

Camilo J. Vergara (1944–), *View South Along John R. St. from Edmund Place*, Detroit, Michigan, 2003. Digital photograph. Courtesy of Camilo J. Vergara.

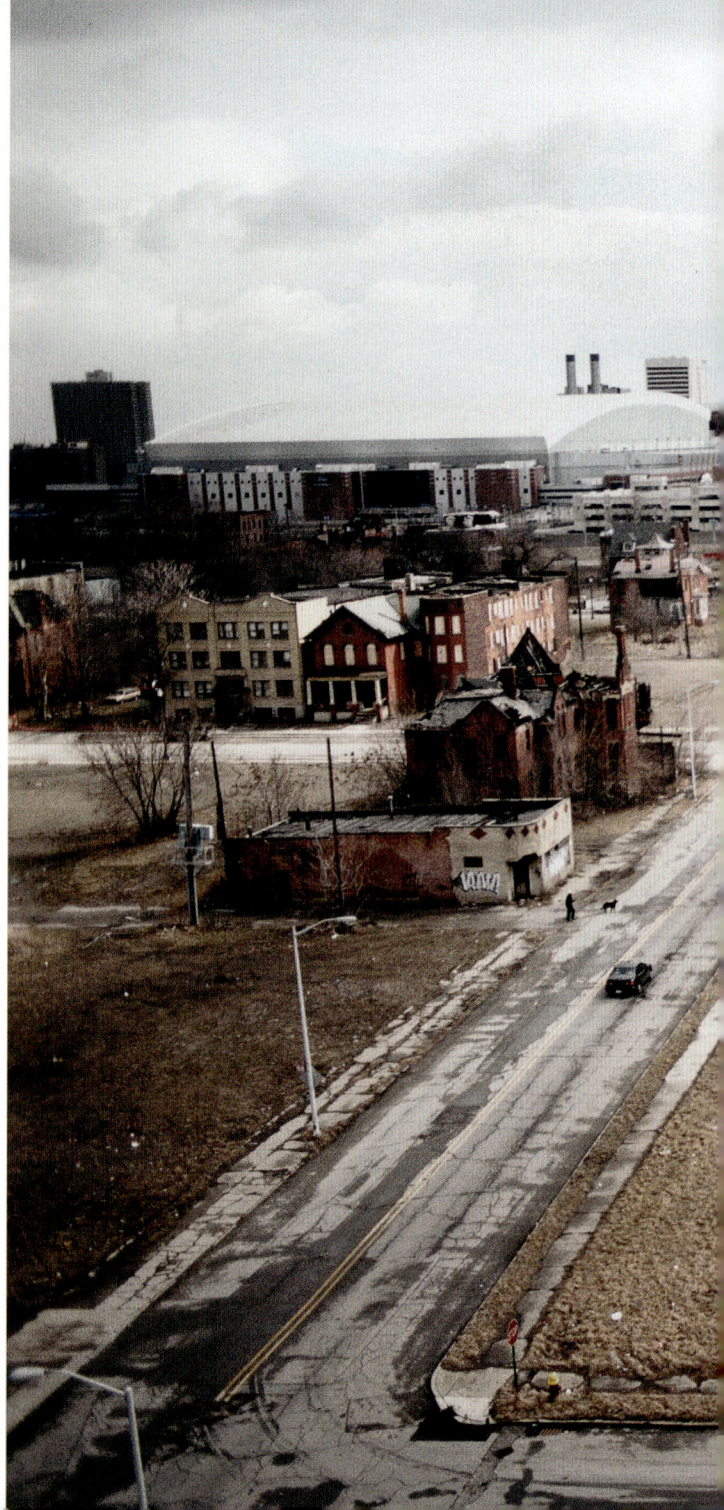

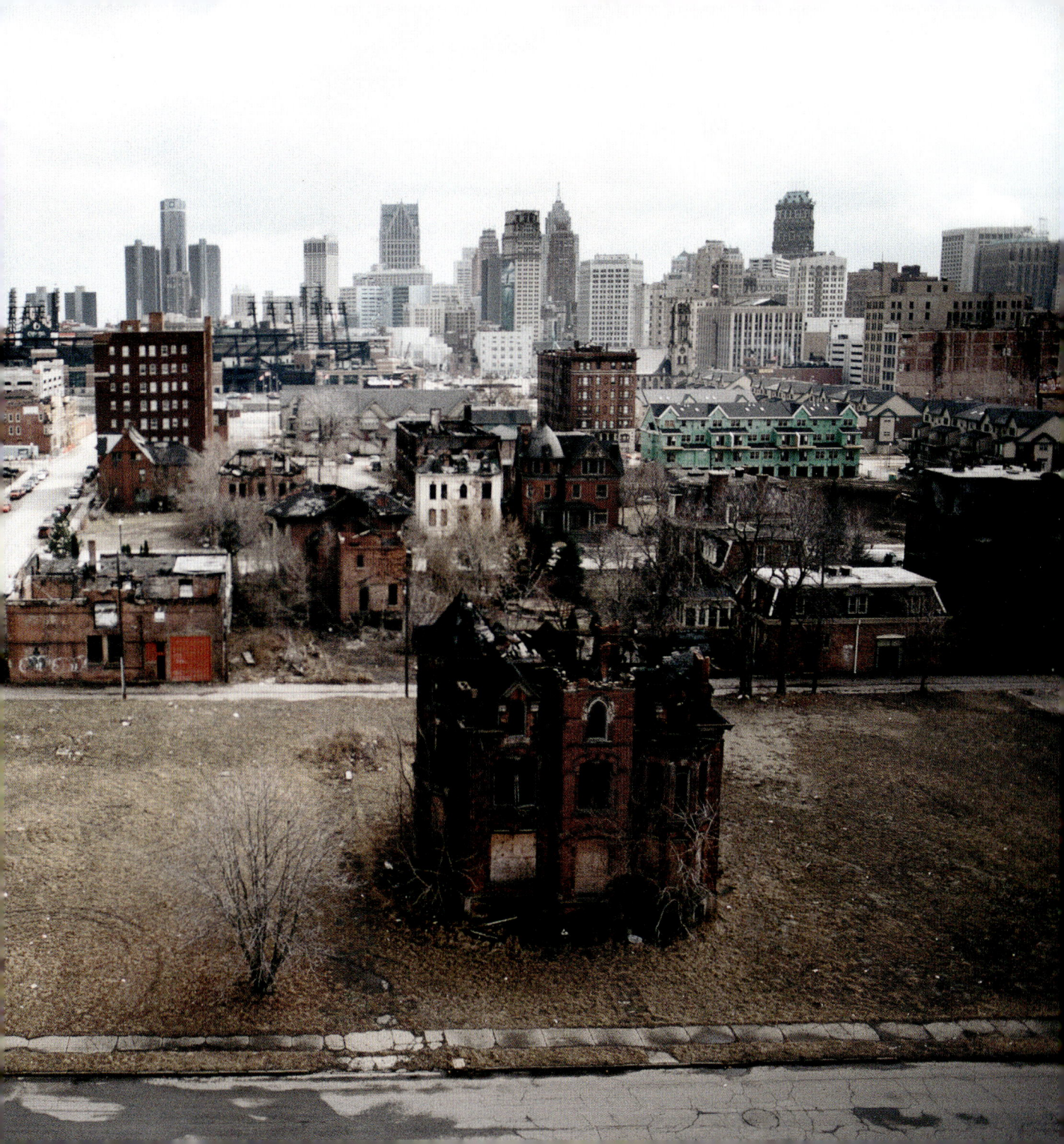

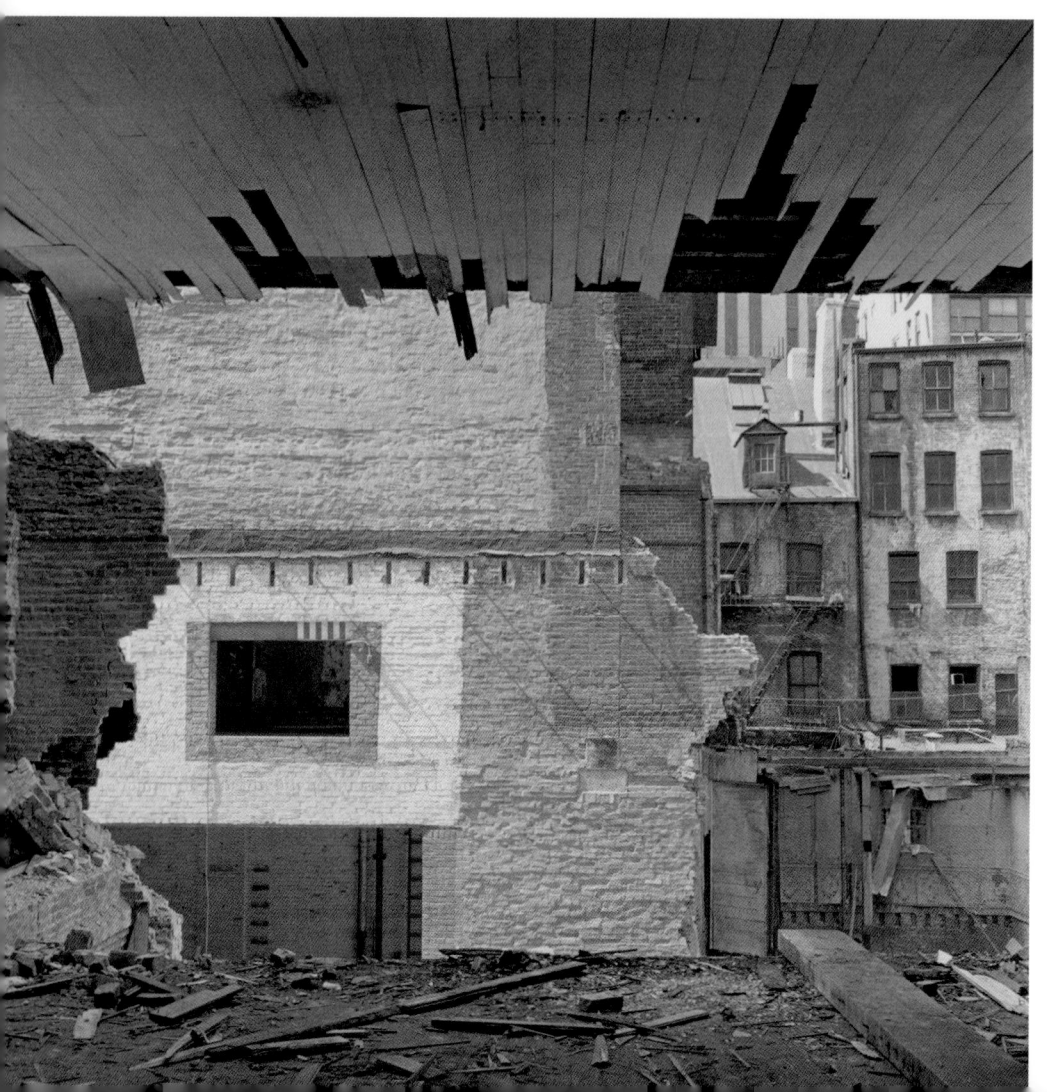

Danny Lyon photographed the extensive redevelopment of Lower Manhattan in the late 1960s, recording the transformation of entire neighborhoods. Here, layers of crumbling brick and beams suggest archaeological layers of building materials, while fire escapes, windows, and chimneys jostle for space in the background.

Danny Lyon (1942–), *View Through the Rear Wall, 89 Beekman Street*, New York City, 1966. Gelatin silver print. Courtesy of Danny Lyon / Magnum Photos.

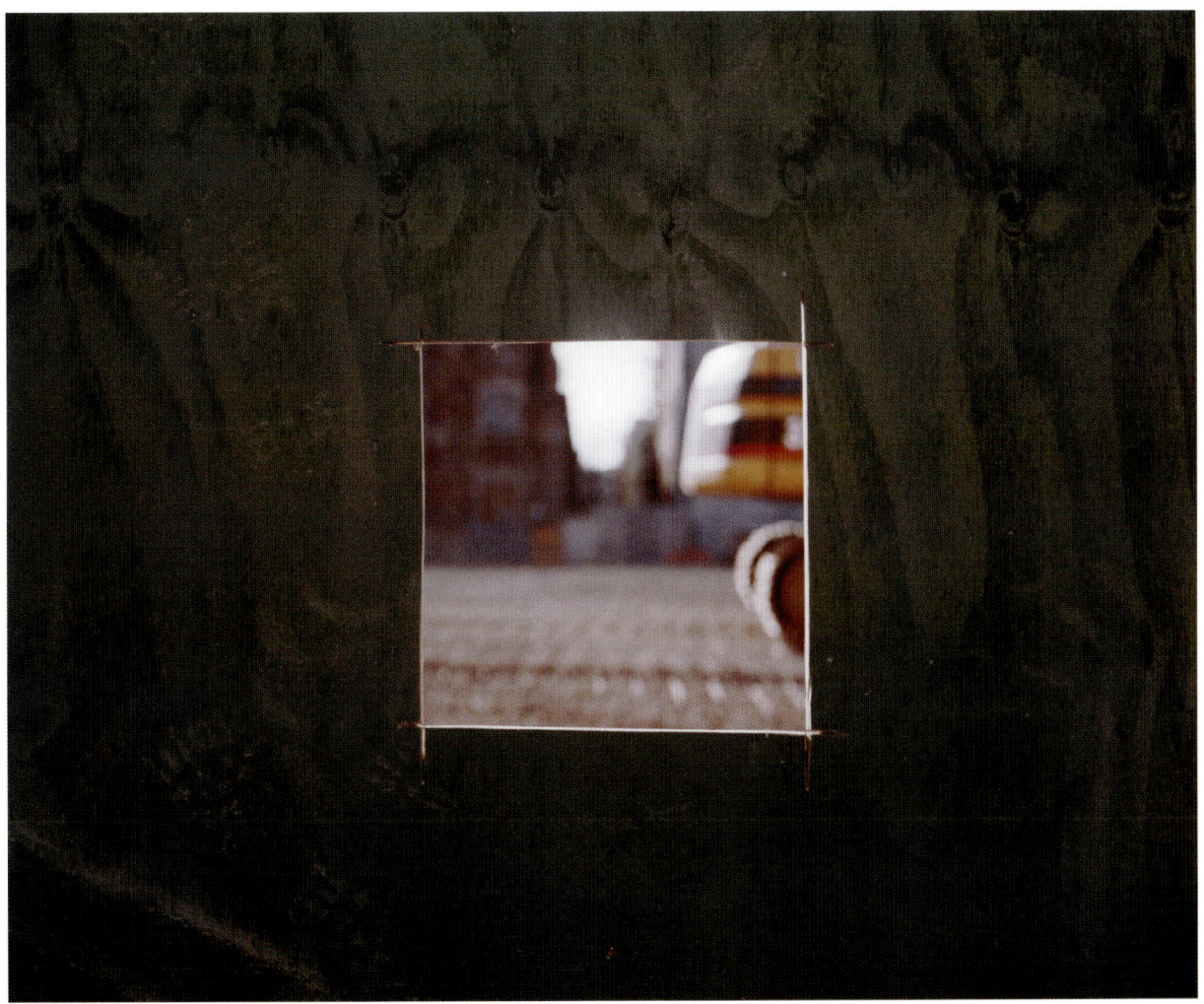

Dawoud Bey (1953–), *Former Renaissance Ballroom Site*, New York City, 2016. Inkjet print. *Harlem Redux* portfolio. Courtesy of Dawoud Bey.

For his *Harlem Redux* series, Dawoud Bey frames the site of the legendary Renaissance Ballroom, a historic center of Black culture that was demolished for new construction, from behind a plywood barrier. The square opening serves as a viewfinder, demanding contemplation of what has been lost amidst rapid gentrification.

Platt D. Babbitt's daguerreotype shows the silhouette of Joseph Avery clinging to a log in the Niagara River after a boating accident that sent his two fellow boaters to their deaths over the falls. Avery weathered the powerful current for eighteen hours before succumbing to the river.

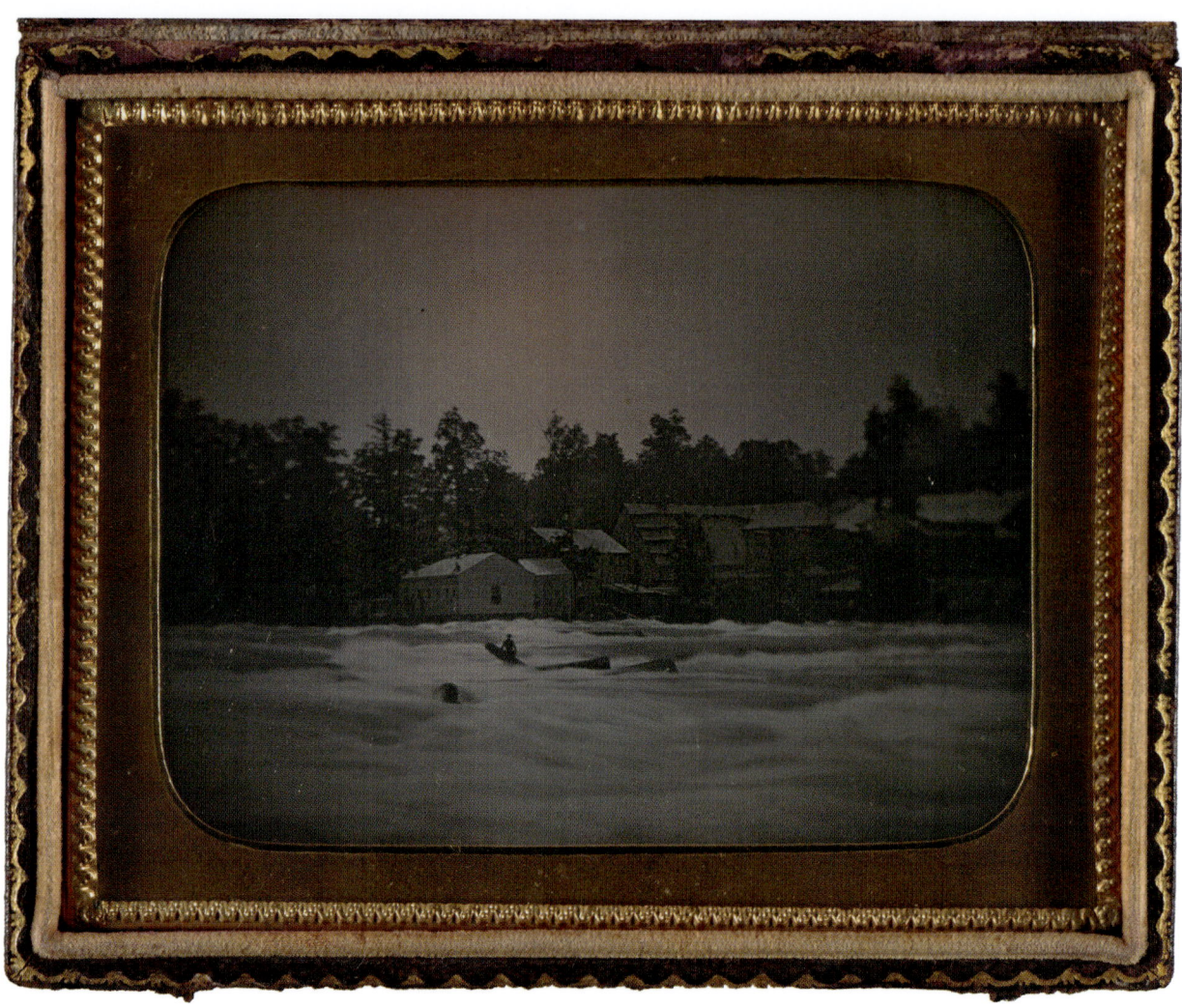

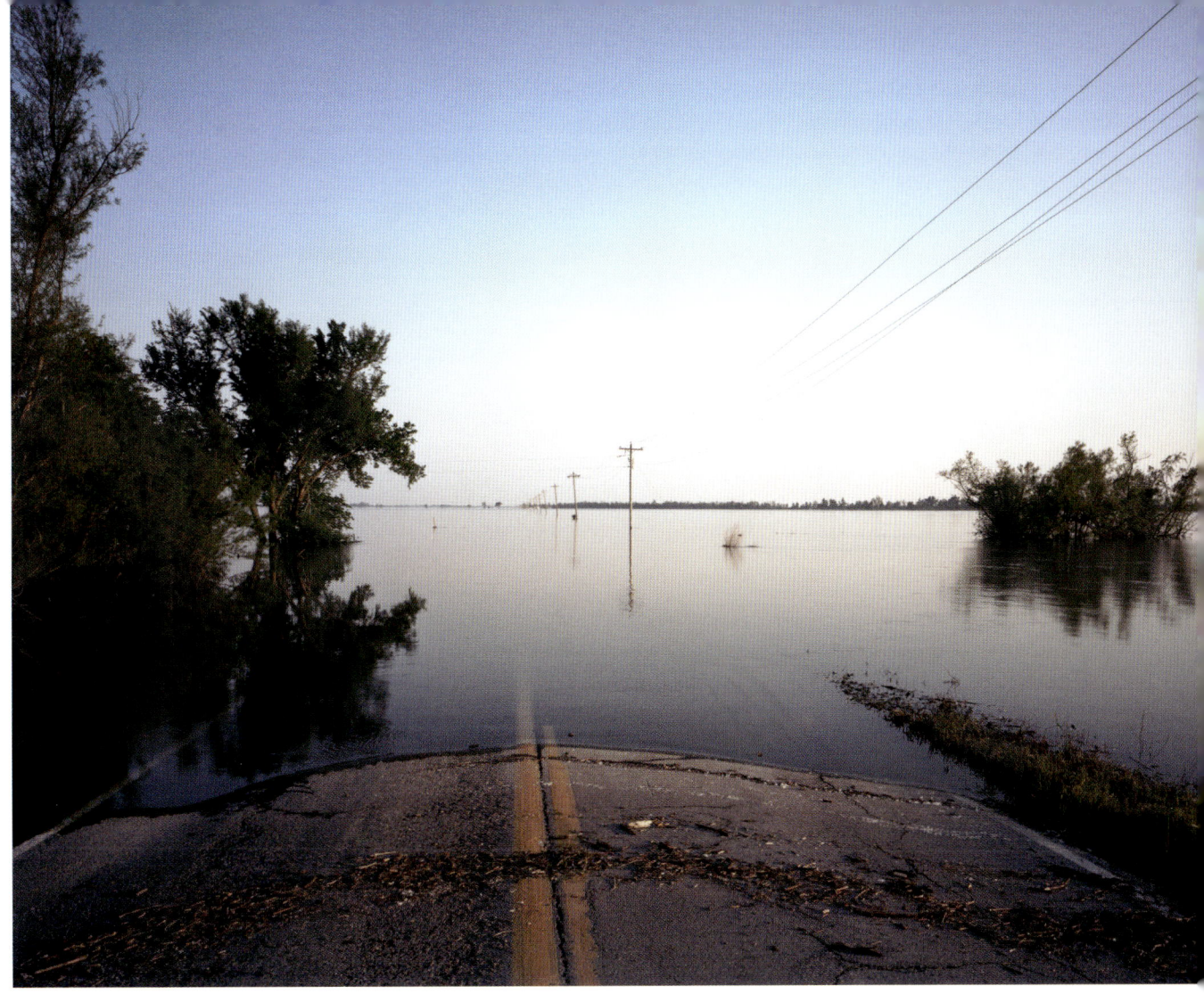

A two-lane road descends into still water that stretches to the horizon in Jeff Rich's deceptively peaceful photograph. Floodwaters inundated 130,000 acres of farmland after the opening of a levee, a measure taken to alleviate extensive flooding of the Mississippi River.

Jeff Rich (1977–), *Birds Point–New Madrid Floodway, During the 2011 Floods, Mississippi River,* Wyatt, Missouri, 2011. Inkjet print. *Watershed* portfolio. Courtesy of Jeff Rich.

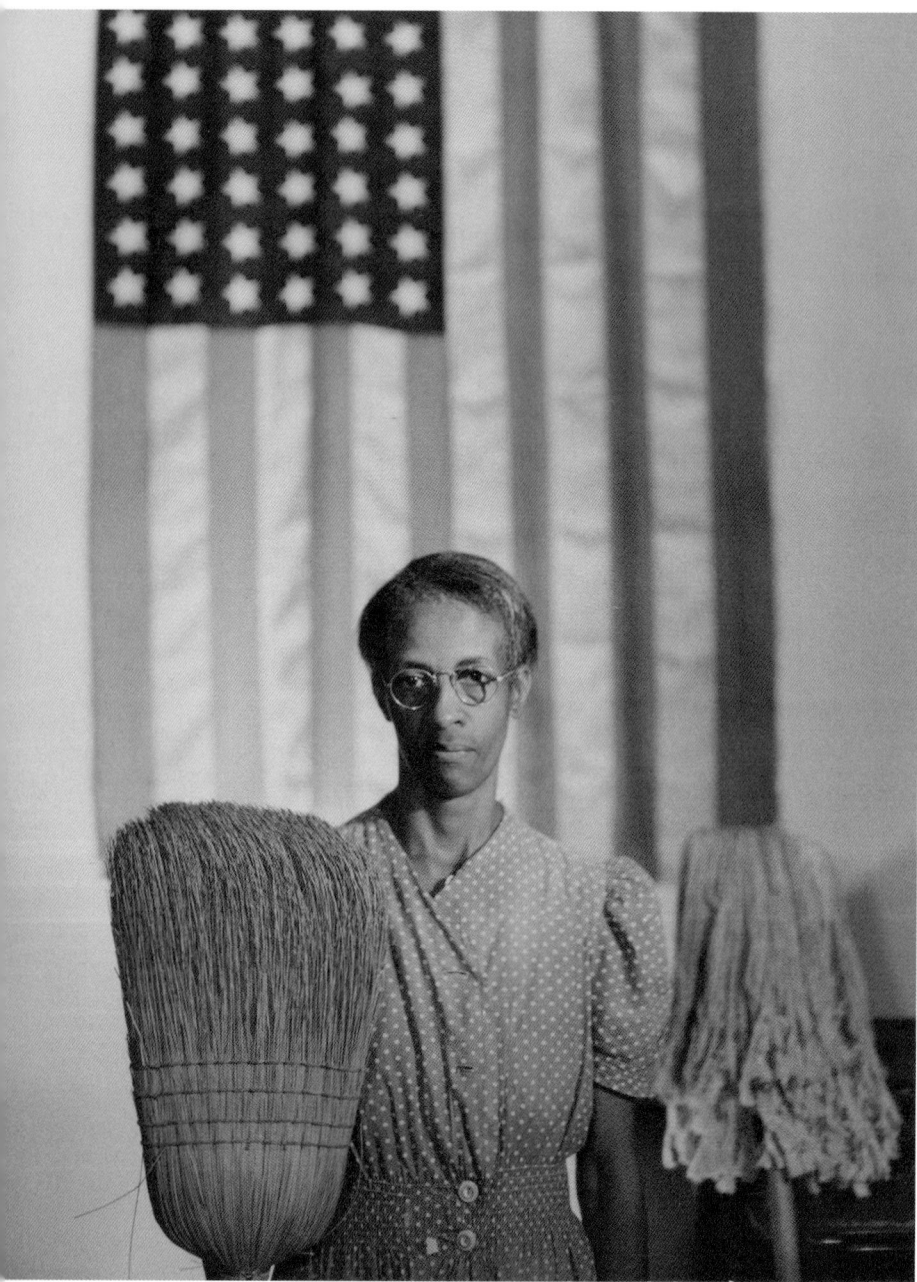

While viewers may be familiar with Gordon Parks's iconic portrait—often called "American Gothic" because of its compositional similarity to the eponymous 1930 Grant Wood painting—few know that Parks took ninety more photographs of Ella Watson.

Watson, a cleaner at the headquarters of the Farm Security Administration in Washington, DC, where Parks worked, welcomed Parks to her modest apartment, where he photographed members of her family squeezed into a small room having dinner. Together, these photos expose the harsh conditions endured by African Americans while also revealing Watson's inner strength and resolve.

| Gordon Parks (1912–2006), *Government Charwoman*, Washington, DC, 1942. Gelatin silver print.

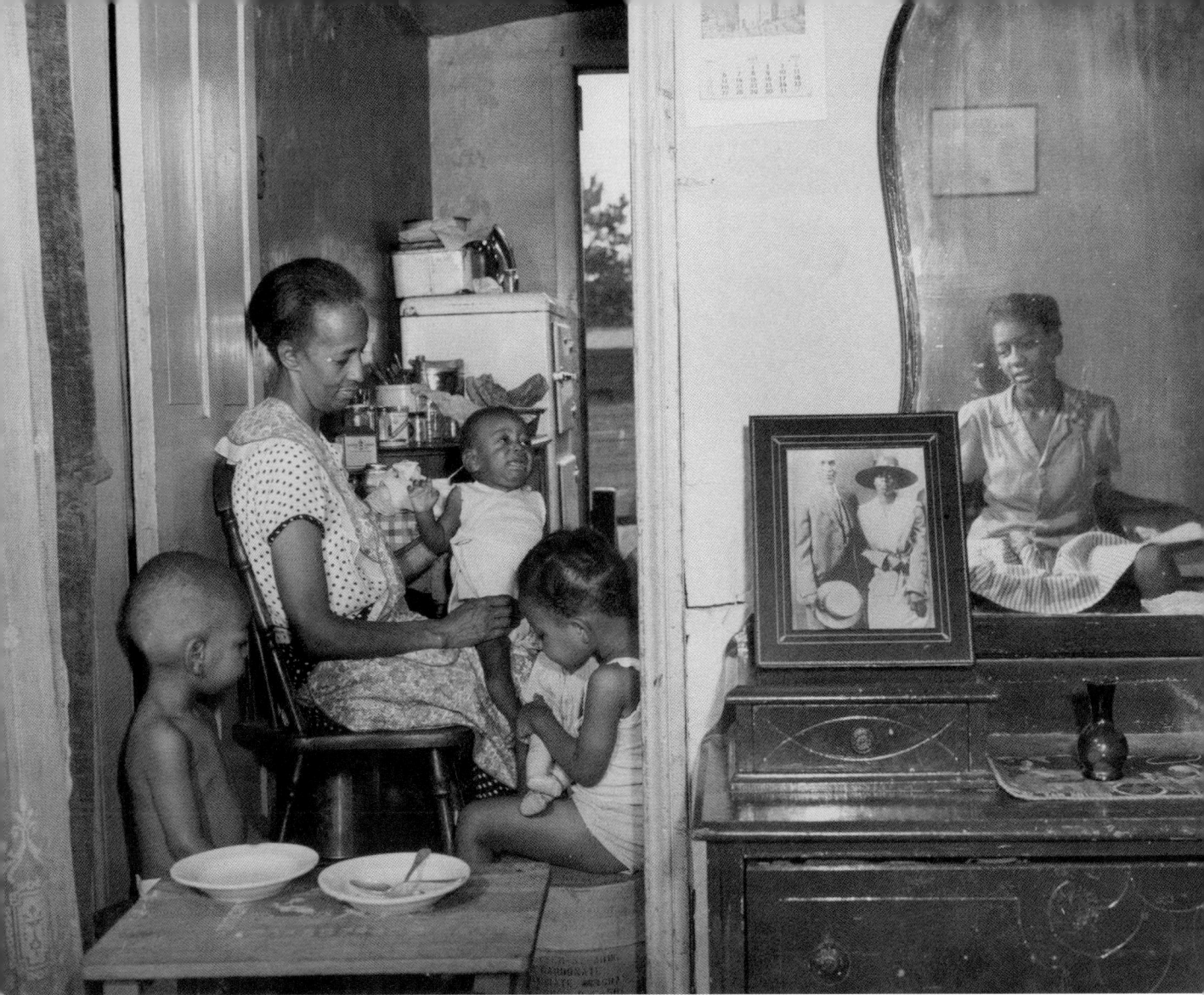

Gordon Parks (1912–2006), *Mrs. Ella Watson,
a Government Charwoman, with Three
Grandchildren and Her Adopted Daughter,*
Washington, DC, 1942. Gelatin silver print.

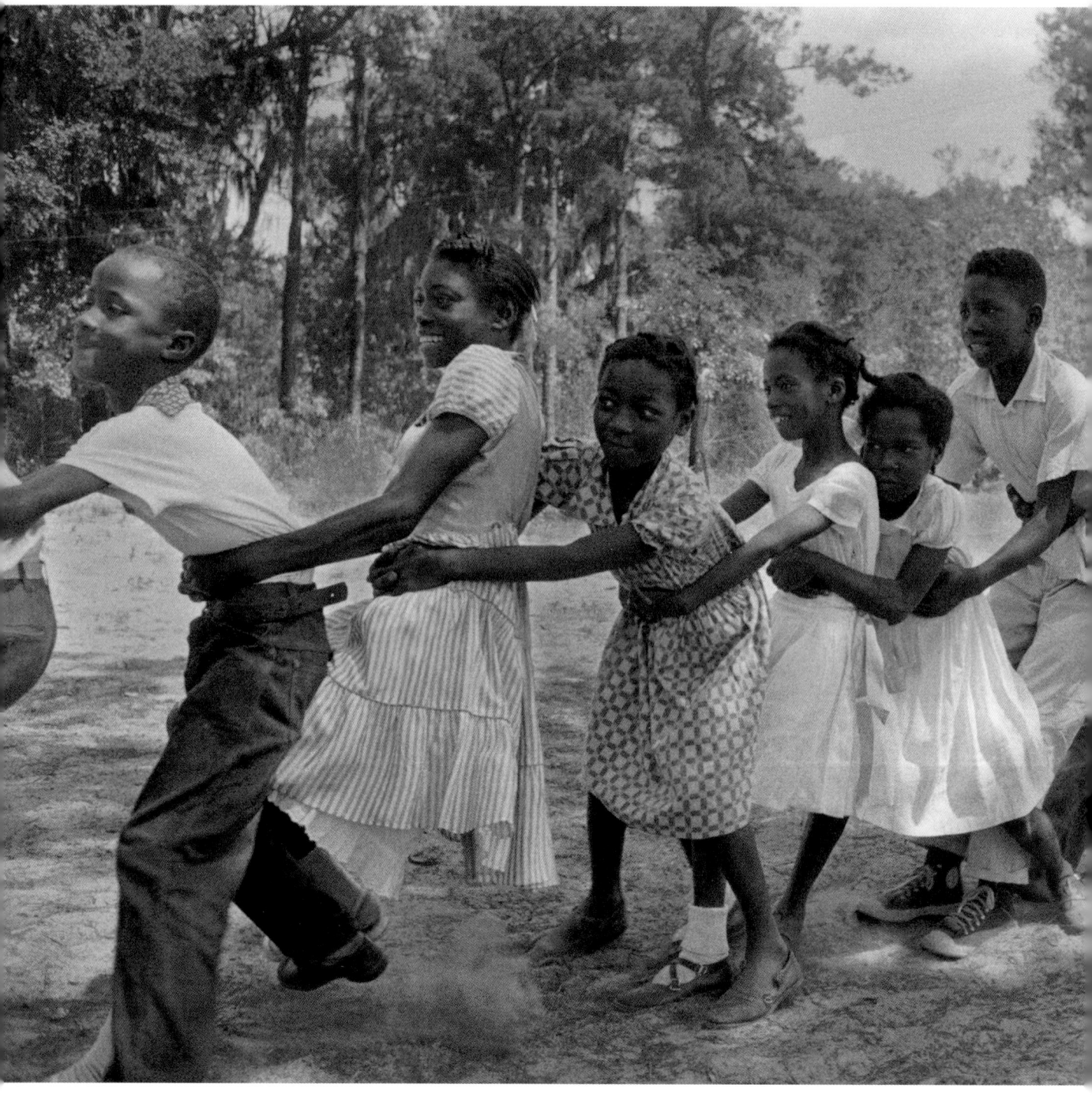

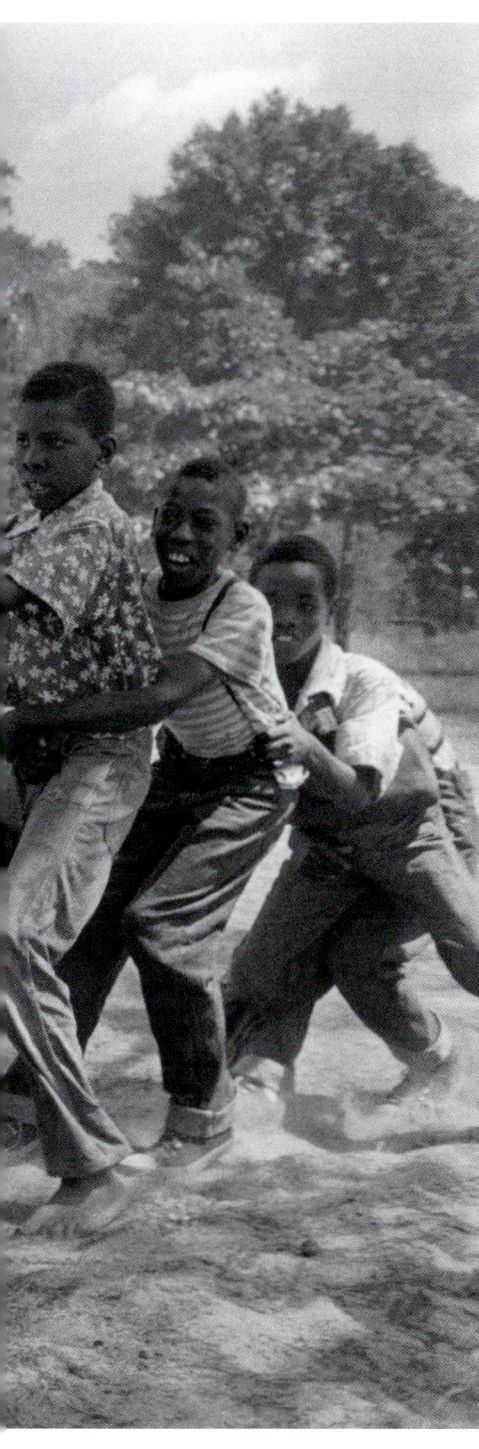

Children play a ropeless tug-of-war game in Constantine Manos's photograph, their expressions exuberant as the line of arms and bodies ripples across the frame. When Manos visited the remote Daufuskie Island, most residents were descended from enslaved people who labored on the island's plantations.

Constantine Manos (1934–), *Daufuskie Island*, South Carolina, 1952, printed later. Inkjet print. Courtesy of Constantine Manos.

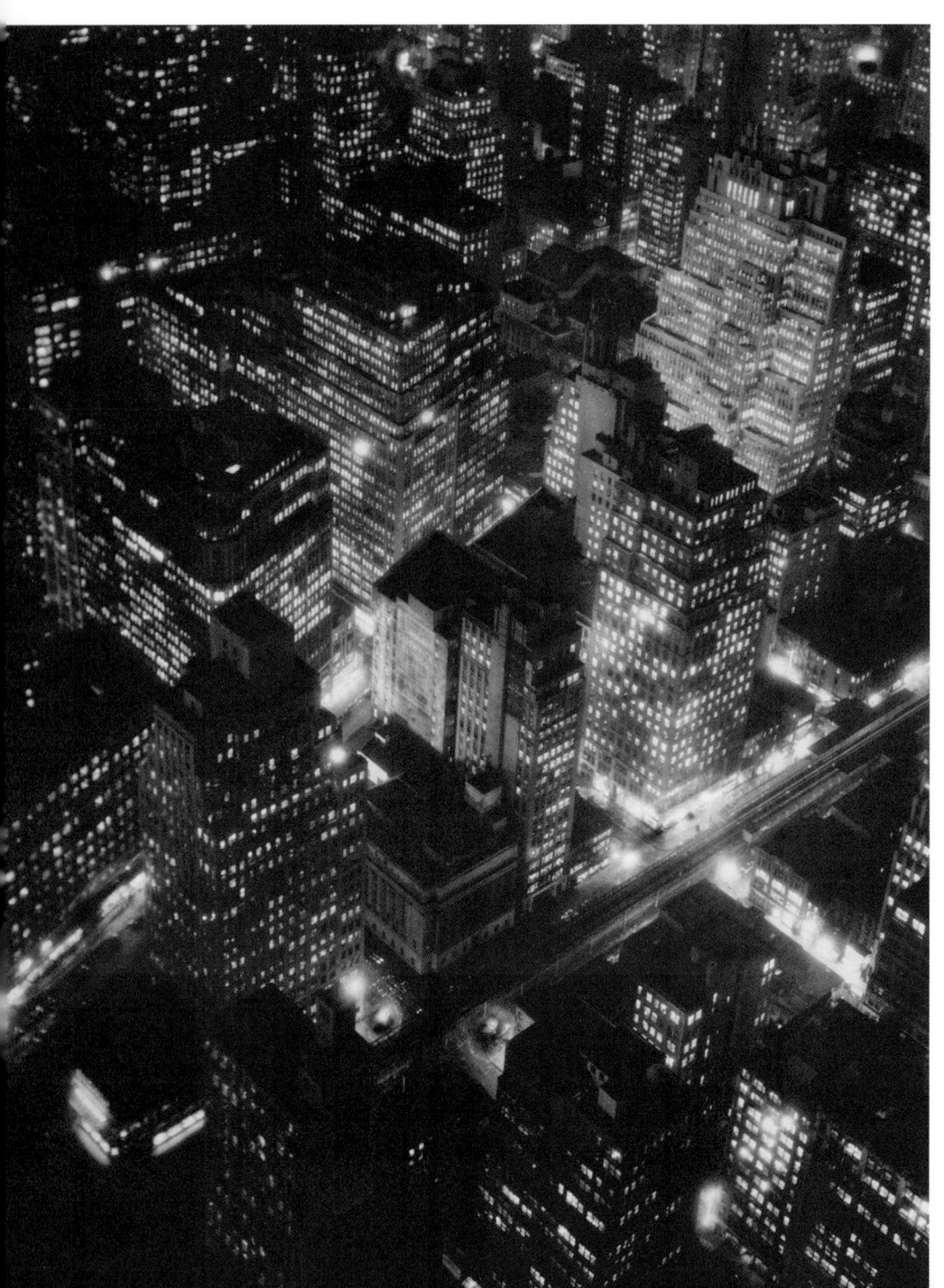

Taken from the Empire State Building, Berenice Abbott's kinetic view of midtown Manhattan captures the metropolis after dark. Previously known for her portraits, Abbott focused her camera on the rapidly changing city when she moved from Paris to New York in 1929.

Berenice Abbott (1898–1991), *Night Scene in Manhattan*, 1934. Gelatin silver print. Courtesy of Berenice Abbott / Premium Archive via Getty Images.

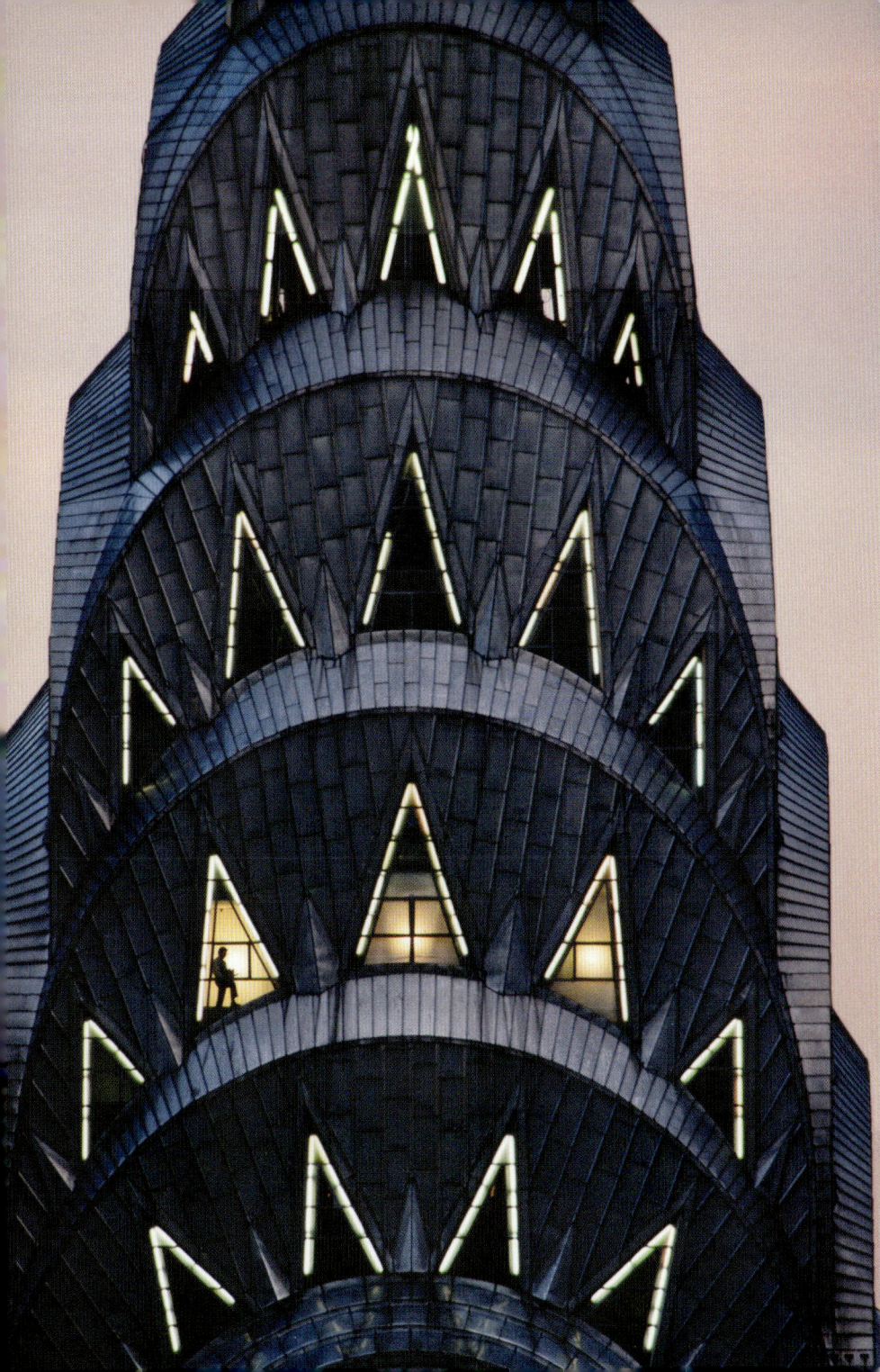

In this photograph for *National Geographic*, Nathan Benn depicts the Chrysler Building in half light, the glittering façade of the stainless steel spire punctuated by triangular windows, including one that features the silhouette of a figure inside.

| Nathan Benn (1950–), *Chrysler Building, Skyscrapers—Above the Crowd*, New York City, 1987. Inkjet print. Courtesy of Nathan Benn.

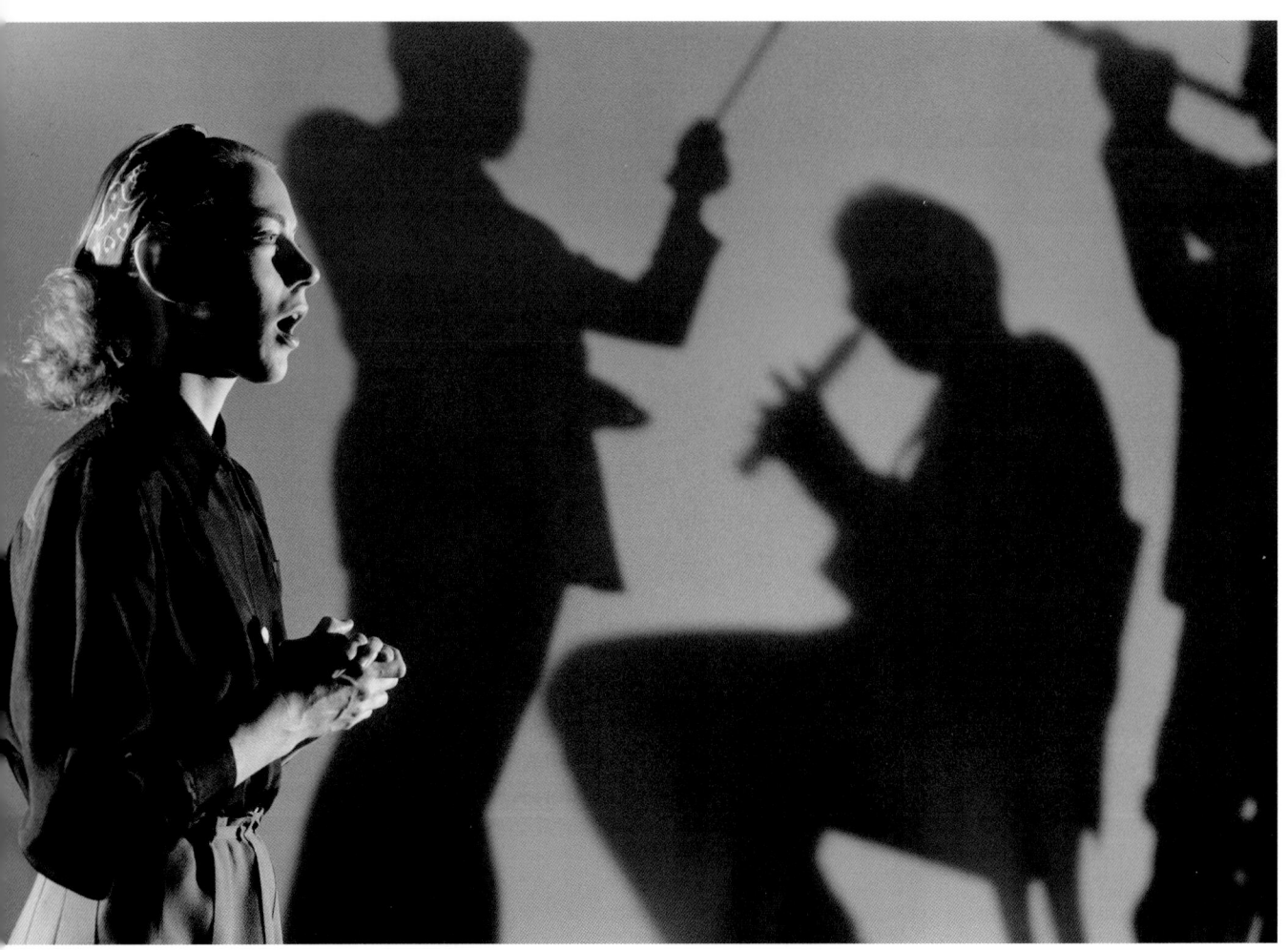

Shadow figures conduct and play instruments behind a starkly lit singer in Stanley Kubrick's dynamic photograph for *Look* magazine, taken long before he became a celebrated filmmaker.

Stanley Kubrick (1928–1999), *Shadow Story*, 1947. Film negative.

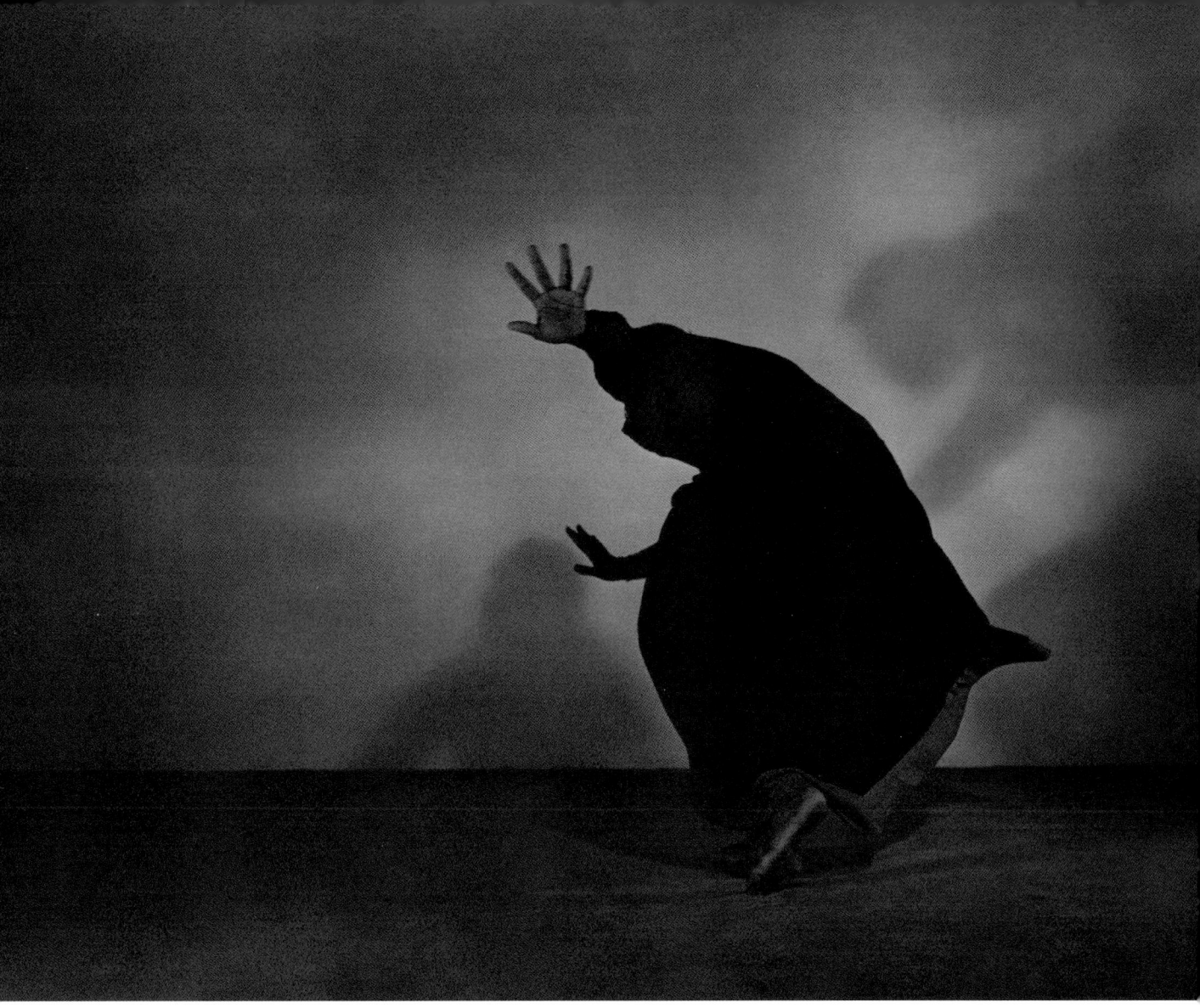

Barbara Morgan captures the energetic movement of dancer Pearl Primus, highlighting the contrast between her silhouette and the shadowy backdrop as well as the tension between her outstretched fingers and contracted form.

Barbara Brooks Morgan (1900–1992), *Pearl Primus—Speak to Me of Rivers*, 1944. Gelatin silver print. Printed with permission from the Barbara and Willard Morgan photographs and papers, Library Special Collections, Charles E. Young Research Library, UCLA.

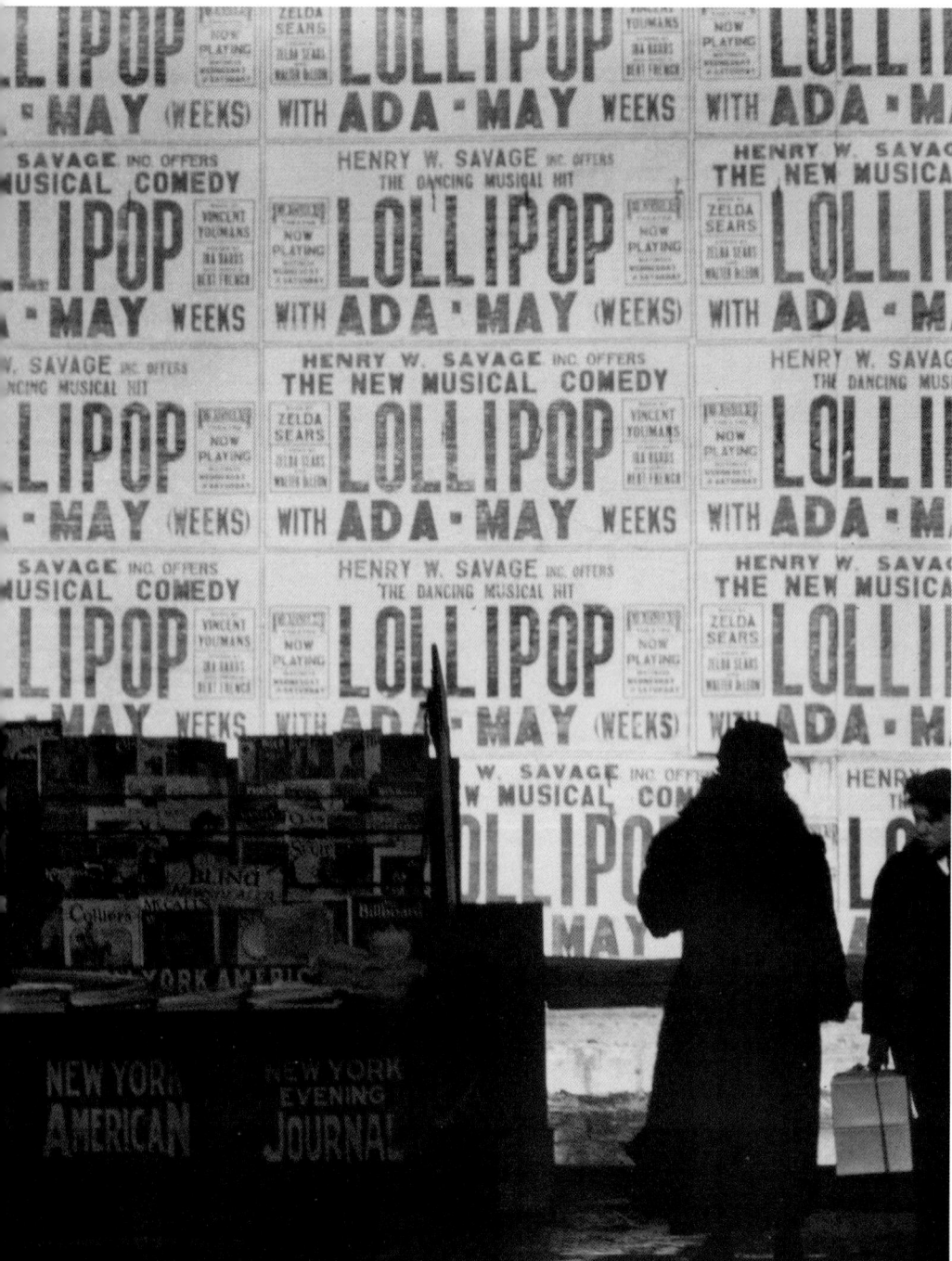

The repeating type in posters advertising the musical *Lollipop* creates an abstract backdrop for the dark newsstand and silhouetted figures in Ralph Steiner's photograph. A student of Clarence H. White, Steiner was a successful commercial photographer and filmmaker.

Ralph Steiner (1899–1986), *Lollipop*, New York City, 1922. Gelatin silver print. Courtesy of the Steiner Estate.

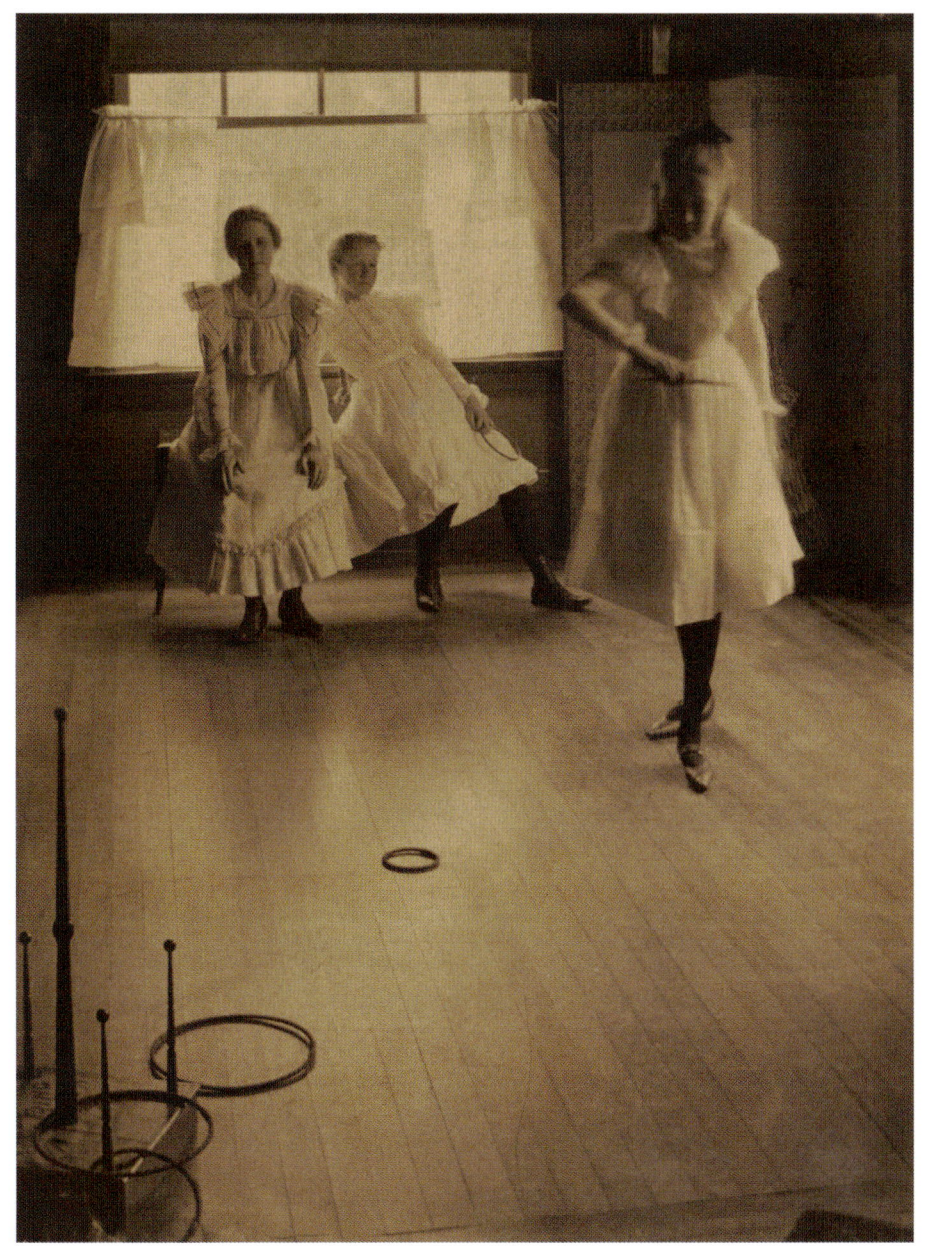

Clarence H. White, a self-taught photographer from Ohio, became a leading advocate for pictorialism, an artistic movement promoting aestheticism and craftsmanship in photography. His school trained a generation of photographers in New York. In *The Ring Toss*, White emphasized the choreography of play, as the diagonal line of rings on the floor draws the viewer's eye to the girl in motion.

Clarence H. White (1871–1925), *The Ring Toss*, Ohio, 1899. Platinum print.

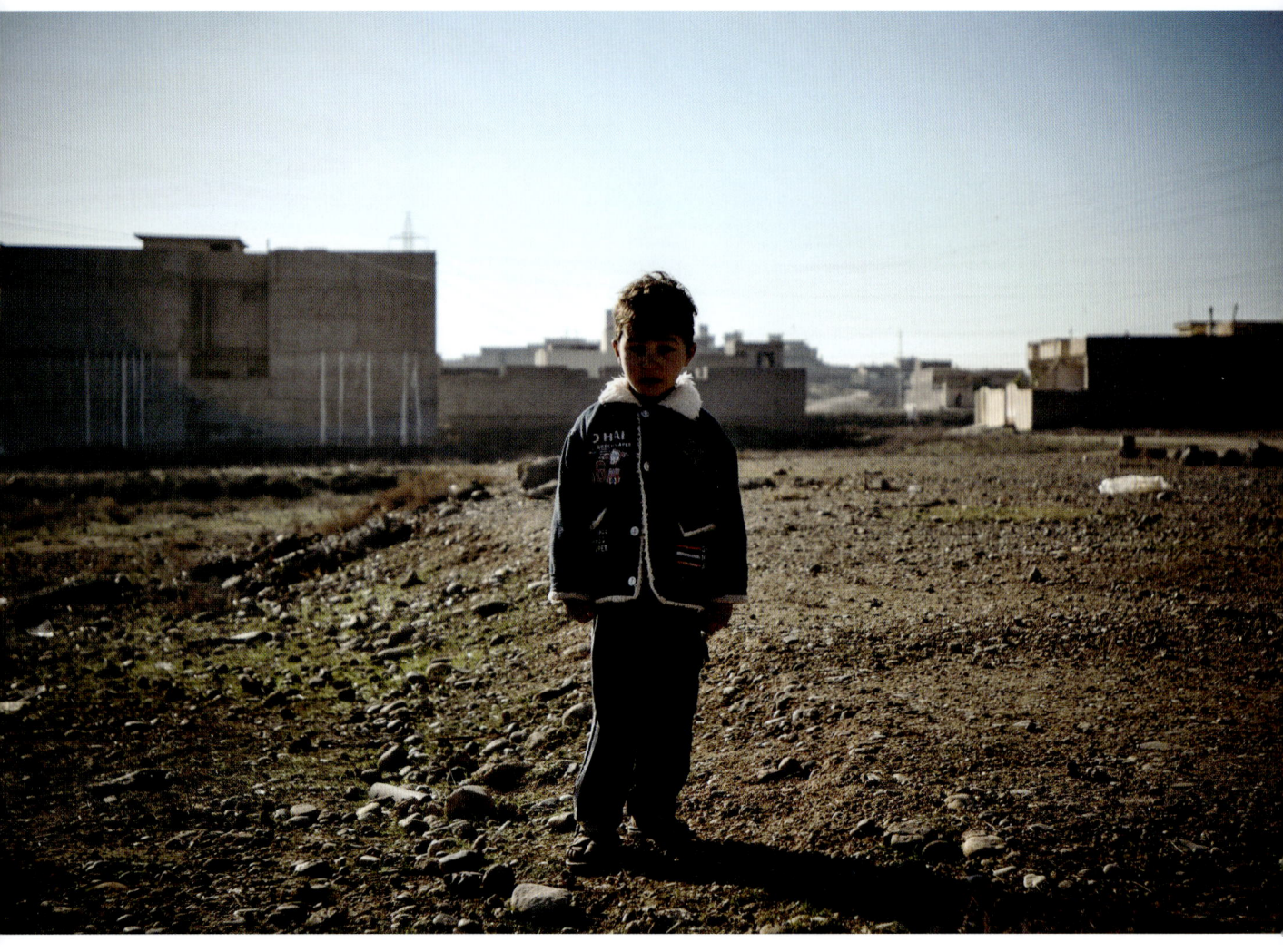

While on a cordon and search mission in Mosul, Army National Guard photographer Shawn Miller noticed a young boy with a forlorn expression. Through the photograph's composition, Miller conveys his observation that the boy, alone on rocky terrain, had spent his entire life only knowing war.

Shawn Miller (1985–), *An Iraqi Boy Watches a Patrol on the Outskirts of Mosul*, Iraq, 2011. Digital photograph.

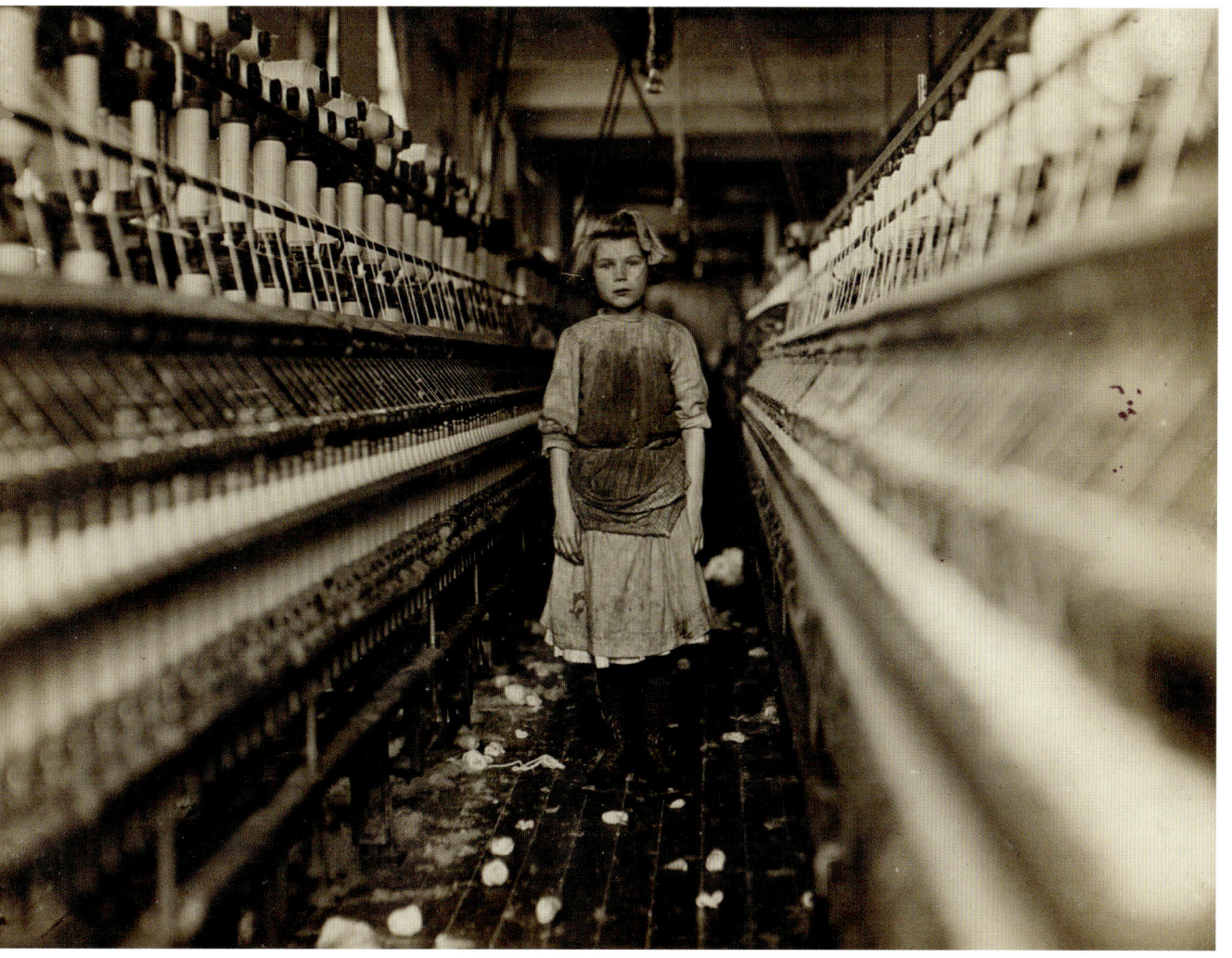

Lewis Hine's effective use of photography made him one of the National Child Labor Committee's greatest publicists in the campaign to ban child labor. Hine documented offenders such as this cotton mill, where a young worker in stained clothing stands between seemingly endless rows of bobbins, the floor littered with cotton balls.

Lewis Hine (1874–1940), *Little Spinner in Globe Cotton Mill. Overseer Said She Was Regularly Employed,* Augusta, Georgia, 1909. Gelatin silver print.

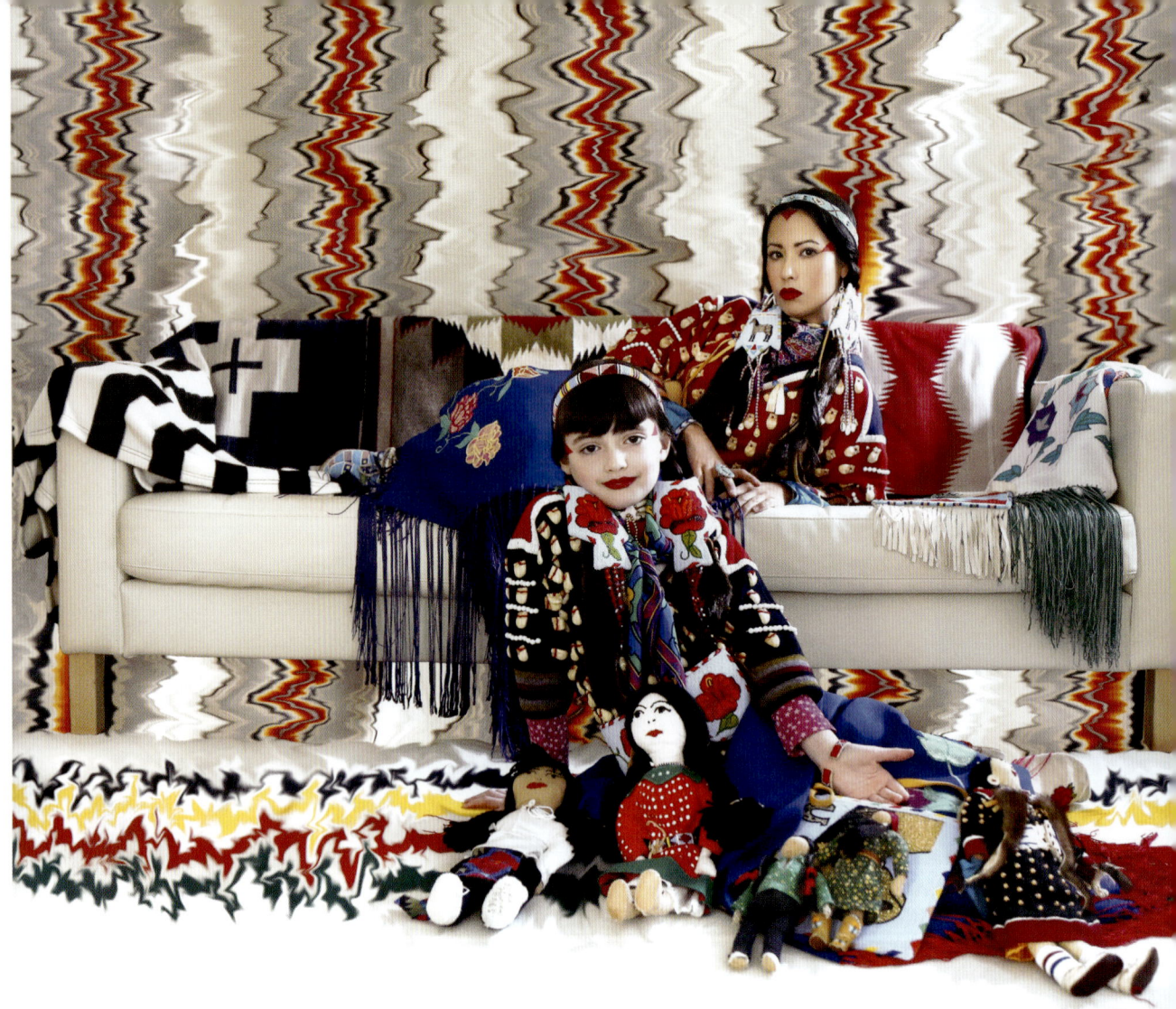

Raised on the Apsáalooke (Crow) reservation in Montana, Wendy Red Star created this self-portrait series with her daughter, Beatrice, blending traditional and contemporary motifs. Their elk tooth dresses signify their Crow heritage, womanhood, and the matrilineal line, connecting them to their ancestors.

Wendy Red Star (1981–), *Apsáalooke Feminist Series #3*, 2016. Inkjet print. Courtesy of Wendy Red Star.

For her *Kitchen Table* series, Carrie Mae Weems photographed herself in a sequence of poses, bringing in others to portray friends, partners, and family members, as well as objects to signify one woman's roles and relationships in the domestic sphere. Here, Weems and a young girl apply makeup, each with their own mirror.

| Carrie Mae Weems (1953–), *Untitled (Putting on makeup)*, 1990. Gelatin silver print. *Kitchen Table* series. © Carrie Mae Weems. Courtesy of the artist and Jack Shainman Gallery, New York.

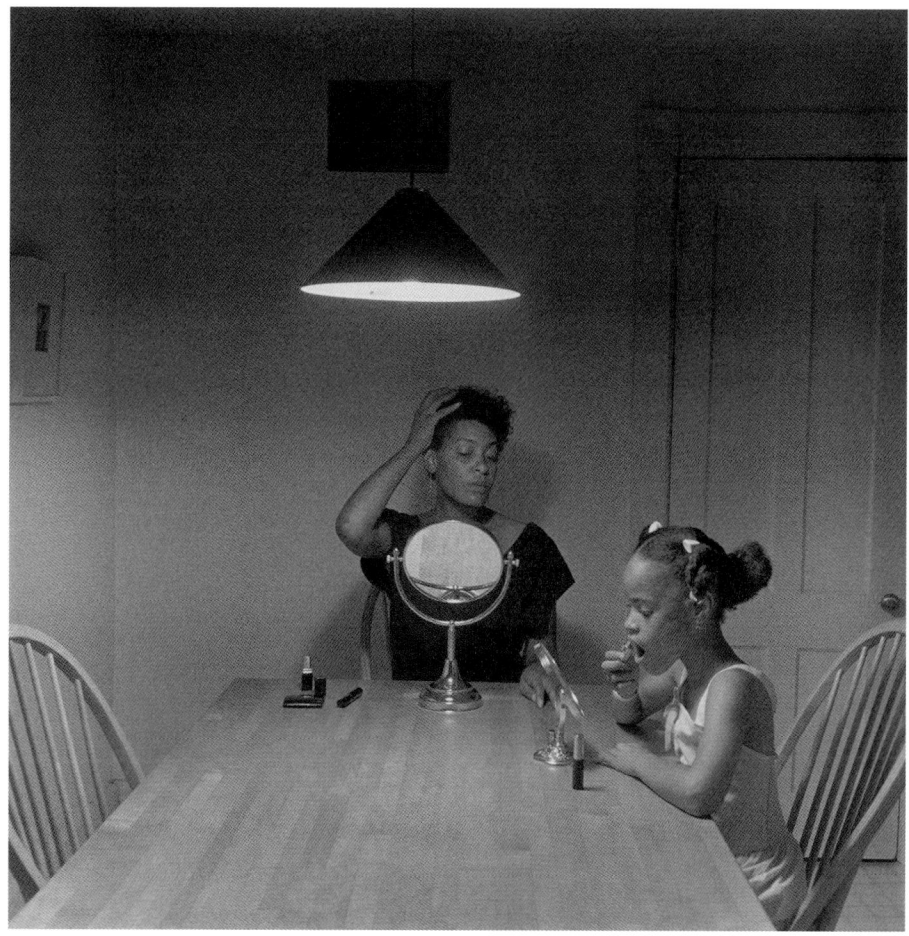

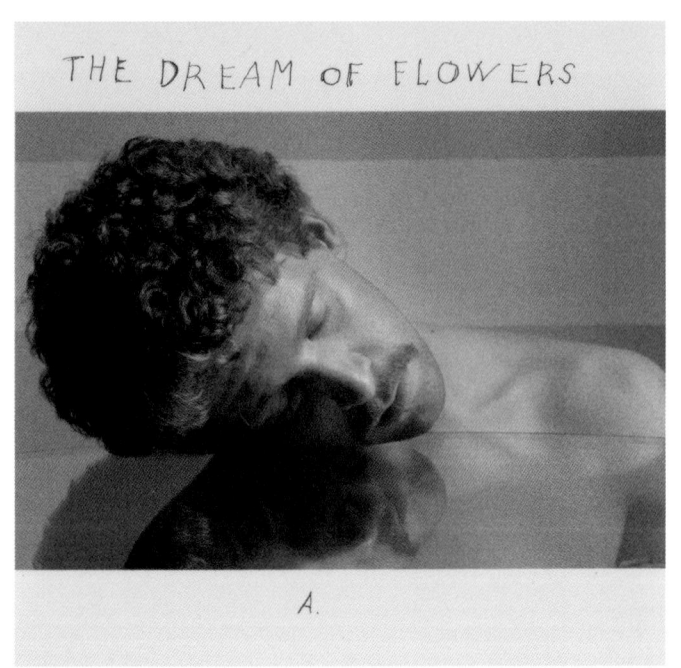

THE DREAM OF FLOWERS

A.

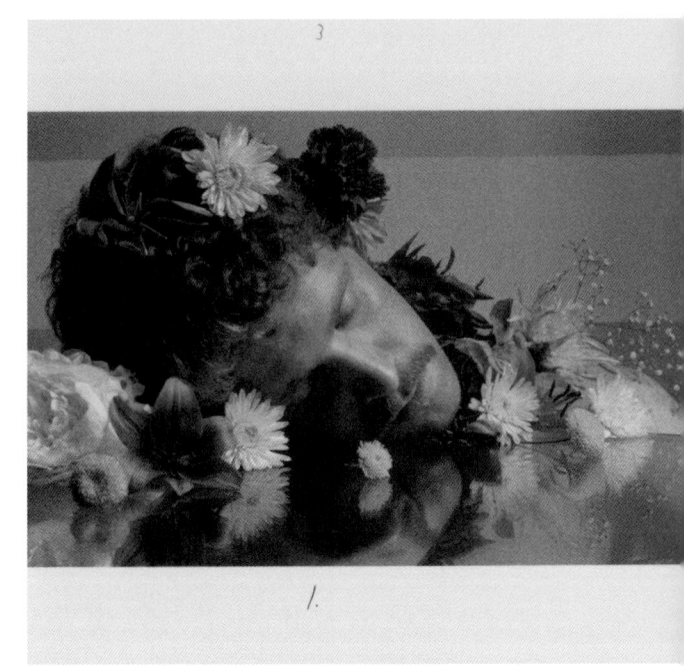

3

l.

As a young man rests his head on a reflective surface, flowers gradually cover him in each image in Duane Michals's series. Each photograph is inscribed with a letter sequentially spelling the word "AIDS," giving the surreal floral imagery a funereal cast, but perhaps suggesting rebirth as well.

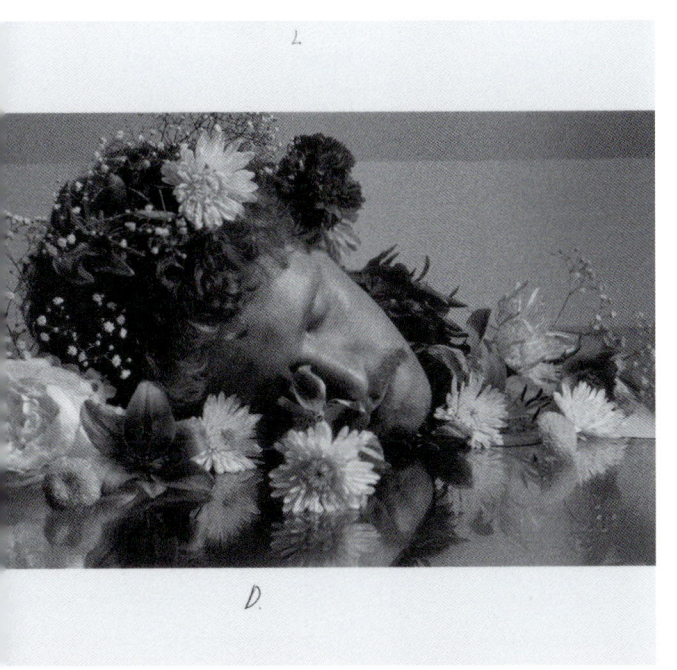
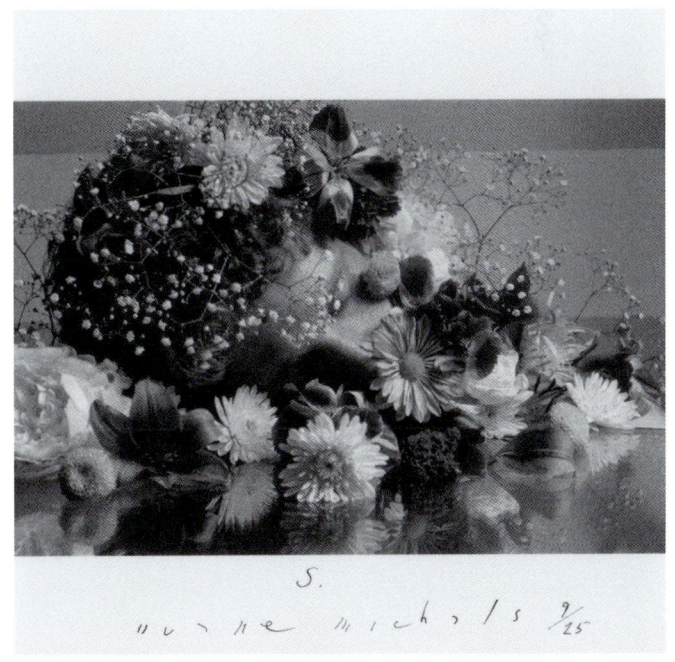

Duane Michals (1932–), *The Dream of Flowers*, 1990. Gelatin silver prints. Copyright Duane Michals, Courtesy of DC Moore Gallery, New York.

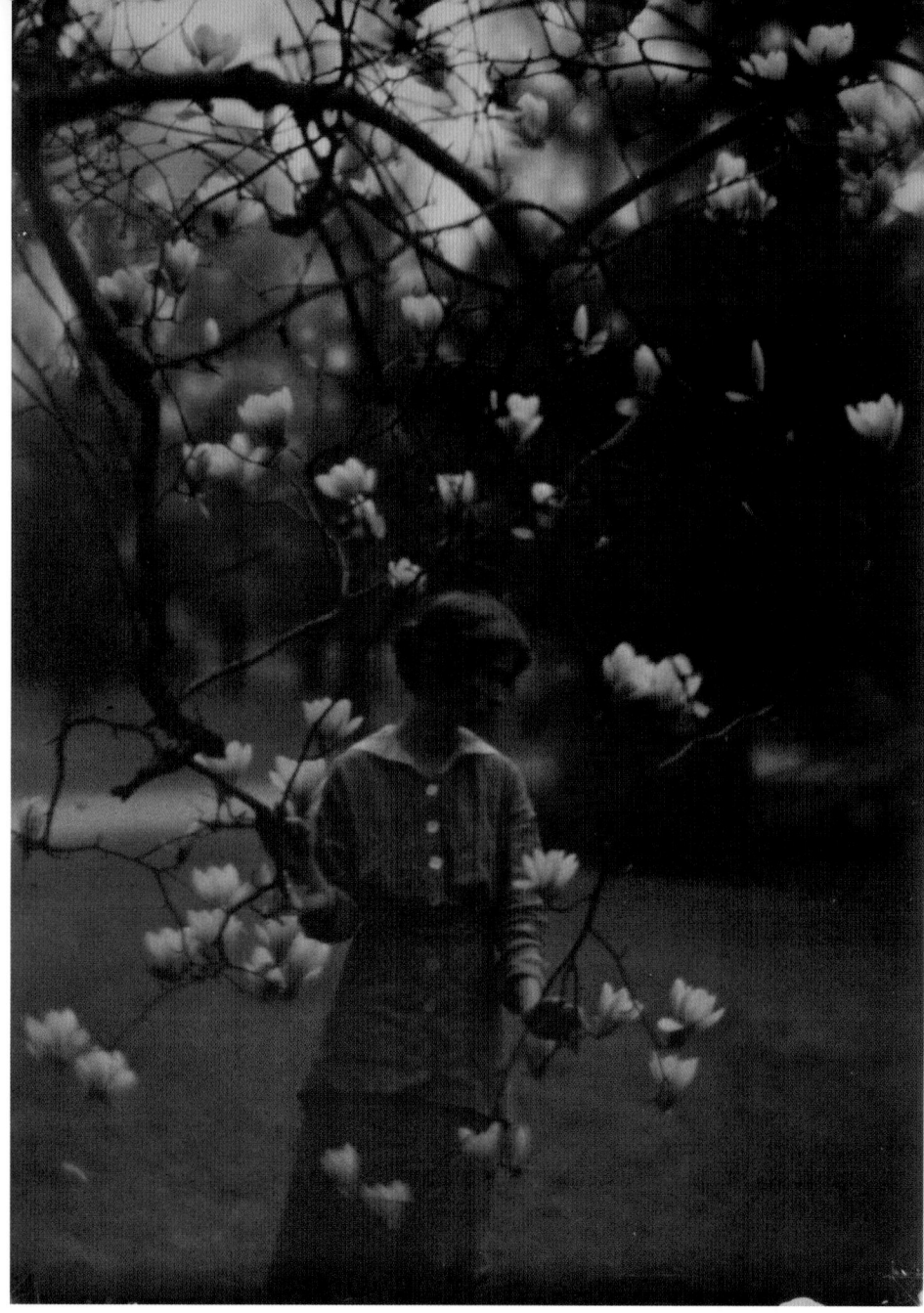

In acclaimed pictorialist photographer Arnold Genthe's portrait of poet Edna St. Vincent Millay, he used the autochrome process to create a unique color transparency in the camera. The pastel tones of the process's dyed potato starch grains contribute to the soft, romantic effect, as does the shallow depth of field and framing of Millay behind the branches of a flowering tree.

Arnold Genthe (1869–1942), *Edna St. Vincent Millay at Mitchell Kennerley's House*, Mamaroneck, New York, 1914. Autochrome.

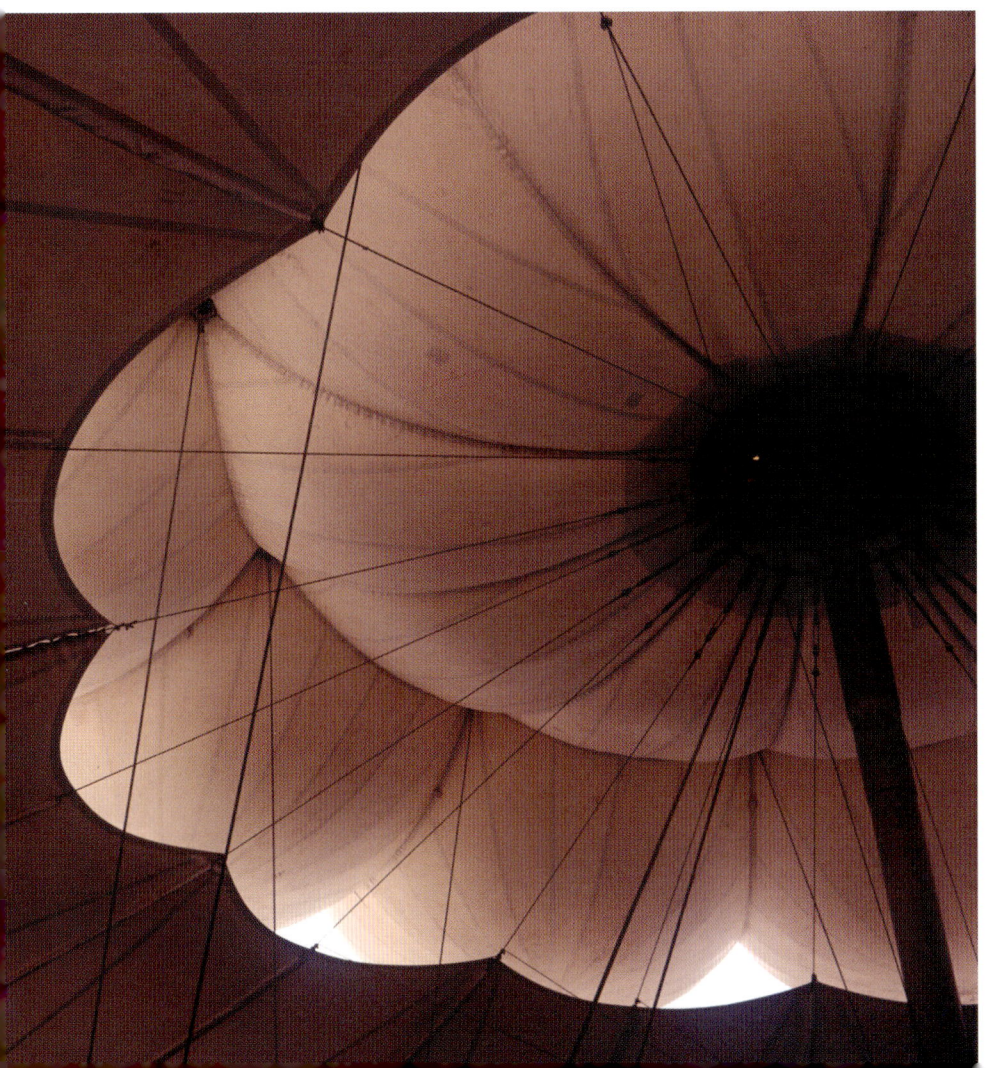

A flower, an internal organ, a hot air balloon? George Cserna's close-up photograph of bulblike shapes does not immediately reveal its subject: one of Victor A. Lundy's inflated "space flower" refreshment stands created for the New York World's Fair.

George Cserna (1919–2003), *Refreshment Stand Ceiling with Mast, Brass Rail Food Service Organization, World's Fair*, New York City, 1964. Color transparency. Victor A. Lundy Archive.

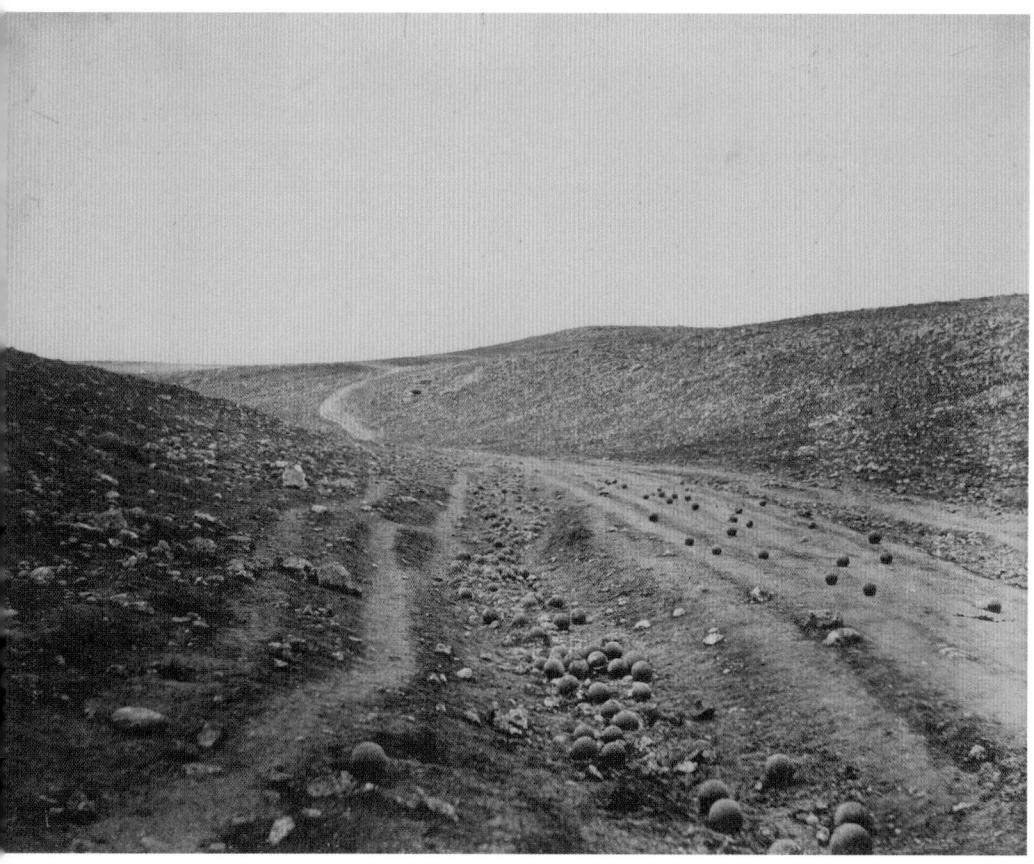

Roger Fenton took this austere image of cannonballs littering a rocky hillside during the Crimean War in one of the first attempts to document war through photography. In this shot—one of the most famous and enduring war photos to date—the absence of any soldiers or vegetation makes the photograph more haunting, suggesting a limitless potential for devastation.

Roger Fenton (1819–1869), *The Valley of the Shadow of Death*, Crimea, 1855. Salted paper print.

elin o'Hara slavick (1965–), *Four A-Bombed Bottles from Hiroshima*, 2013. Cyanotype print.

Contemporary artist elin o'Hara slavick created this cyanotype photograph by placing deformed bottles from the Hiroshima Peace Memorial Museum on sensitized paper and exposing them to the sun. Their ghostly images evoke the white nuclear shadows cast as the city and its residents were incinerated by the atomic bomb.

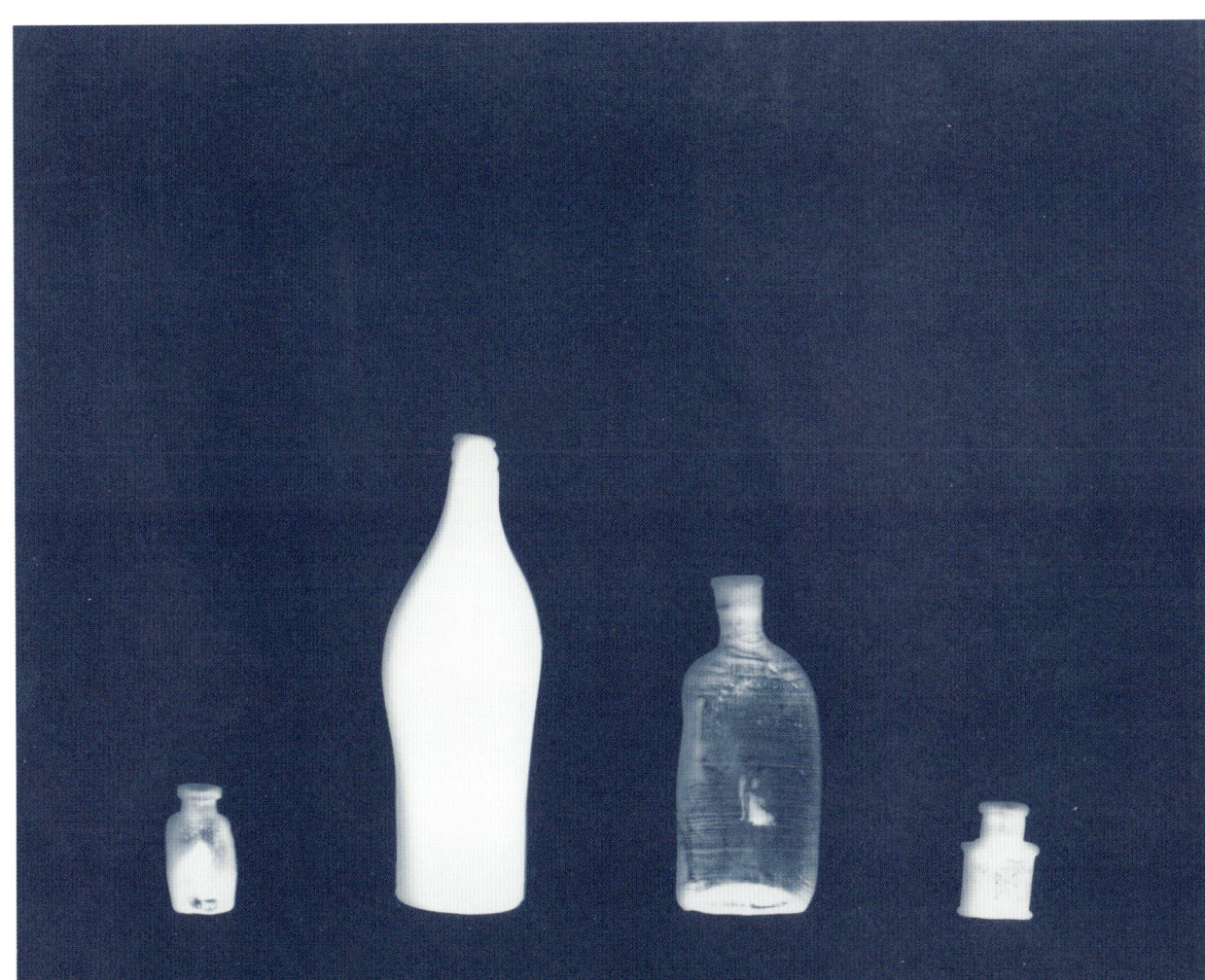

US Army photographer Emil David Edgren took this dramatic shot while under German fire with the 82nd Airborne Division at the Battle of the Bulge. Edgren was hugging the ground with a machine gunner behind him yelling, "don't get up!" when he photographed another soldier running across the field to aid his compatriots.

Emil David Edgren (1919–2020), *An 82nd Airborne Soldier Running Across a Field Holding a Thompson Machine Gun During a German Ambush in Belgium, Christmas Day*, 1944. Gelatin silver print.

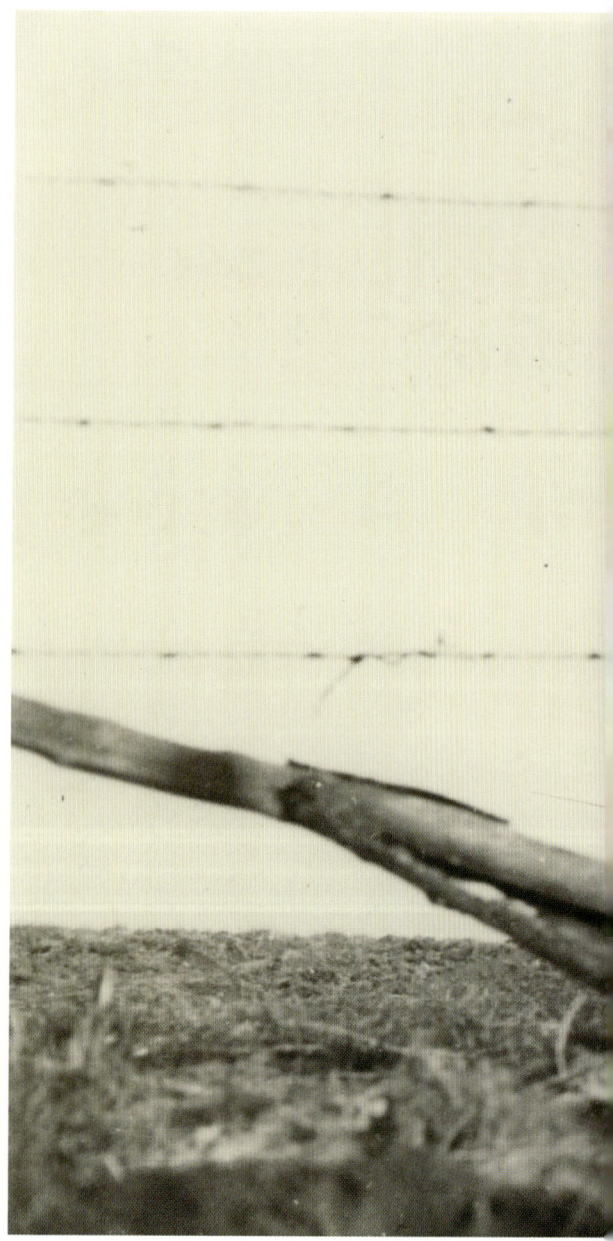

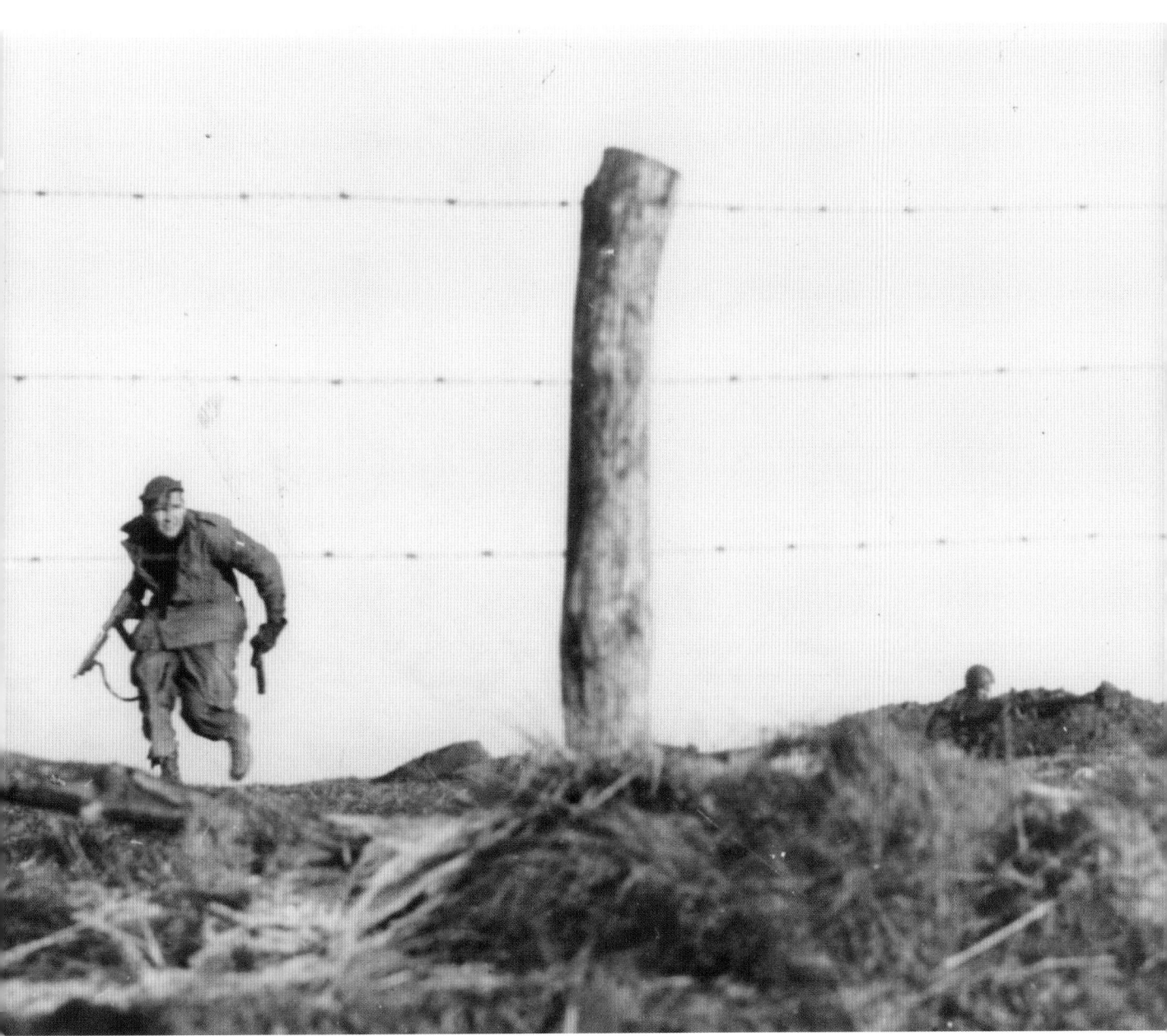

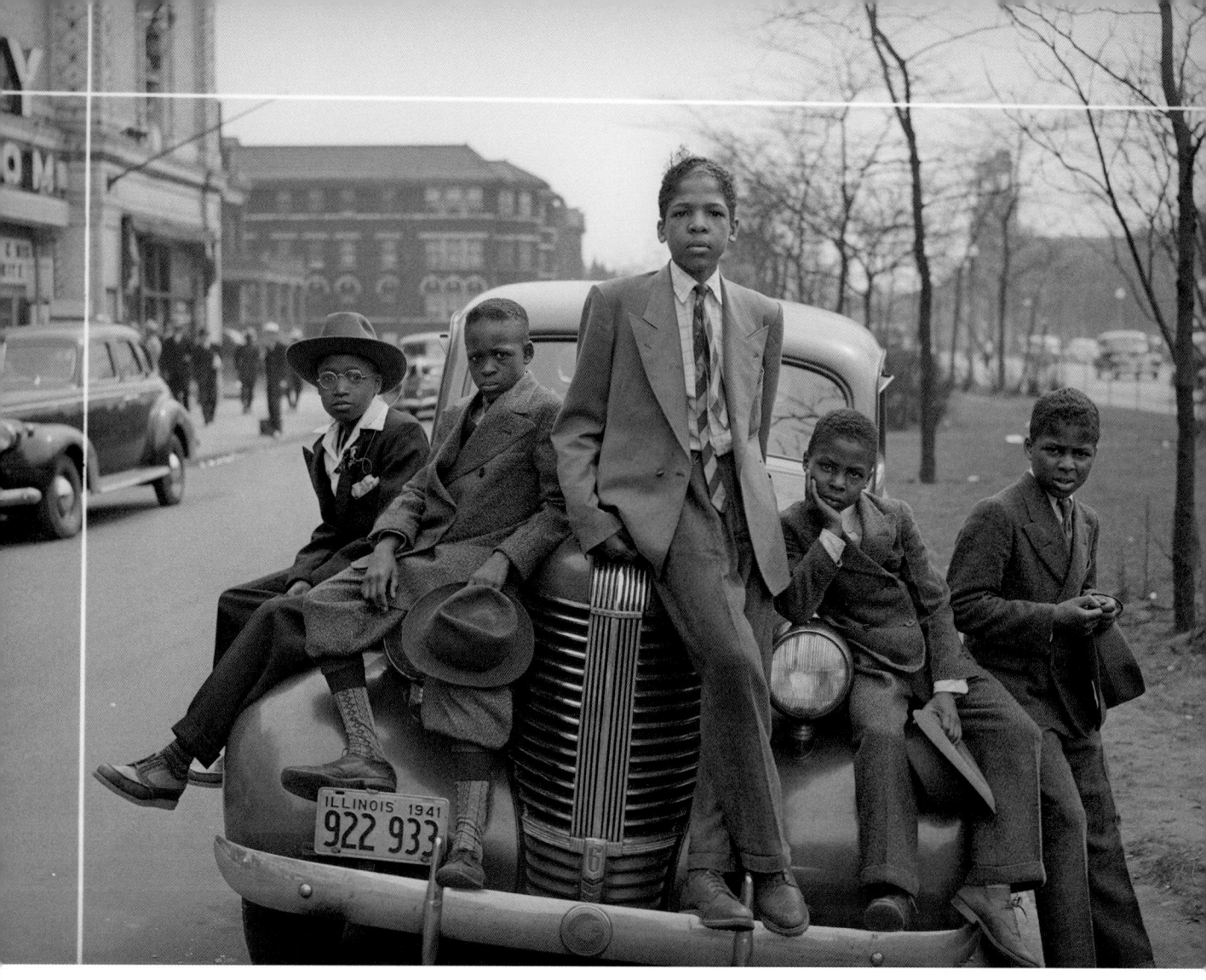

Russell Lee (1903–1986), *Negro Boys on Easter Morning*. Southside, Chicago, Illinois, 1941. Safety film negative.

Russell Lee, the most prolific of the Farm Security Administration's photographers, took this arresting portrait of five boys in the Bronzeville neighborhood of Chicago while photographing African Americans for Richard Wright's *12 Million Black Voices* (1941). The confident stance of the central figure, Spencer Lee Readus Jr., and that of his unnamed companions, demonstrates their claim on their neighborhood. The white lines on the negative are crop marks, reflected in the eventual print.

Zig Jackson, *Indian Man on Bus*, San Francisco, 1994, printed later. Inkjet print. *Indian Man in San Francisco* series. Courtesy of Zig Jackson.

Riding a San Francisco city bus, Zig Jackson wears a feather headdress along with sunglasses, jeans, and sneakers. Jackson, a member of the Mandan, Hidatsa, and Arikara Nation, creates performative work that juxtaposes traditional Native iconography with contemporary urban settings to invite reflection on the long history of Native American displacement.

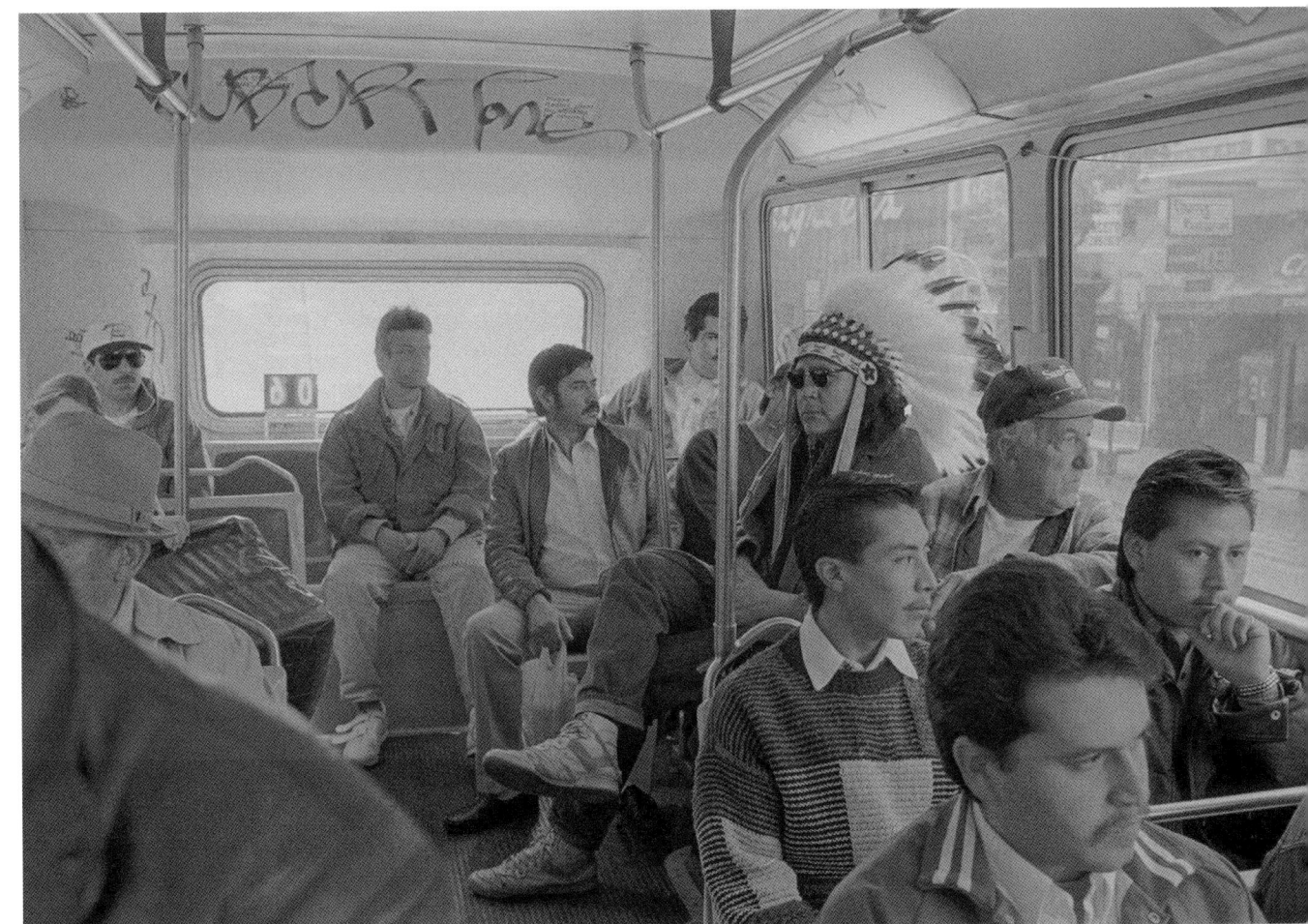

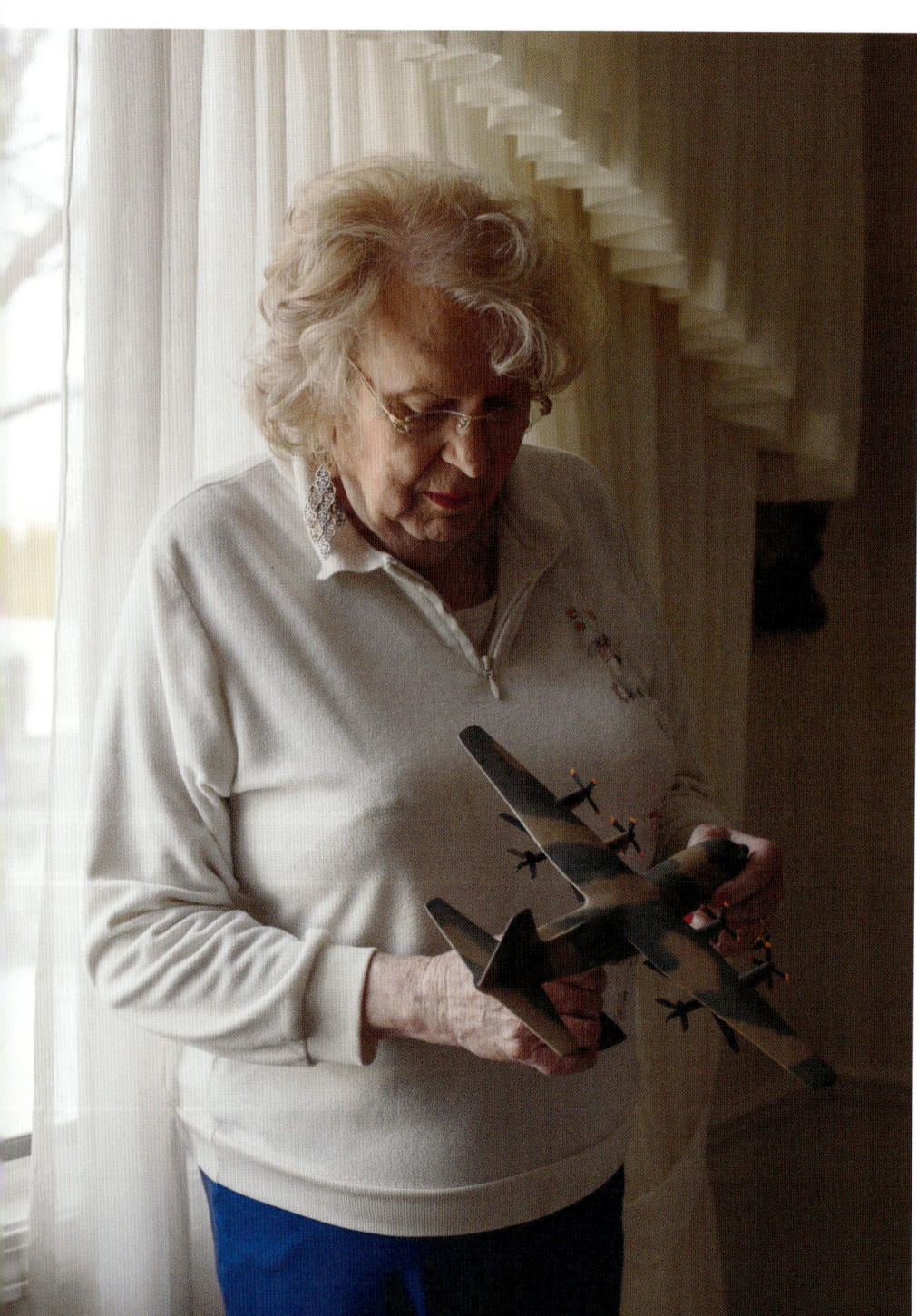

This portrait is part of a poignant series featuring transgender and gender nonconforming older adults, a group that photographer Jess T. Dugan felt had not been properly represented. Shown here, Bobbi began transitioning around age 70 after a high-profile career with the Air Force. "I'm proud of both me's," she reflected in an interview. "And I feel it has been a remarkable thing to have happened to a person. I'm grateful."

Jess T. Dugan (1986–), *Bobbi, 83*, Detroit, Michigan, 2014. Inkjet print. *To Survive on This Shore* portfolio. Courtesy of Jess T. Dugan.

Ka-Man Tse's photograph, created in Manhattan's Chinatown, depicts a figure holding a tray of tomato plants, looking directly at the viewer. Flanked by an elderly cobbler's colorful drawings, the young man holds the scene much like he holds the plants.

Ka-Man Tse (1981–), *Untitled*, New York City, 2017. Inkjet print. *Narrow Distances* series. © Ka-Man Tse, 2017.

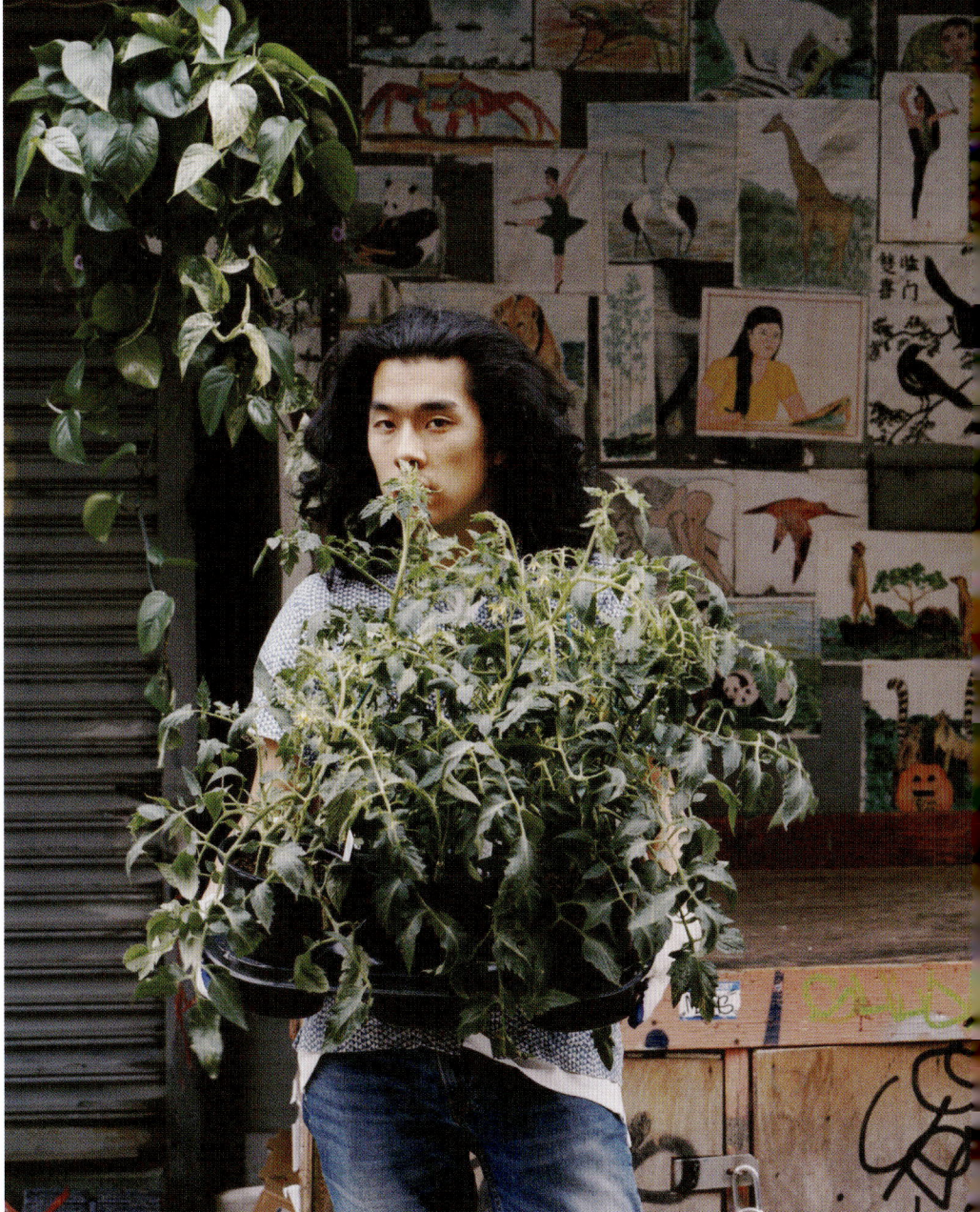

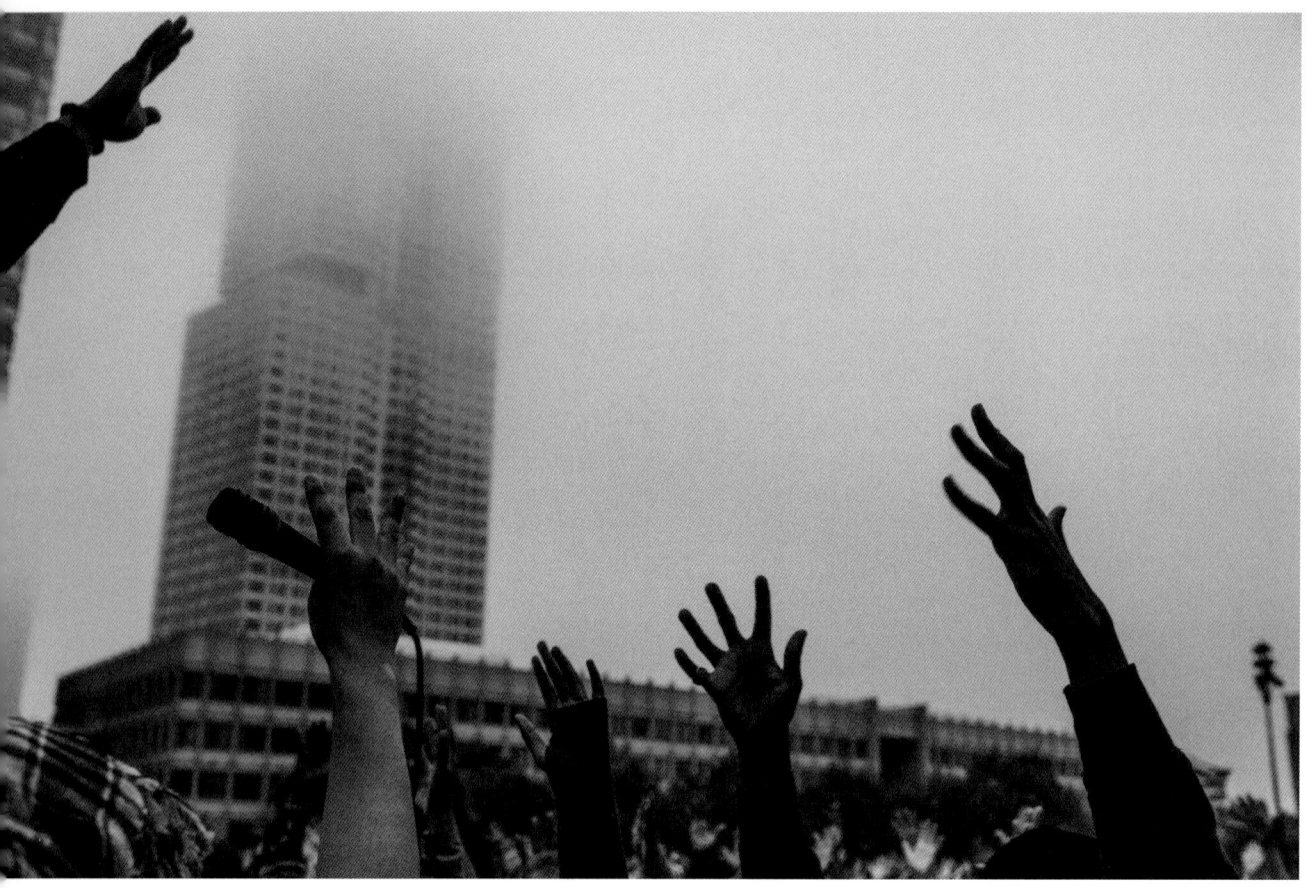

During a Black Lives Matter protest in June 2020, local photographer Harry Scales captured a moving scene in Boston in which demonstrators were taught to sign words of peace and unity. Gesturing upward, their hands appear silhouetted against the foggy sky.

Harry Scales (1990–), *Protesters Learning Sign Language*, Boston, 2020. Inkjet print. Courtesy of Harry Scales.

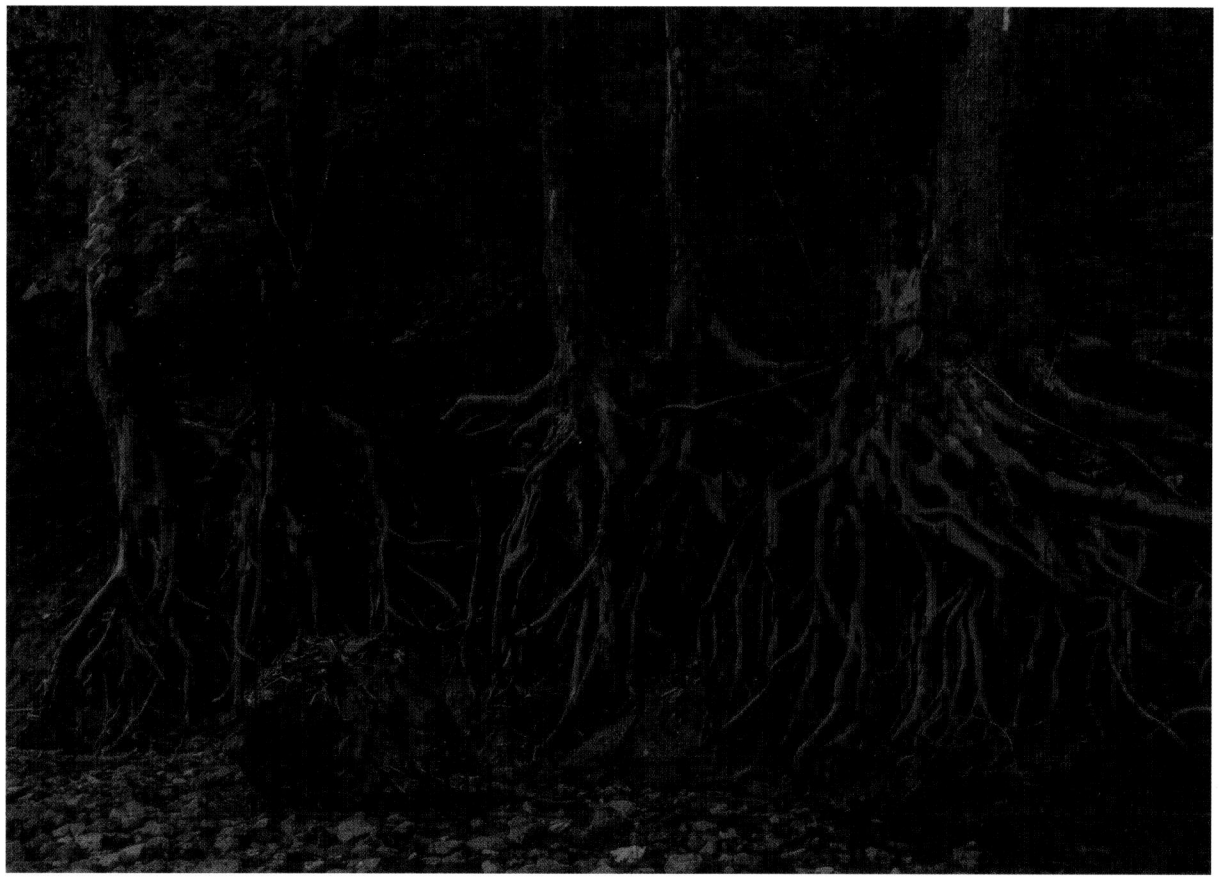

Jeanine Michna-Bales researched accounts of people who had escaped slavery and made photographs inspired by their descriptions of the 1,400-mile path from Louisiana to Canada. To evoke the emotional resonance of their journeys, she set all of the photos at night—the least dangerous time to travel. The intertwined tree roots emerge from darkness, contributing a sense of unease to the photograph.

Jeanine Michna-Bales (1971–), *Eagle Hollow from Hunter's Bottom*, Indiana, 2014. Digital chromogenic print. *Through Darkness to Light: Photographs Along the Underground Railroad* portfolio. Courtesy of Jeanine Michna-Bales.

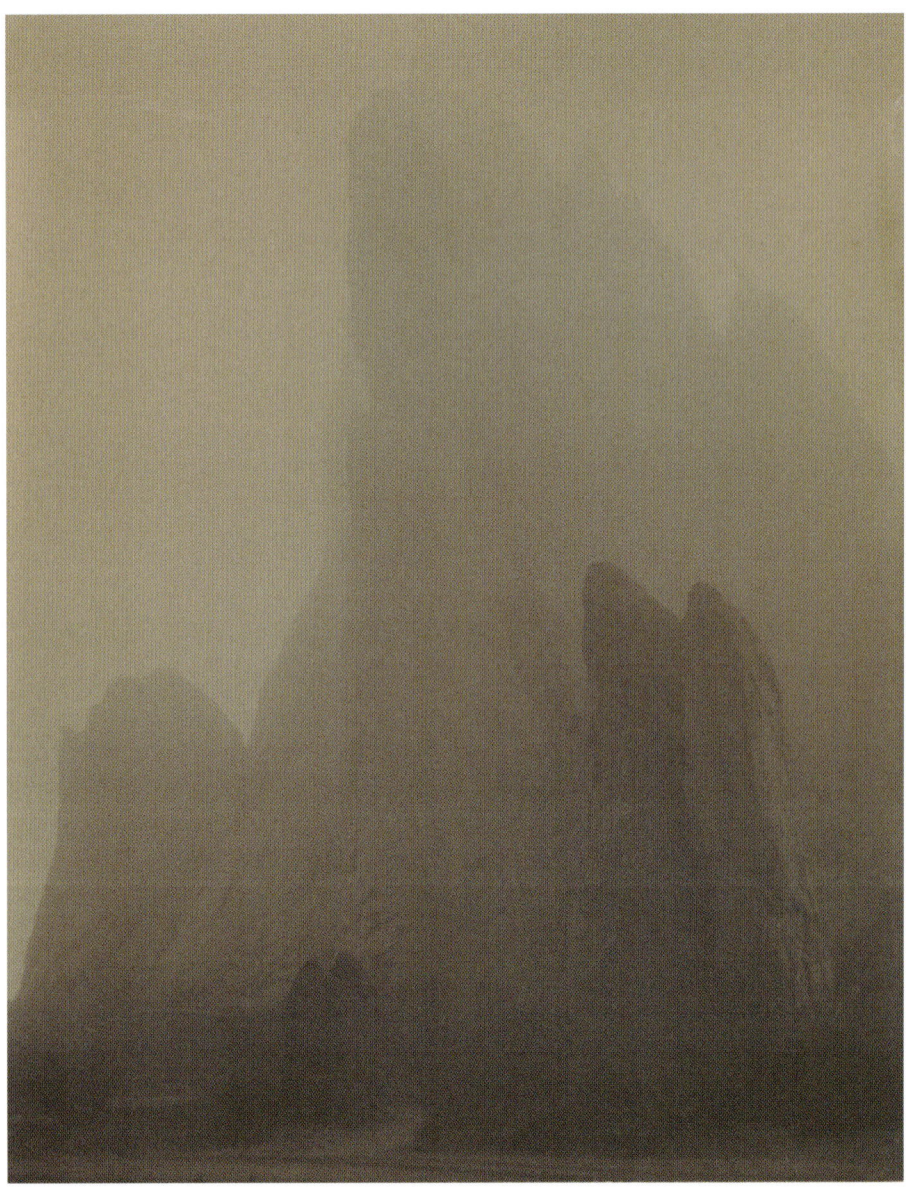

Colorado photographer Laura Gilpin studied with pictorialist Clarence H. White and turned her camera toward the landscapes of her American southwest home. Massive rock formations take on an ethereal quality in this photograph as their amorphous shapes emerge from the fog.

Laura Gilpin (1891–1979), *The Ghost Rock*, Garden of the Gods, Colorado, 1919. Platinum print. © 1979 Amon Carter Museum of American Art.

Clouds of locusts darken the daytime sky in Lewis Larsson's moody photograph of the plague that swept Jerusalem and the surrounding region in 1915, devastating vegetation and threatening food supplies. Swedish-born Larsson was a member of the American Colony, a Christian utopian society, and head of its American Colony Photo Department, a commercial studio that took iconic images of the Middle East in the early twentieth century.

| Lewis Larsson (1881–1958), *Swarming Locusts*, Jerusalem, 1915. Gelatin silver print, hand-colored. Locust Plague of 1915 Photograph Album.

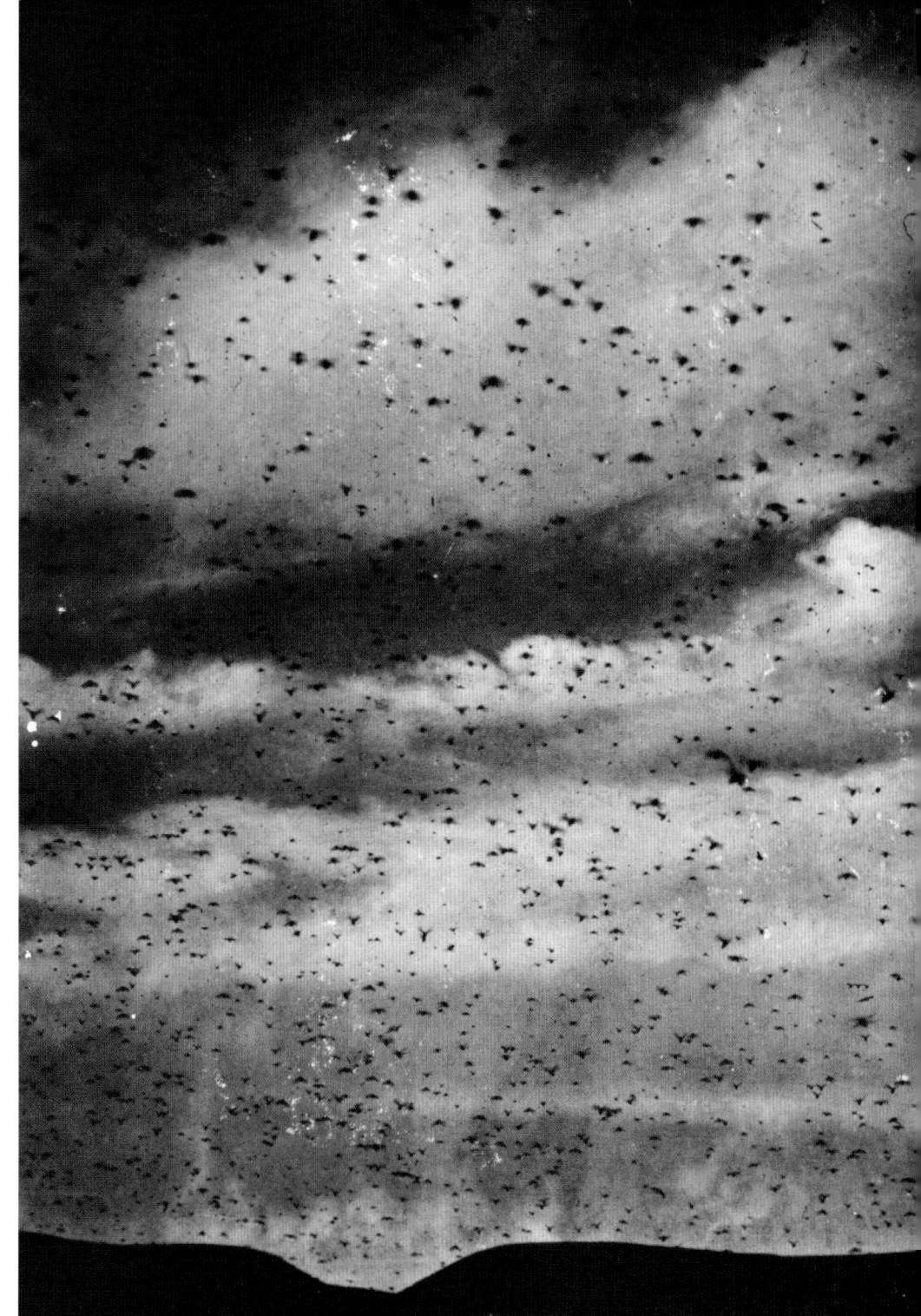

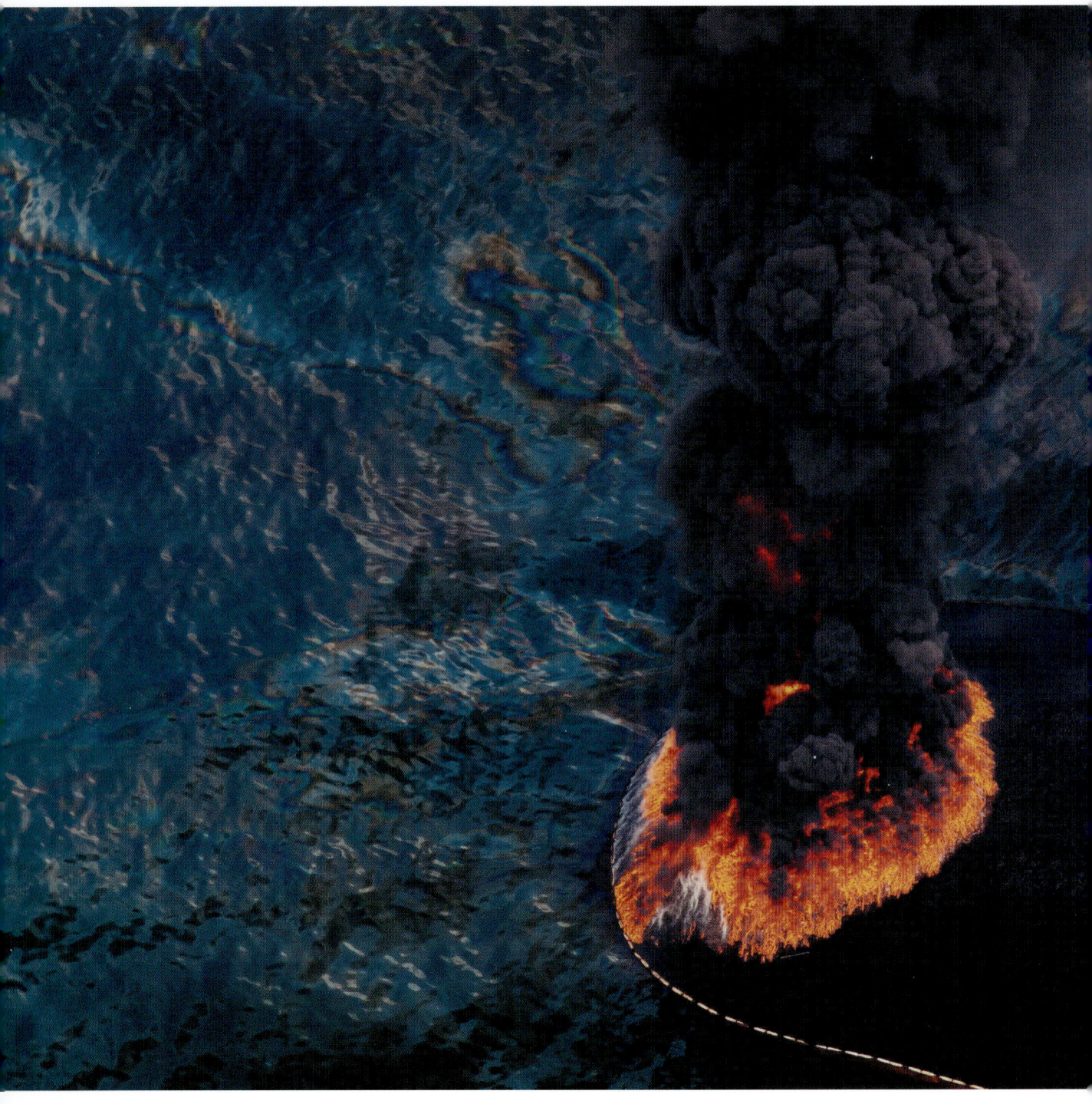

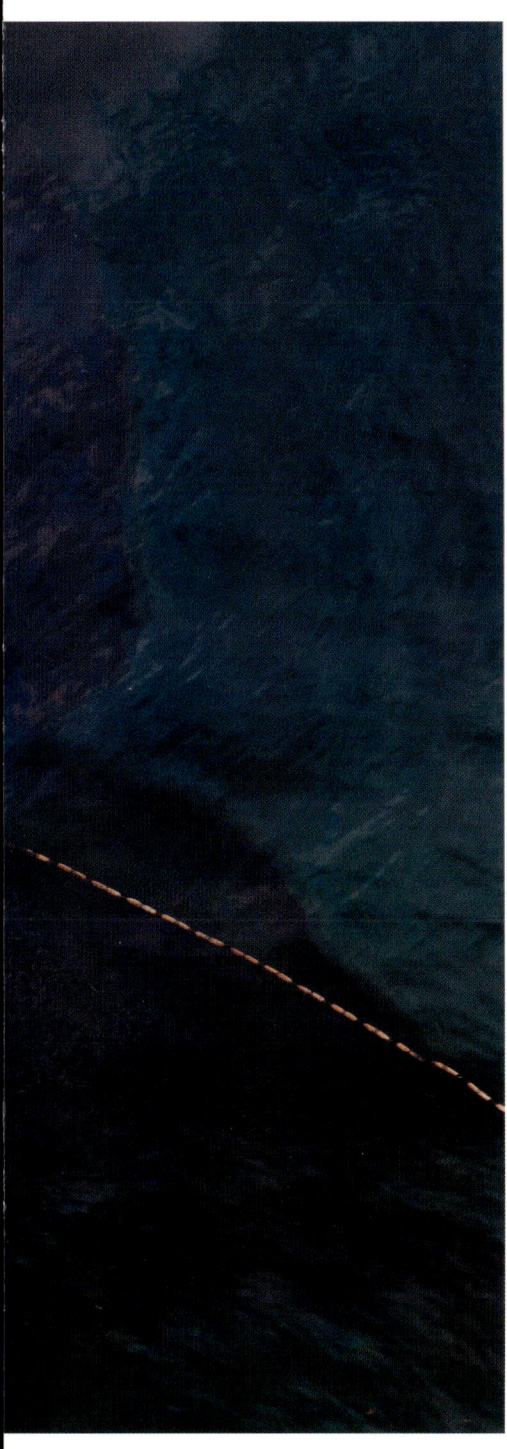

In Daniel Beltrá's aerial photographs of the BP Deepwater Horizon oil spill, he shows the vast impact on the Gulf of Mexico with disturbing beauty, as iridescent colors emerge from the oil-drenched waters. Here, a burn of collected oil intended to remove it from the water's surface sets the ocean aflame.

Daniel Beltrá (1964–), *Gulf Oil Spill #1*, 2010. Digital chromogenic print. Courtesy of Daniel Beltrá.

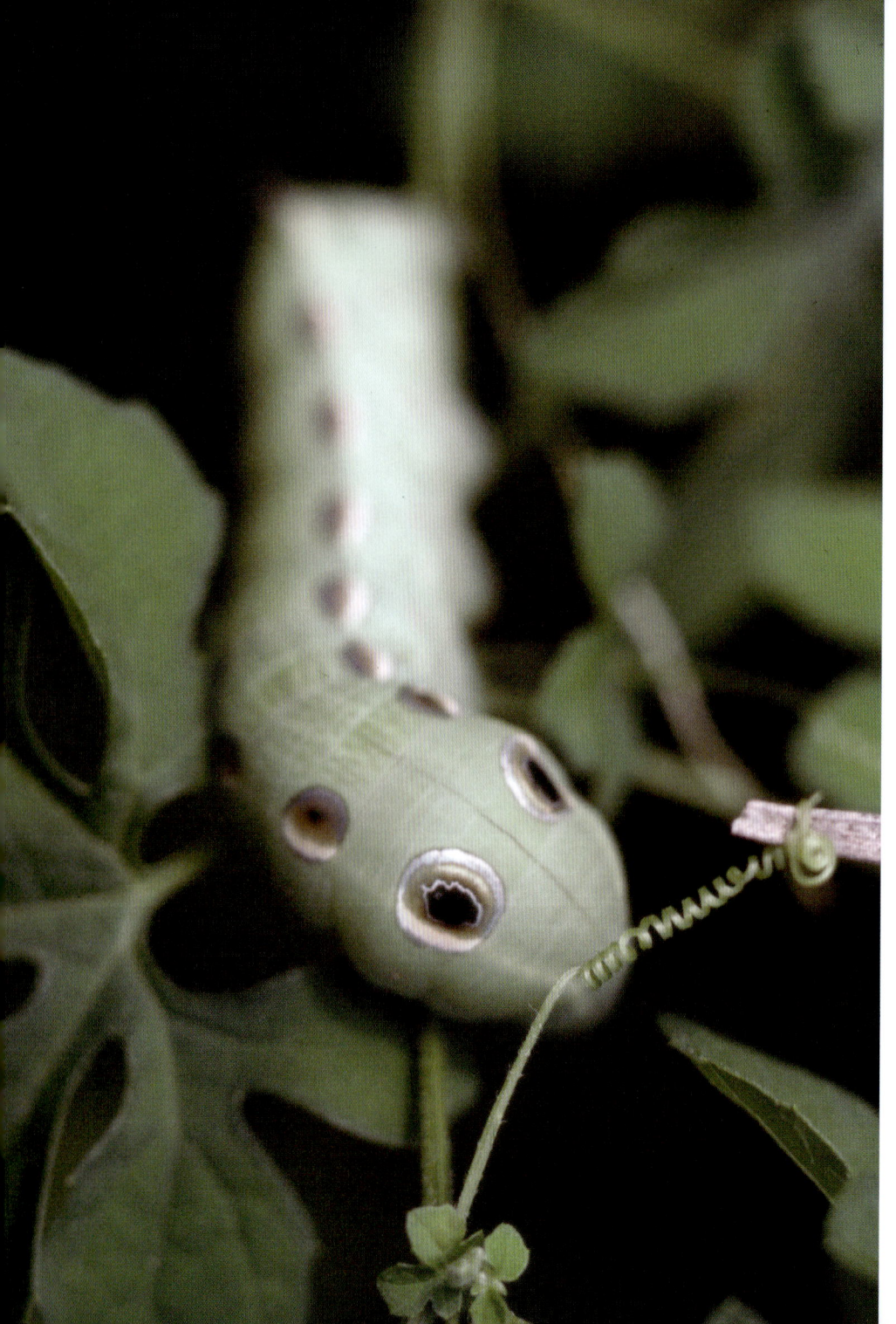

Working closely with his wife, Maria, pioneering entomologist Thomas Eisner developed new macro-photography techniques to capture the chemical defense mechanisms and other characteristics of insects. He used this image of the posterior false eyespots of the caterpillar *Pholus satellitia* in his lectures to illustrate adaptive coloration.

Thomas Eisner (1929–2011), *Pholus Satellitia*, ca. 1986. Color slide. Courtesy of Maria Eisner.

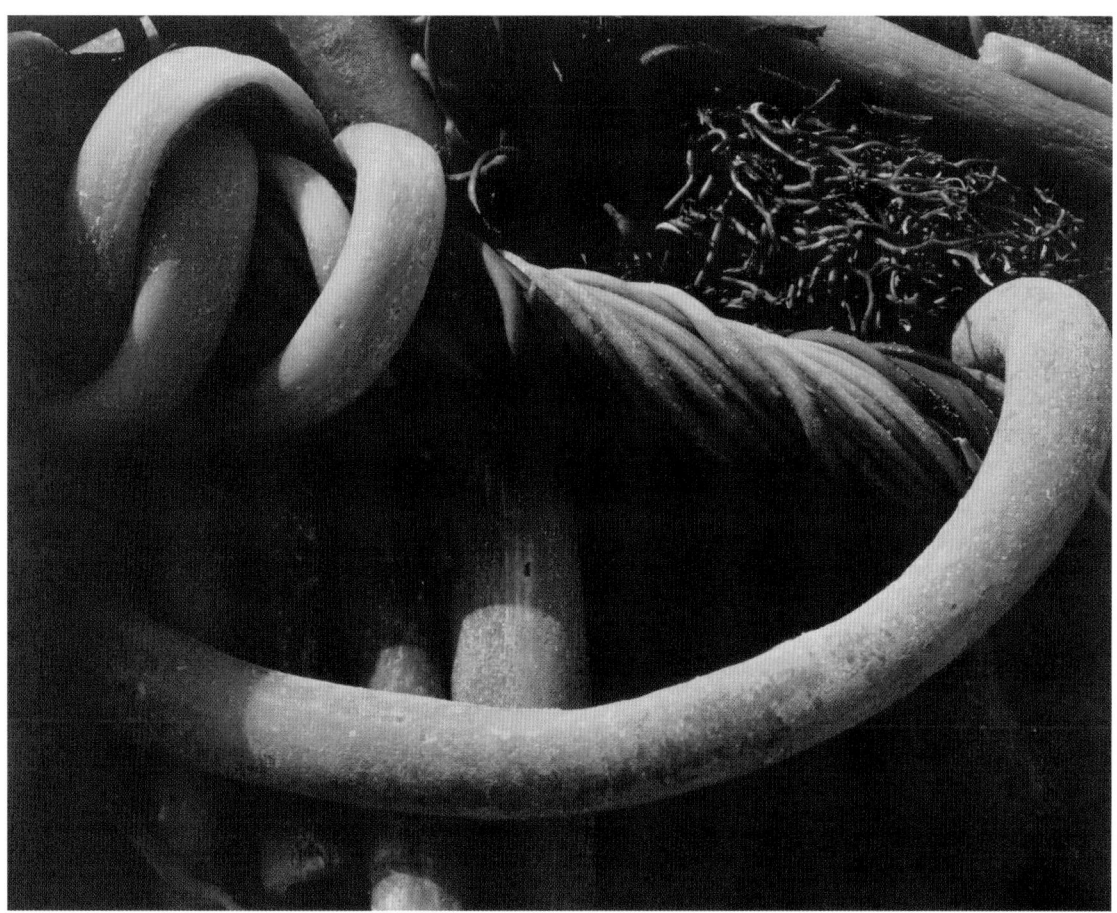

Edward Weston (1886–1958), *Kelp*, 1930. Gelatin silver print. © Center for Creative Photography, Arizona Board of Regents.

Born in Illinois, photographer Edward Weston lived most of his adult life in California, where the local landscape provided countless interesting subjects for his sharp, often abstract photography. Here, he trained his camera on the curved, ropy lines of the ocean plant kelp.

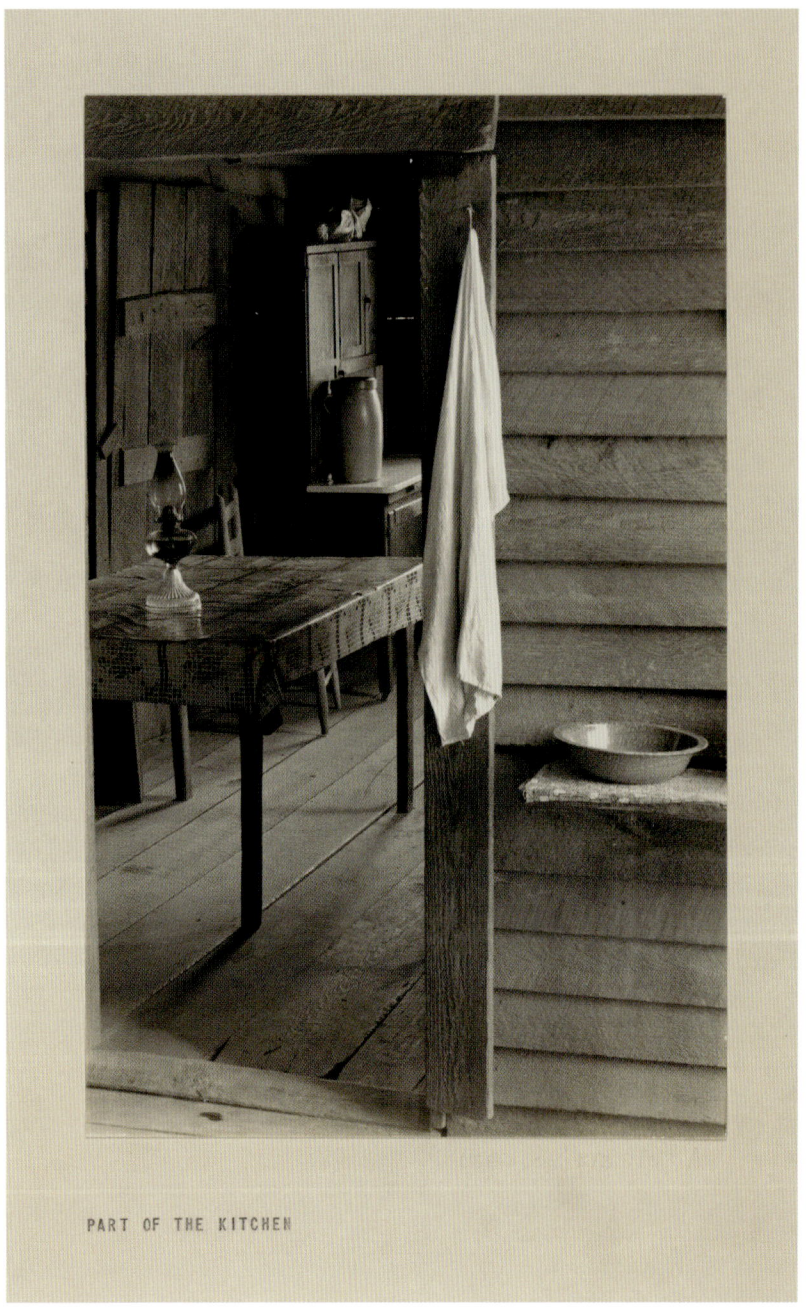

PART OF THE KITCHEN

Walker Evans took this view of a tenant farmer's kitchen, bisected by the door frame and hanging towel. He included this print in a set of albums that laid out the images for the book, *Let Us Now Praise Famous Men* (1941), a collaboration with writer James Agee. Evans's direct style capturing quintessential American scenes influenced documentary photographers throughout the twentieth century.

Walker Evans (1903–1975), *Part of the Kitchen*, Alabama, ca. 1935. Gelatin silver print. *Pictures of the House and Family of an Alabama Cotton Sharecropper* album.

Known as "Migrant Mother," Dorothea Lange's portrait of Florence Owens Thompson and three of her children for the Farm Security Administration became an iconic photograph of the Great Depression. Many saw Thompson's wearied and pensive expression as embodying the precarious existence of agricultural workers during this era, though Thompson herself contested Lange's use of her image.

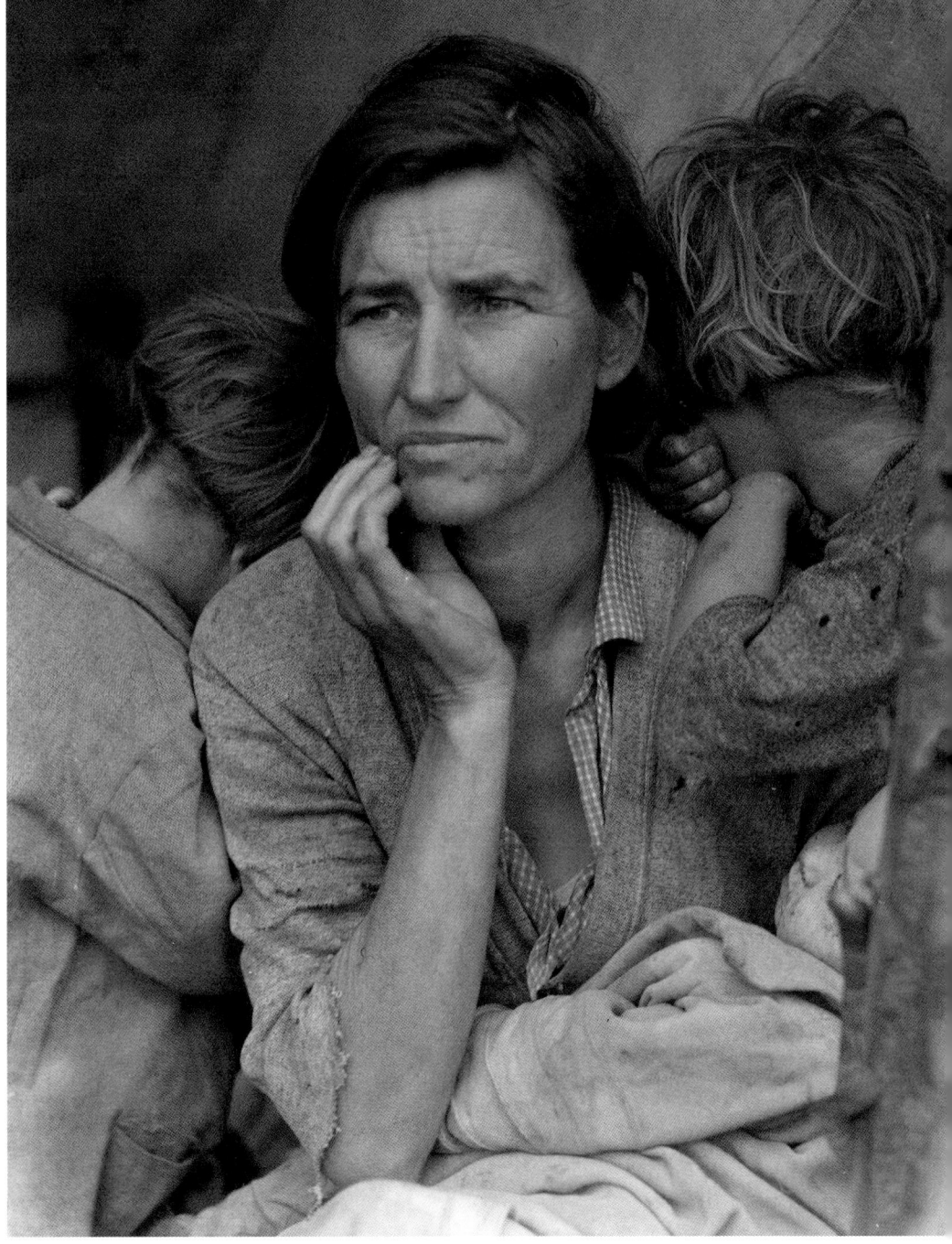

Dorothea Lange (1895–1965), *Destitute Pea Pickers in California. Mother of Seven Children. Age Thirty-two*, Nipomo, California, 1936. Nitrate negative.

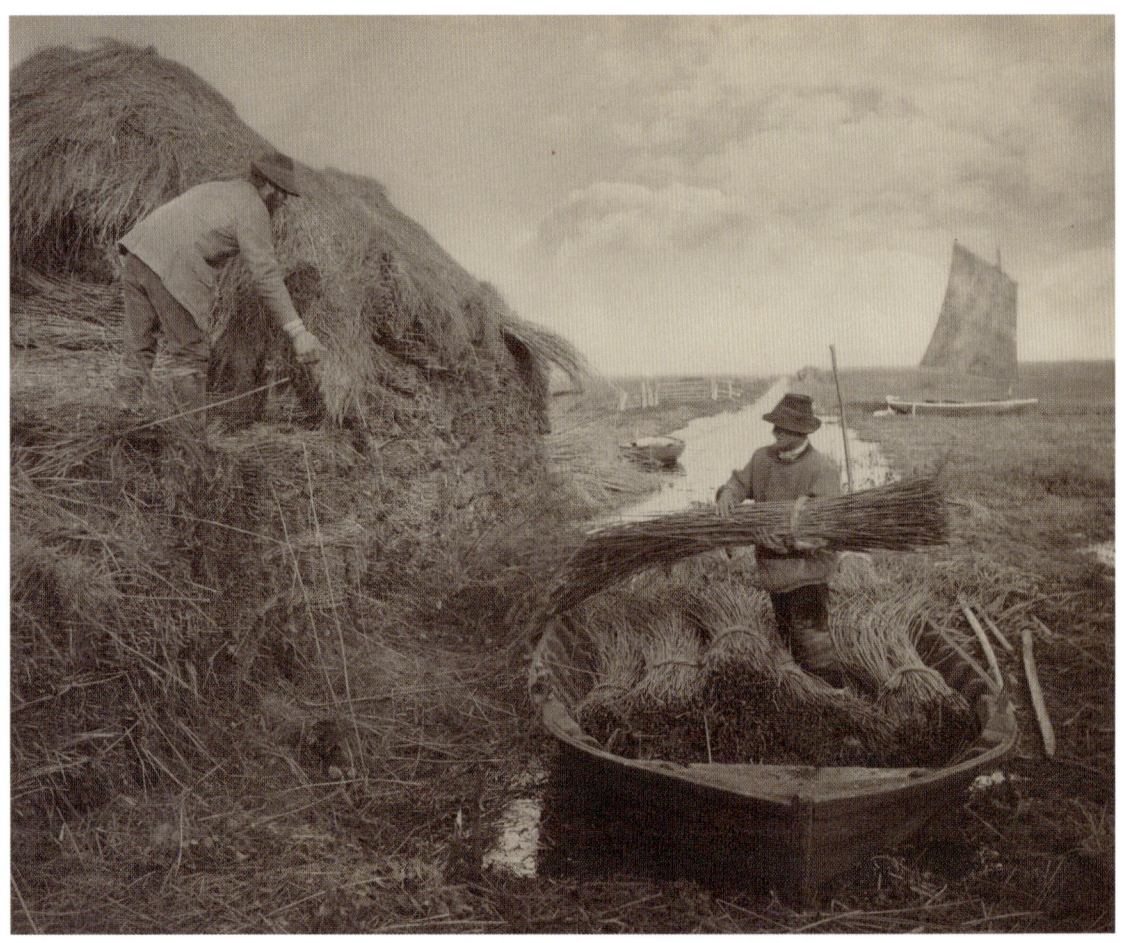

With photographs like this one, Peter Henry Emerson sought to document and celebrate what he saw as disappearing British agrarian traditions. Emerson advocated for photography as an art form and theorized that the way focus could be controlled with the camera's lens, leaving some areas sharp and others falling into blurriness, closely mirrored human vision.

P. H. (Peter Henry) Emerson (1856–1936), *Ricking the Reed*, England, 1886. From *Life and Landscape on the Norfolk Broads*. Platinum print.

Known for her fashion photography and photojournalism, Toni Frissell snapped this charming shot for an edition of Robert Louis Stevenson's *A Child's Garden of Verses* illustrated entirely with her photographs (1944). Frissell focuses on a young girl, the large triangle of the rake emphasizing her small stature. The swirling dust creates movement in an otherwise quiet moment.

Toni Frissell (1907–1988), *Girl Raking Leaves*, between 1939 and 1944. Gelatin silver print.

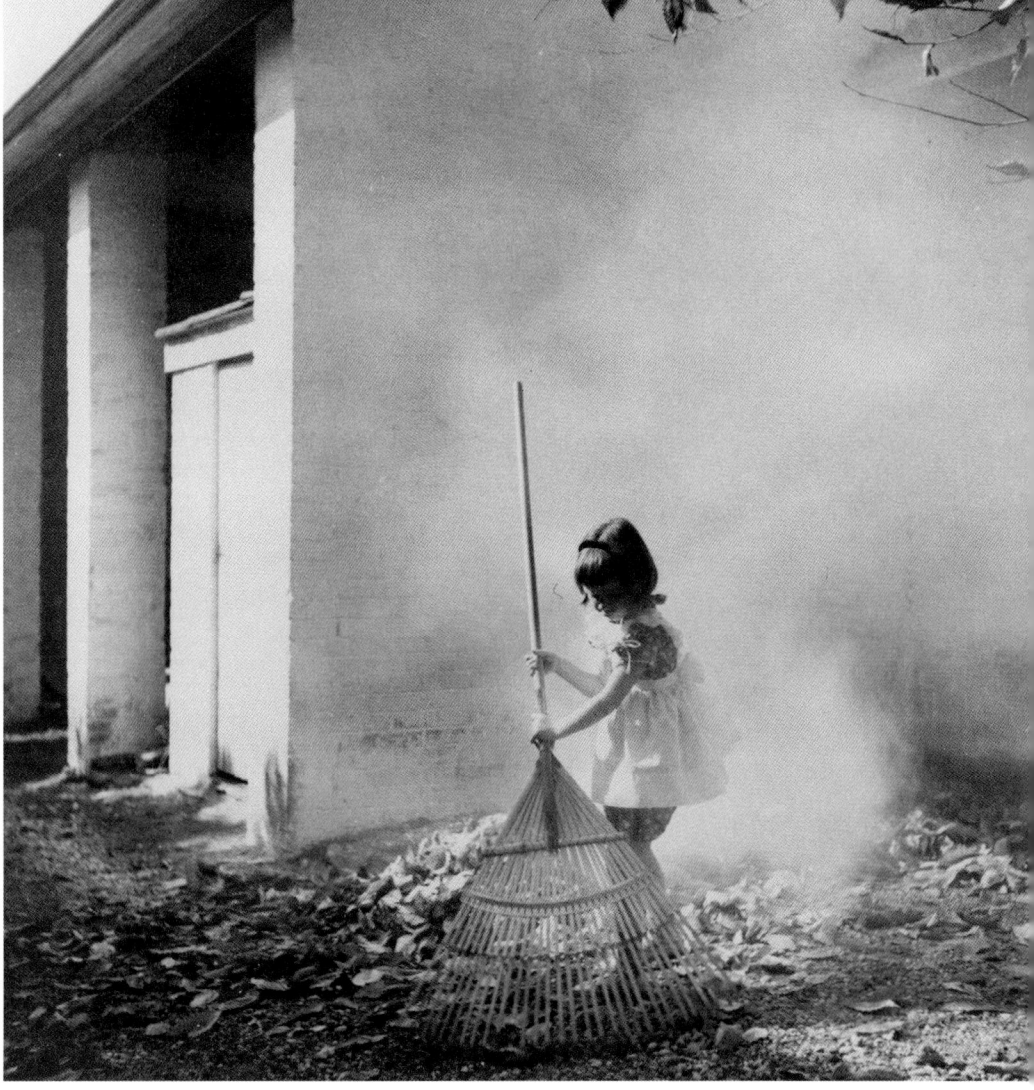

Prominent landscape photographer George Barker took this vivid image of a steamboat in Florida, documenting the state's burgeoning tourist trade in the last quarter of the nineteenth century. Undulating steam, moss dripping from tree branches, and dramatic clouds—printed in from another negative—all evoke the lush, alluring scenery sought out by visitors.

George Barker (1844–1894), *Steamboat Approaching Dock, View from the Morgan House*, Silver Springs, Florida, 1886. Albumen silver print.

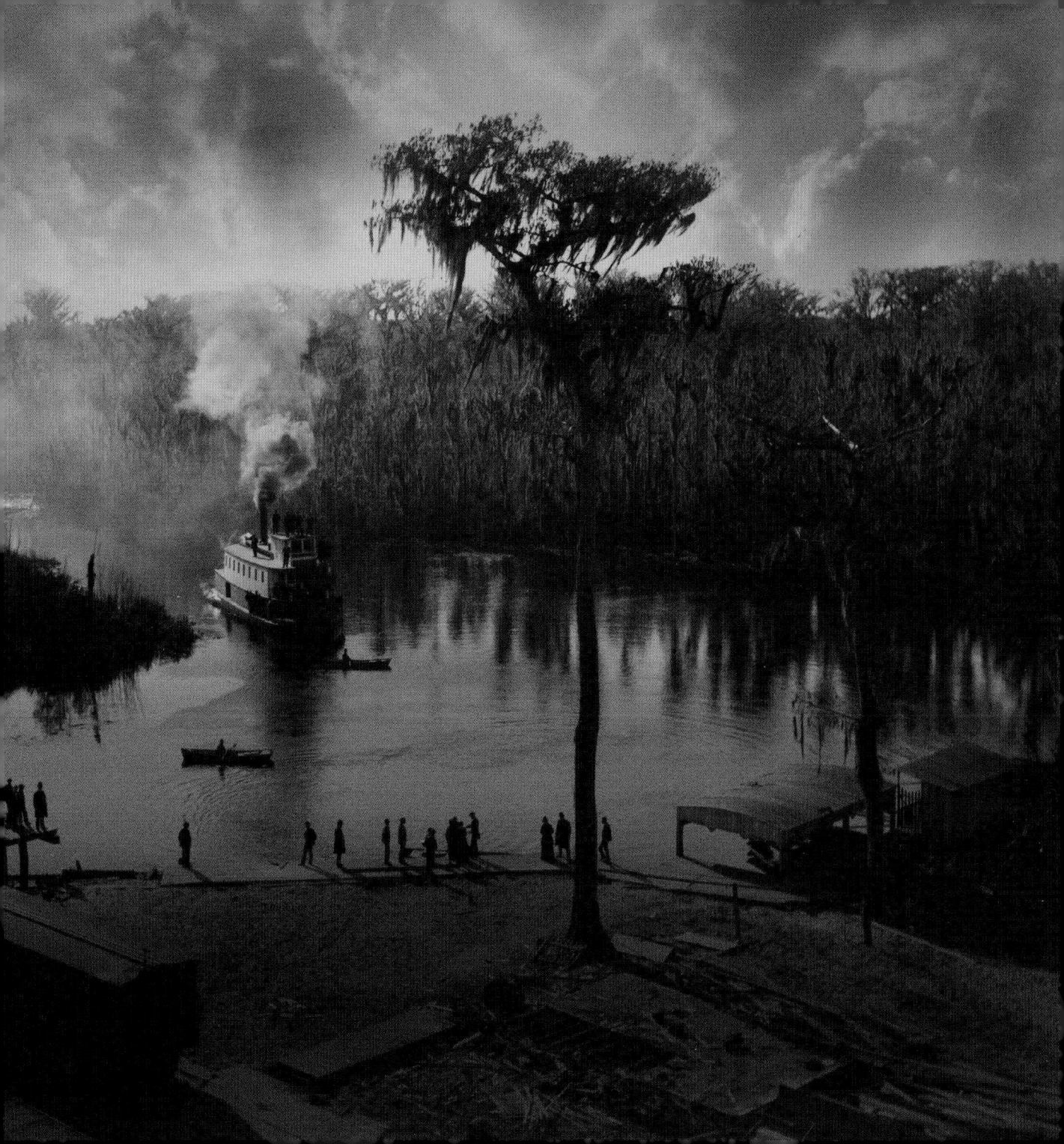

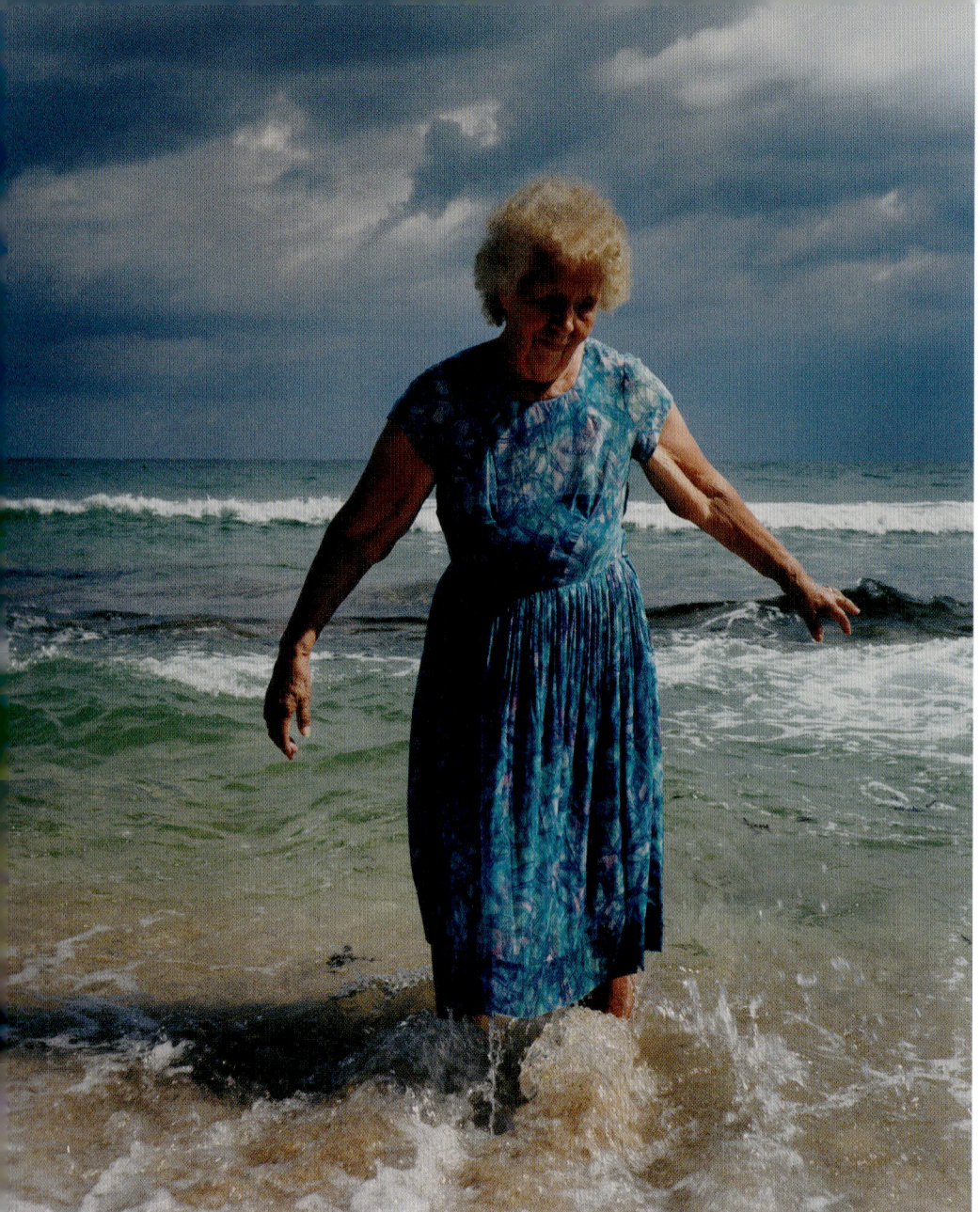

Nina Korhonen depicts her "Amerikan mummu" (American grandma), Anna, who came to the United States alone from Finland at age 40, wading in the Atlantic Ocean. Anna's soft hair and smiling face are offset from the blues and greens of the cloudy sky, boisterous waves, and the abstract pattern of her dress.

Nina Korhonen (1961–), *The Sea*, Lake Worth, Florida, 1997. Chromogenic color print. Courtesy of Nina Korhonen.

American photographer Maggie Steber photographed Haiti for over twenty-five years, seeking out scenes of beauty and resilience in daily life. Here, Steber captures a young girl's joyful moment flouncing her blue lace dress, in contrast with her arid surroundings on the outskirts of Gonaives.

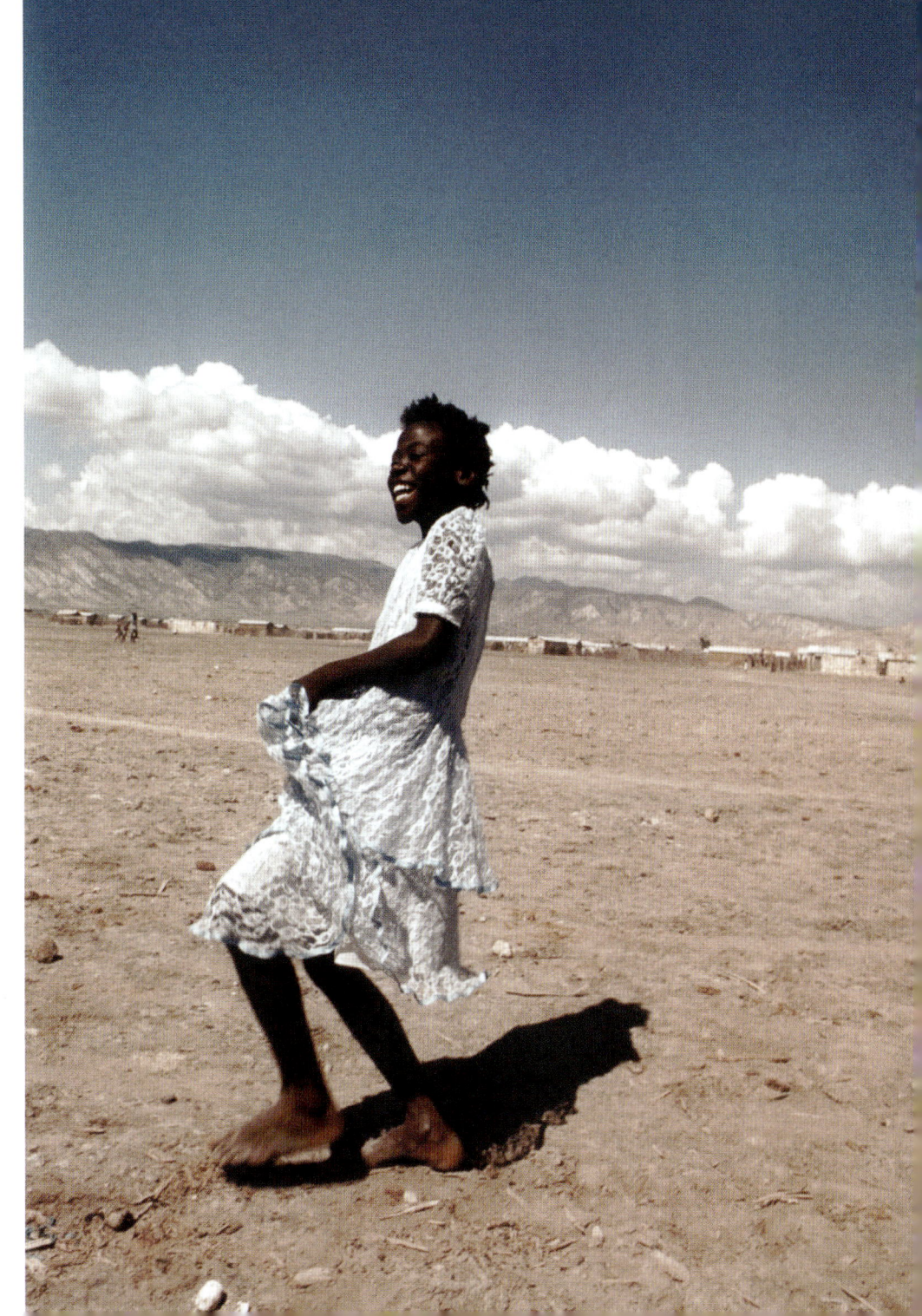

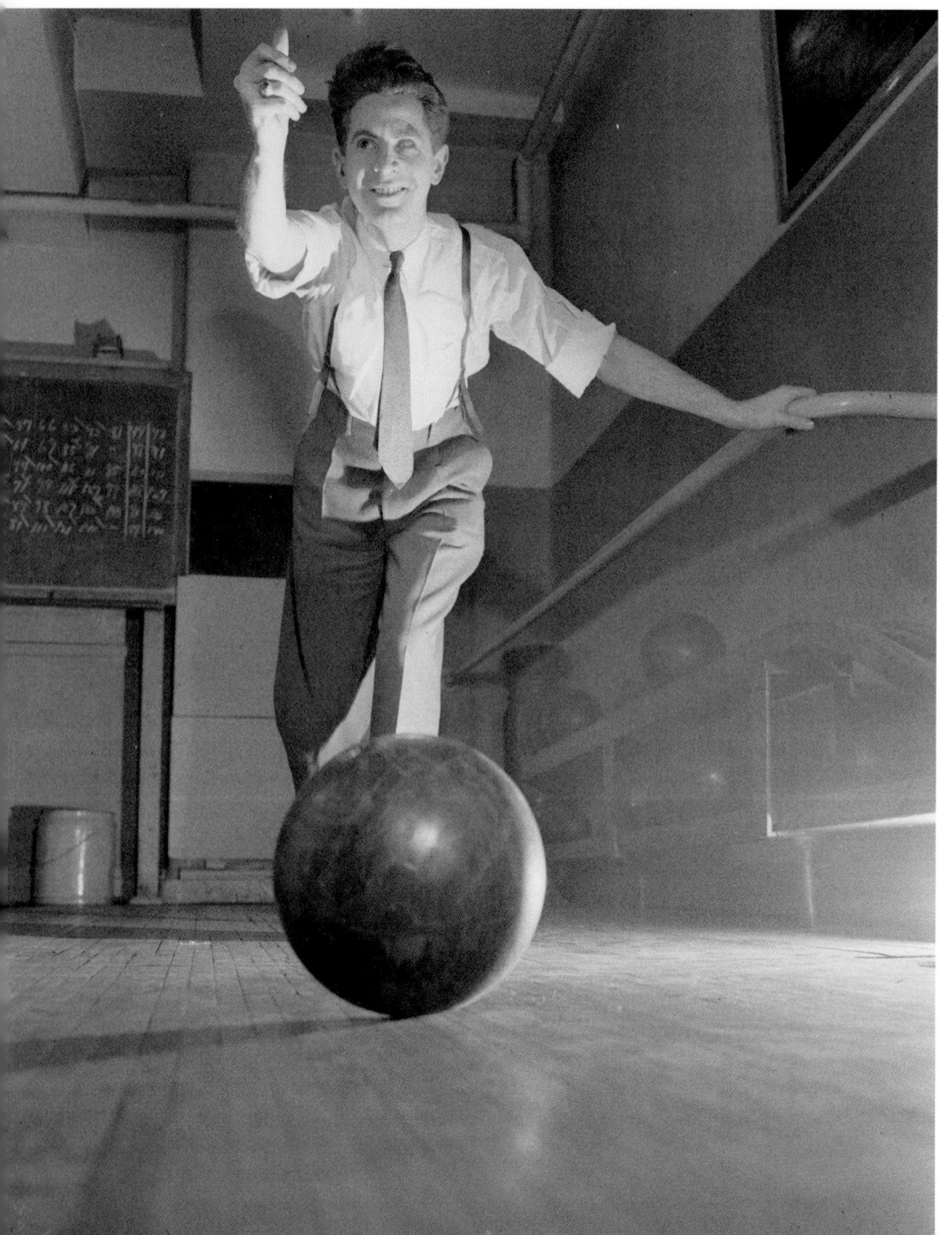

Both shot and lit from below, Richard Boyer's dynamic photograph captures Thomas Gilmartin's evident delight in bowling. Sight impaired, Gilmartin holds onto a rail on his left as a guide to the foul line. Boyer photographed Gilmartin at the Lighthouse, an institution for the blind in New York City.

Richard Boyer (1911–1997), *Thomas Gilmartin Bowling*, New York City, 1944. Safety negative.

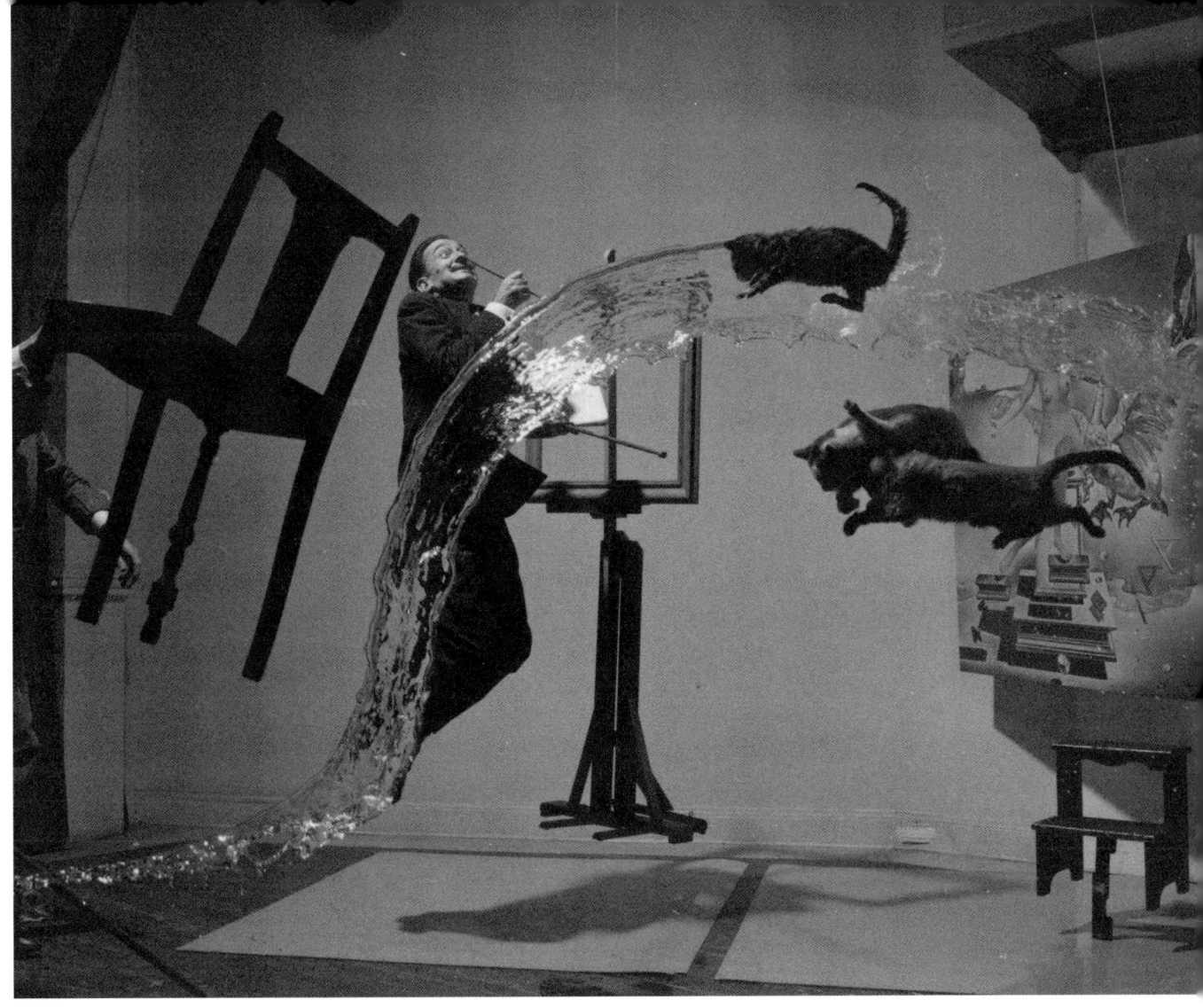

Philippe Halsman's assistants threw three cats and a bucket of water for each of the roughly twenty takes it took to get this fanciful shot, one of many collaborations between Halsman and surrealist painter Salvador Dalí. The props visible in this photo—the arm holding the chair, the lift under the stool, the wires holding up the painting and easel—were removed in the published version of the photograph.

Philippe Halsman (1906–1979), *Salvador Dalí A*, 1948. Gelatin silver print.

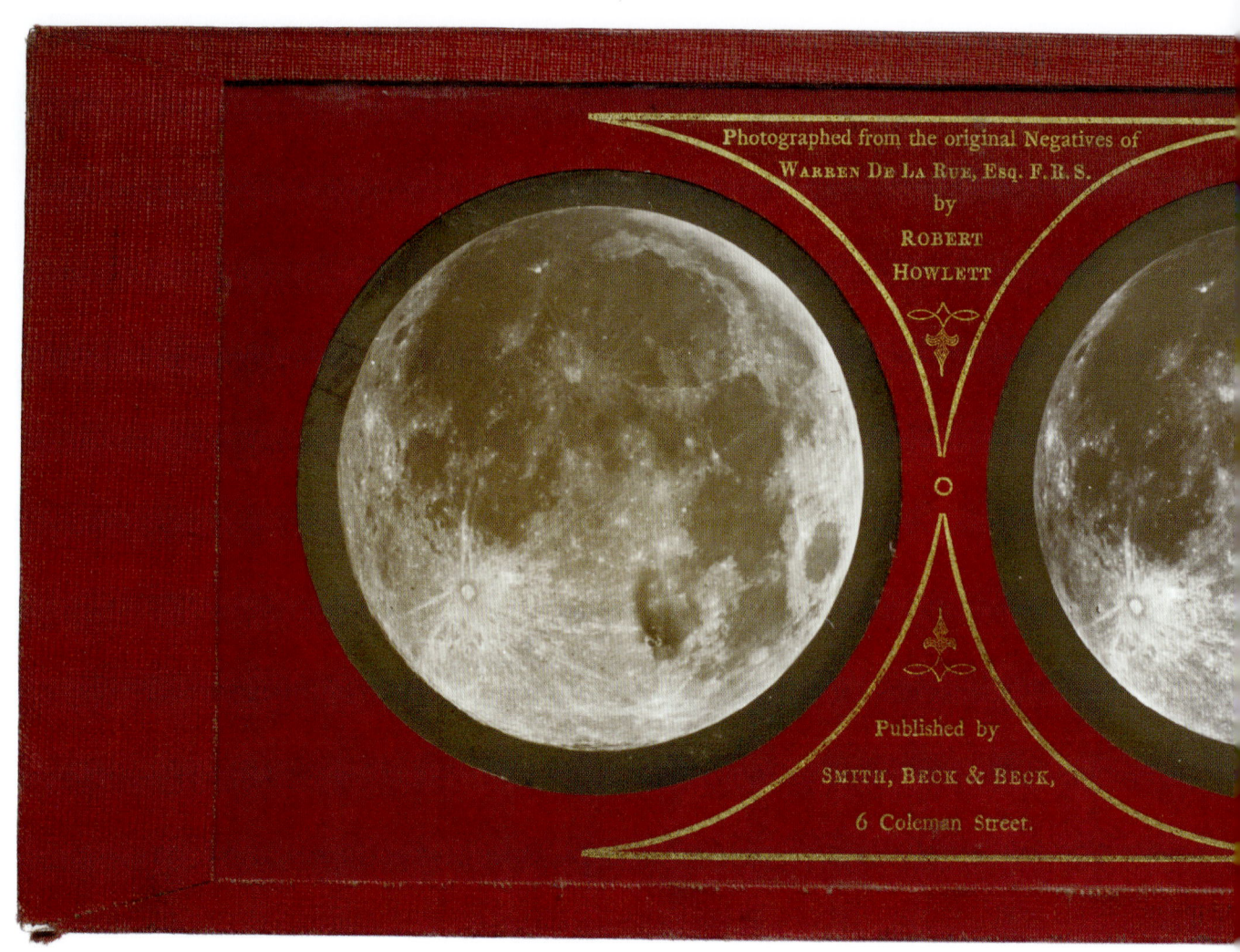

Photographed from the original Negatives of
WARREN DE LA RUE, Esq. F.R.S.
by
ROBERT
HOWLETT

Published by
SMITH, BECK & BECK,
6 Coleman Street.

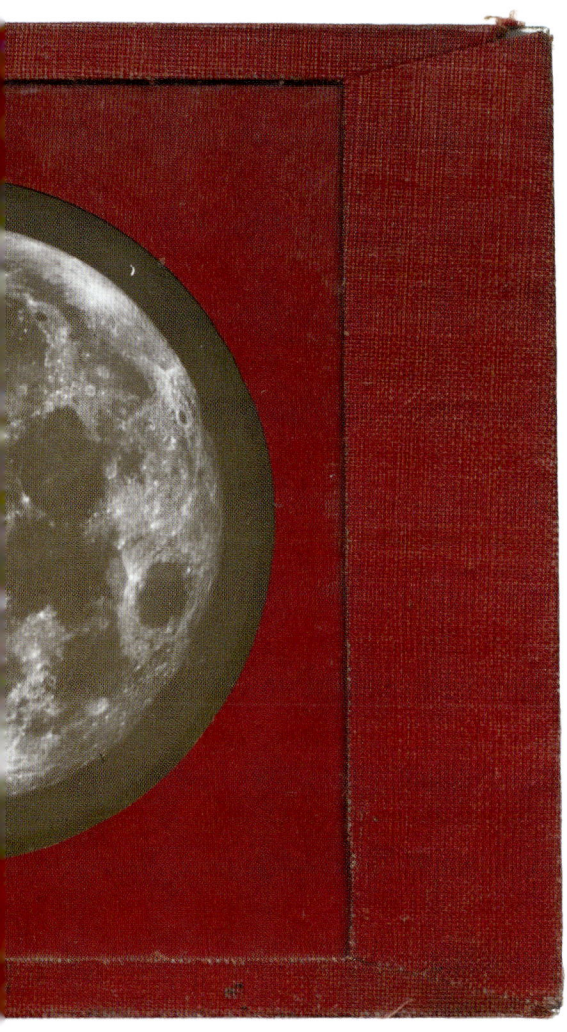

Early efforts to photograph the moon were limited by technological shortcomings. Using a telescope of his own design, British amateur scientist Warren De la Rue made this stereo view, determining the rotation of the moon needed to simulate a stereo effect from two individual photographs made over an interval of twenty-four hours. When seen through a stereoscope, the image appears three dimensional, giving viewers an unprecedented up-close view of the moon.

Warren De la Rue (1815–1889), *The Moon*, London, 1858. Stereoscopic diapositive on glass. Printed by Robert Howlett, published by Smith, Beck & Beck.

Acknowledgments

This book was compiled by Aimee Hess and Hannah Freece with significant contributions from Library of Congress Prints & Photographs Division curators Beverly Brannan, Micah Messenheimer, Mari Nakahara, and Adam Silvia.

In addition, the editors gratefully acknowledge the assistance and scholarship of their Library of Congress colleagues: Matt Barton, Mike Mashon, David Pierce (Motion Picture, Broadcast & Recorded Sound); Katherine Blood, Ryan Brubacher, Phil Michel, Barbara Natanson, Helena Zinkham (Prints & Photographs); Barbara Bair, Michelle Krowl, Joshua Levy, Janice Ruth, Pang Xiong, Margaret McAleer (Manuscript); Mark Dimunation, Mark Manivong (Rare Book & Special Collections); Megan Harris, Rachel Meares (Veterans History Project); John Fenn (American Folklife Center); David Mandel (Center for Exhibits & Interpretation); Mike Munshaw, Jessica Epting (Design Office); Becky Clark, Pete Devereaux, Zach Klitzman, Porsha Perry, Susan Reyburn; interns Samantha Baine, Jane Brinley, Polina Lopez, Juliet Machado, Jude Souazoube (Publishing Office).

Image Credits

Some photograph titles have been modified for consistency.

All images in this book are from the Prints & Photographs Division of the Library of Congress unless otherwise noted. Image identification numbers are noted below, and images can be located by searching for those numbers at www.loc.gov/pictures.

Cover: Clockwise from upper left: LC-DIG-ds-15679; Gift/Purchase, Nathan Benn, 2020; LC-DIG-ds-12025; Look Magazine Photograph Collection; Gift, Cowles Communications, 1971; LC-DIG-ppmsca-09633; Transfer, US Copyright Office, 1948.

ii: LC-DIG-ppmsc-05776; Photochrom Print Collection; Purchase, Galerie Muriset, 1985.

vi: LC-DIG-ppss-01044; Beverly Willis Architectural Photograph Collection; Gift, Beverly Willis, 2018.

2–3: LC-DIG-ds-15677; Bob Adelman Photograph Archive; Gift, Anonymous, 2016, 2018.
4: LC-DIG-ds-15670; Gift/Purchase, Sandra Tepper Sgarro, 1991.
5: LC-DIG-ppmsca-54502; Purchase, 2017.
6: LC-DIG-ppmsca-40464; Marion S. Carson Collection; Daguerreotype Collection; Gift, Marian S. Carson, 1996.
7: LC-DIG-ds-15675; Gift, Cheryl and Robert Zider, 2020.
8: LC-DIG-ds-15671; Gift of Encyclopedia Britannica, 1954 and 1956.
9: LC-DIG-ppmsca-19857; Farm Security Administration/Office of War Information Photograph Collection. Transfer, Office of War Information, 1944.
10–11: LC-DIG-ds-15691; Purchase, Lynsey Addario, 2014.

12: LC-DIG-fsac-1a35371; Farm Security Administration/Office of War Information Color Photograph Collection. Transfer, Office of War Information, 1944.

13: LC-DIG-ds-04496; Daguerreotype Collection; Purchase, 1991.

14: LC-DIG-ppmsca-57433; Frances Benjamin Johnston Photograph Collection; Gift, Frances Benjamin Johnston, 1948.

15: LC-DIG-ds-15689; Purchase/Gift, Sam Comen, 2019.

16: LC-DIG-ds-15676; Purchase, Keith De Lellis Gallery, 2011.

17: LC-DIG-ds-12025; Look Magazine Photograph Collection; Gift, Cowles Communications, 1971.

18–19: LC-DIG-ppprs-00369; Manzanar War Relocation Center Photographs; Gift, Ansel Adams, 1965–1968.

20: LC-DIG-ppmsca-36454; Liljenquist Family Collection of Civil War Photographs; Gift, Tom Liljenquist, 2010.

21: LC-DIG-ppmsca-40838; Purchase/Gift, William Wilson, 2014.

22: LC-DIG-ppss-00855; The Public Library: An American Commons Photographic Survey Collection; Purchase, Robert Dawson, 2015.

23: LC-DIG-ppem-02102; Prokudin–Gorskiĭ Photograph Collection; Purchase, 1948.

24: LC-DIG-highsm-04874; Carol M. Highsmith's America Project in the Carol M. Highsmith Archive; Gift and purchase, Carol M. Highsmith, 2009.

25: LC-DIG-ppprs-00626; Glass Negatives from the Papers of Wilbur and Orville Wright; Gift, Wright Brothers Estate, 1948.

26: LC-DIG-ppmsca-51810; Purchase, Jamey Stillings, 2014.

27: LC-DIG-krb-00609; Balthazar Korab Collection; Gift, Balthazar Korab, 2007.

28–29: LC-DIG-ds-15701, LC-DIG-ds-15702, and LC-DIG-ds-15703; Gift, David Stephenson, 2019.

30: LC-DIG-ds-15678; Purchase, Mexico/Central America Fund, Graciela Iturbide, 2000.

31: LC-DIG-ds-15696; Purchase/Gift, Brian Adams, 2021.

32: LC-DIG-ppmsca-37853; Purchase, Steven Kasher Gallery, 2010.

33: LC-DIG-ppmsca-19599; Gift/Purchase, Bruce Davidson and Sandra Berler Gallery of Photography, 2008.

34: LC-GLB23-0285; William P. Gottlieb/Ira and Leonore S. Gershwin Fund Collection, Music Division; Purchase, William P. Gottlieb, 1995.

35: Box 3, Photographs from the Mary Margaret McBride Collection, Motion Picture,

Broadcasting & Recorded Sound Division. Gift, Cynthia Lowry, 1977.

36–37: LC-DIG-ds-15698; Gift/Purchase, Alicia Vera, 2021.

38: LC-DIG-ppmsca-53168; Gift, Anonymous, 1934.

39: LC-DIG-ppmsca-68723; Papers of O. M. Poe; Gift, Eleanor Carroll Poe, Mrs. Henry Fitzhugh, and Mary F. Bell, 1910–1995; Transfer from Manuscript Division, 1985.

40: LC-DIG-fsa-8c11683; Farm Security Administration/Office of War Information Photograph Collection. Transfer, Office of War Information, 1944.

41: LC-DIG-ds-15687; Purchase, Anastasia Photo, 2010.

42: LOT 15069 (OH size); Purchase, 19th Century Rare Book & Photograph Shop, 2018.

43: LC-DIG-ppmsca-02130, LC-DIG-ppmsca-02131; Purchase, Ariel Meyerowitz, 2002.

44: LC-DIG-thc-5a38942; Theodor Horydczak Collection; Gift, Norma and Francis Reeves, 1973.

45: LC-DIG-ds-15672; Purchase, Joseph Bellows Gallery, 2019.

46: LC-DIG-ppmsca-69392; Anthony Angel Collection; Bequest, Angelo A. Rizzuto, 1967.

48: Sylvester and Orphanos Archive, Rare Book & Special Collections Division; Gift, Stathis Orphanos, 2015.

49: LC-DIG-ds-15680; Purchase, 1999.

50: LC-DIG-ds-15695; Purchase, Salwan Georges, 2018.

51: LC-DIG-ds-15692; Gift/Purchase, Joana Toro, 2020.

52: LC-DIG-ds-15688; Gift/Purchase, Brian Ulrich, 2018.

53: LC-DIG-ppmsca-22695; Milton Rogovin Photograph Collection; Gift, Milton Rogovin, 1999.

54–55: LC-DIG-ds-15668; Panoramic Photograph Collection; Acquired by copyright deposit, F. W. Sheelor, 1915.

56: Albert K. Fisher Papers, Manuscript Division. Gift, Anne B. Fisher, 1955 and 1960.

57: LC-DIG-ppmsca-32160; Purchase, Galerie f5,6, 2011.

58: LC-DIG-ppmsca-09982; Transfer, US War Department, 1915.

59: LC-DIG-ppmsca-11680; Gift, John Medveckis, 2006.

60: LC-DIG-ppmsc-07885; Photochrom Print Collection; Purchase, Galerie Muriset, 1985.

61: LC-DIG-ppmsca-51816; Daguerreotype Collection; Purchase, 1972.

62: LC-DIG-ppmsca-69289; Purchase, Mexico/Central America and Huntington Funds, 2000.

63: LC-DIG-fsa-8b35942; Farm Security Administration/Office of War Information Photograph Collection. Transfer, Office of War Information, 1944.

64–65: LC-DIG-vrg-00344; Camilo J. Vergara Photograph Collection.

66: LC-DIG-ppmsca-51510; Purchase; Danny Lyon; 2009.

67: LC-DIG-ds-15697; Purchase, Stephen Daiter Gallery, 2017.

68: LC-DIG-ppmsca-77373; Daguerreotype Collection; Purchase, 1973.

69: LC-DIG-ppmsca-69153; Purchase, Jeff Rich, 2018.

70–71: LC-DIG-ds-11802, LC-DIG-ppmsca-55830; Farm Security Administration/Office of War Information Photograph Collection. Transfer, Office of War Information, 1944.

72–73: LC-DIG-ds-15673; Gift, Constantine Manos, 2017.

74: LC-DIG-ds-00188; Purchase, Rizzuto Fund (Witkin–Berley Limited), 1976.

75: LC-DIG-ds-15679; Gift/Purchase, Nathan Benn, 2020.

76: LC-DIG-ppmscd-00556; Look Magazine Photograph Collection; Gift, Cowles Communications, 1971.

77: LC-DIG-ppmsca-31882; Purchase, 1977.

78: LC-DIG-ppmsca-07432; Warren and Margot Coville Collection; Purchase, Coville Photographic Art Foundation, 2002.

79: LC-DIG-ppmsca-49539; Purchase, 1926.

80: Shawn Miller (AFC 2001/001/99678), Photograph (PH27), Veterans History Project Collection, American Folklife Center.

81: LC-DIG-nclc-01641; National Child Labor Committee Collection; Gift, NCLC, 1954; Transfer, Manuscript Division.

82: LC-DIG-ppmsca-69176; Purchase, Wendy Red Star, 2017.

83: LC-DIG-ds-15685; Purchase, Jack Shainman Gallery, 2014.

84–85: LC-DIG-ds-15681, LC-DIG-ds-15682, LC-DIG-ds-15683, LC-DIG-ds-15684; Purchase, Sidney Janis Gallery, 1990.

86: LC-G41-CT-0341; Arnold Genthe Photograph Collection; Gift, Norma Millay Ellis, 1969.

87: LC-DIG-ds-11082; Victor A. Lundy Archive; Gift, Victor A. Lundy, 2008–2019.

88: LC-DIG-ppmsca-35546; Roger Fenton Crimean War Photograph Collection; Purchase, Frances M. Fenton, 1944.

89: LC-DIG-ppmsca-39711; Gift, elin o'Hara slavick, 2014.

90-91: Emil Edgren (AFC 2001/001/65358), Photograph (PH46), Veterans History Project Collection, American Folklife Center.

92: LC-USF34-038825-D; Farm Security Administration/Office of War Information Photograph Collection. Transfer, Office of War Information, 1944.

93: LC-DIG-ds-15700; Purchase, Andrew Smith Gallery, 2021.

94: LC-DIG-ds-15694; Purchase, Catherine Edelman Gallery, 2019.

95: LC-DIG-ppmsca-69177; Gift/Purchase, Ka-Man Tse, 2019.

96: LC-DIG-ds-15699; Purchase, Harry Scales, 2021.

97: LC-DIG-ds-15693; Purchase, Arnika Dawkins Gallery, 2018.

98: LC-DIG-ppmsca-69154; Purchase, Laura Gilpin, not after 1933.

99: American Colony in Jerusalem Collection, Manuscript Division; Gift, American Colony of Jerusalem, Ltd., 2004–2009.

100–101: LC-DIG-ds-15690; Purchase, Catherine Edelman Gallery, 2012.

102: Thomas Eisner Papers, Manuscript Division; Gift, Thomas Eisner and Maria Eisner, 2010–2012.

103: LC-DIG-ds-15669; Purchase, 1930.

104: LC-DIG-ppmsca-19407; US Resettlement Administration Photograph Collection; Transfer, Office of War Information, 1944.

105: LC-DIG-fsa-8b29516; Farm Security Administration/Office of War Information Photograph Collection. Transfer, Office of War Information, 1944.

106: LC-DIG-ds-15667; Case Book Collection; Gift; Peter Henry Emerson.

107: LC-USZ62-131238; Toni Frissell Collection; Gift, Toni Frissell, 1971.

108–109: LC-DIG-ppmsca-09548; Acquired by copyright deposit, 1886.

110: LC-DIG-ds-15686; Purchase, Lee Marks Fine Art, LLC, 2010.

111: LC-DIG-ppmsca-65189; Gift, Maggie Steber, 2011.

112: LC-USW3-041481-C; Farm Security Administration/Office of War Information Photograph Collection. Transfer, Office of War Information, 1944.

113: LC-DIG-ppmsca-09633; Transfer, US Copyright Office, 1948.

114–115: LC-DIG-ppmsca-69207; Purchase, Hans P. Kraus Jr. Fine Photographs, 2020.

Index